Also by Harry Browne

HOW YOU CAN PROFIT FROM THE COMING DEVALUATION (1970)

HOW I FOUND FREEDOM IN AN UNFREE WORLD (1973)

You Can Profit
from a Monetary Crisis

You Can
PROFIT
from a
Monetary Crisis

HARRY BROWNE

Macmillan Publishing Co., Inc.

NEW YORK

Publisher's Note: The purpose of this book is to give an economic analysis and general investment guidance and not provide legal advice. In dealing with any transaction whose legality may be questionable, the reader should obtain the advice of a lawyer.

Library of Congress Cataloging in Publication Data

Browne, Harry, 1933–
    You can profit from a monetary crisis.

    Bibliography: p.
    1. Investments—United States. 2. Currency question—United States. I. Title.

HG4921.B77   332.6   73-16686

ISBN 0-02-517460-6

Macmillan Publishing Co., Inc.
866 Third Avenue
New York, N.Y. 10022
Collier-Macmillan Canada Ltd., Toronto, Ontario

FIFTH PRINTING 1974

PRINTED IN THE UNITED STATES OF AMERICA

to my friend
whose presence doubles the enjoyment
I receive from my wealth

&

to the poor souls
who failed to heed the advice three years ago;
may they have the courage to do so now

Contents

Part IV—*Investments of the Past*

Part V—*Recommended Investments*

Epilogue

Appendix

Prologue

1

A Time of Opportunity

IN THE FALL OF 1970, Peter Panic read a book that frightened him. The book forecast the collapse of the American dollar and the U.S. economy.

In a state of mild hysteria, Peter withdrew his $5,000 savings from the bank (the book suggested that U.S. banks might close again) and sent them to a Swiss bank to be kept in Swiss francs. He sold his few other investments and scraped together all the cash he had—providing $10,000 more to go with the $5,000 he'd already sent to Switzerland.

He put $5,000 into South African gold stocks and bought pre-1965 U.S. silver coins with the remaining $5,000 (if the U.S. dollar failed, he wanted to have money with intrinsic value to spend).

He told his friend Tom Trueblue what he was doing, but Tom laughed at his anxiety. "The dollar's as good as gold," said Tom. "It's backed by the wealthiest, most productive economy in the world. Don't panic, Panic; the sky isn't going to fall."

And to prove his point, Tom immediately bought $15,000 worth of blue-chip industrial stocks.

As it turned out, Tom Trueblue was literally correct. As of August 1973, the stock market hadn't crashed, the banks hadn't closed, the sky hadn't fallen; it was business as usual in the U.S.A.

But strangely enough, although Peter may have been over-anxious, his actions proved to be extremely prudent and profitable.

3

From 1970 to 1973, the value of his Swiss francs increased by 42% (through upvaluations, devaluations, and floating currencies) from $5,000 to $7,100. His gold stocks tripled in price (due to runaway gold prices) from $5,000 to $15,000. And his silver coins went up in price by 45%, increasing their value from $5,000 to $7,250.

All told, his original investment of $15,000 had grown to $29,350—an increase of 96%—in just three years. And his objective had been safety, not profit.

Meanwhile, calm and cool Tom Trueblue's blue-chip stocks went up only 18%—so that his $15,000 investment was now worth $17,700. And he was lucky at that. Had he bought his stocks eighteen months earlier, he would have been in a loss position in 1973. Fortunately, he bought during a temporary low in the stock market.

As it was, Tom's 18% profit was far too small to offset the major losses in purchasing power that occurred during the three-year period. His dividends could only partially cover a normal rate of inflation. And the early 1970s saw *more* than a normal rate of inflation.

Imports increased 10–40% in price. Higher food prices, accompanied by shortages, required far greater purchasing power to remain even with the situation.

Peter had that necessary purchasing power—and more. Tom lagged far behind.

Peter Panic and Tom Trueblue are fictional characters. However, they represent a composite of many individuals I've known and talked with during the past three years. The book that scared Peter was my *How You Can Profit from the Coming Devaluation*, published in 1970.

In it, I said that any currency not backed by gold is doomed to disaster. I suggested that the time had come to get out of the traditional investments—the stock market, mutual funds, real estate, bonds, etc.—and place your funds where they'd be protected against a crashing dollar, a new depression, and runaway inflation.

Although there's much more to come, it's obvious that we're already in the transition period. Change isn't ahead; it has already arrived. This is demonstrated by the lackluster performance of the traditional investments and the great flight to real money (gold, silver, and currencies backed by gold) as havens of safety.

As recently as January 1973, an individual could have put his savings in Swiss francs in a Swiss bank and been over 25% ahead of the game by the fall of 1973. Whoever did that had the purchasing power to cope with the explosive price problems that developed during 1973.

The charts on pages 6 and 7 show the changing climate we're in now. Traditional investments were the place to be during the 1960s—but no longer. Meanwhile, gold, silver, and foreign currencies were stagnant during the 1960s—but are already turning upward.

MORE TO COME

Despite the dramatic changes that have already occurred, we've seen only the first act of a lengthy three-act drama. In this book, I intend to demonstrate the reasons for expectations such as these:

1. It will be much harder during the 1970s to make a decent living in the traditional ways. Business conditions will get worse, and we'll see a more difficult depression than that of the 1930s.

2. Retail prices have only begun to move upward. The chances are now far better than 50% that we'll see a classic runaway inflation in the United States.

But while it will be a time of severe crisis for many, it will also be a time of opportunity for those who foresee these things. Not only is protection still possible, but the opportunities for profit are many. These expectations can be added to the more grim ones already listed:

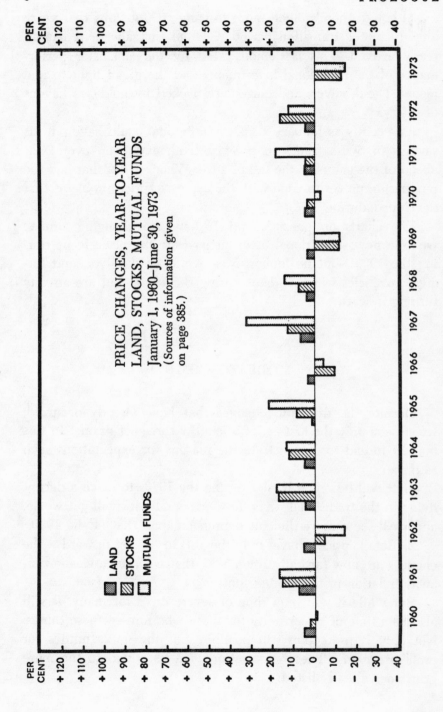

PRICE CHANGES, YEAR-TO-YEAR
LAND, STOCKS, MUTUAL FUNDS
January 1, 1960–June 30, 1973
(Sources of information given
on page 385.)

LAND
STOCKS
MUTUAL FUNDS

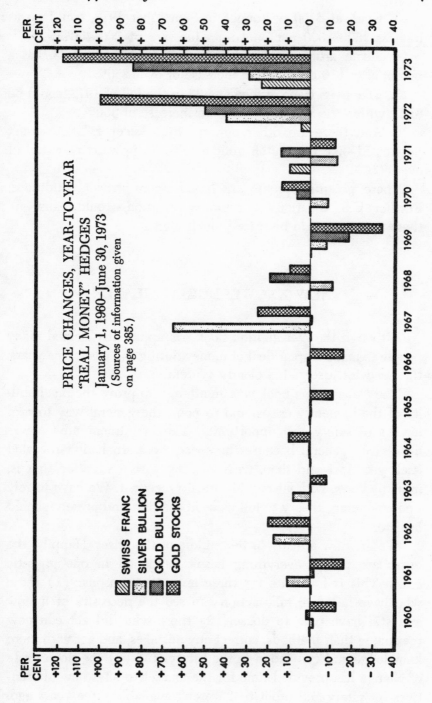

PRICE CHANGES, YEAR-TO-YEAR
"REAL MONEY" HEDGES
January 1, 1960–June 30, 1973
(Sources of information given
on page 385.)

SWISS FRANC
SILVER BULLION
GOLD BULLION
GOLD STOCKS

3. Gold, at $100 per ounce in September 1973, could go as high as $300–$500 per ounce—an increase of 200–400%.

4. Silver, around $2.70 per ounce in September 1973, has a potential of $10 or more—an increase of over 250%.

5. The Swiss franc, priced at $.33 in the fall of 1973, could be $1.50 within the next few years—an increase of 350%.

6. And there are other opportunities—"sleepers" that aren't publicized—like the Dutch guilder with an upward potential of over 500%.

These potential profits are based upon *present* conditions. Further U.S. inflation—or runaway inflation—would cause all these investments to be priced much higher.

NEW KNOWLEDGE AVAILABLE

Although the *Devaluation* book has apparently helped many people to make a great deal of money during the past three years, the need for a sequel is clearly evident.

The *Devaluation* book was an attempt to prove the inevitability of the monetary crises, and to point the general way toward havens of safety and opportunity. The investment advice was necessarily general because the specific pattern hadn't revealed itself yet. As I said then, we're dealing with a situation that is, in many ways, without any historical precedent. We have to rely upon monetary theory to tell us what the past and present should lead to.

We are now already in the middle of the crises. Happily, the crises are plural; everything hasn't happened in one gigantic crash. This is fortunate for three important reasons: (1) those who have failed to take action can see the necessity of it now and still have time to do so; (2) those who did act can now reexamine their methods, correct any mistakes, and act with more knowledge and conviction in the future; and (3) the slower rate of change has provided time for the market to offer new alternatives for safety and profit that weren't available three years ago.

UNDERSTANDING NECESSARY

It may seem that there's far less need now to prove the inevitability of further crises. But too few people truly understand the magnitude of the present situation and what it will lead to.

Most people read the news, hear about short-term trends— a declining dollar or a rising dollar, upturns in some investments, decreases in others. But they have no grasp of what's coming beyond a few months ahead. Where can they turn for help and understanding? To stock brokers, bankers, financial analysts, Swiss bankers?

Hardly. These are the people who three years ago were saying that the dollar wouldn't be devalued because it was the reserve currency of the world—that the Dow Jones averages were ready to burst through 1,000—that what the U.S. needed to control inflation was wage and price controls. Clearly, better understanding than that is needed to cope with today's crises.

You won't be protected by the superficial knowledge of short-term variables indicated by news items, current statistics, etc. What is needed is an understanding of the basic economic problems that afflict the United States—a firm grasp of the underlying market forces that are driving the world inexorably in one direction. Only then can you act with conviction to protect yourself.

Then you will know that the events of the past three years weren't mysterious accidents. They were the inevitable consequences of previous causes. And you won't be surprised by the events of the next few years; they'll seem obvious to you, and you may even wonder why others can't see them coming.

CONTENTS

The first part of the book will be concerned with those principles. The first section will be perhaps the most important part of the book—for it will demonstrate *why* we are where we are today, and what must follow.

Some readers may think that economic principles are boring and skip over them to get to the investment recommendations. That will be unfortunate because the recommendations won't be self-evident then. And relying upon specific recommendations only won't give you the understanding to adjust your investments wisely should market conditions change.

Others may recognize, at the outset, similarities to college textbooks and assume they know the rest. But traditional economics textbooks too often start with true premises and leap to impossible conclusions—assuming that human beings will act in inhuman, unrealistic ways.

Most readers, I hope, will find the economics exciting. For the study of economics is an attempt to understand how and why human beings act—how they attempt to get what they want and what they'll go through to accomplish that. And those individuals who understand these basic principles can approach their investments with conviction.

The principles will be presented in this book in a different way from that of the *Devaluation* book. There the emphasis was on the monetary aspects of the market; here the whole range of marketplace action will be encompassed. The two presentations will be complementary to each other.

The second part will review the events of the past that have led inexorably to the present situation and will attempt to sum up where we are now. It will include an explanation of the international monetary system. And it will show, in general, what kind of a future we can expect—including what must happen before you can believe the crises have ended.

The third part will state several investment principles that are often overlooked, and which I believe must be used to create an investment program that will work for you.

The fourth part will review the traditional investments that have worked so well in the past and demonstrate why they are no longer appropriate.

The fifth, and longest, part will cover in detail all the investments I'm aware of that can provide safety and profit in the years to come. It will include explanations of various ways to invest in gold, silver, and foreign currencies, specifics for opening a Swiss bank account, the tactics of speculation for those so inclined, and analyses of the major currencies of the world.

There will be guidelines for designing your own investment program, together with fourteen sample programs—each fitted to the objectives of a different kind of investor.

It will also include methods of protecting your savings through life insurance and annuities denominated in foreign currencies, a method for protecting the purchasing power of a pension, lists of Swiss banks and other suppliers that can help you, guidelines for determining when to sell the recommended investments, and other considerations such as tax matters, privacy, what to do if you think you're too late, etc.

The recommendations will assume that you're a U.S. citizen with U.S. dollars to invest. If you aren't, it should be easy to convert the information to fit your own situation. The principles involved are universal; they apply everywhere.

If, anywhere along the way, you come across a word whose meaning isn't clear, check the Glossary on page 369. It includes definitions of all important economic, monetary, and investment words.

LET US BEGIN

Every crisis is an opportunity. Those who recognize that a thirty-year inflationary cycle is ending will be prepared to act profitably in the future. They'll take the initiative to rearrange their lives so as to be invulnerable to the worst and prepared to take advantage of the best. New fortunes have already been made—just since 1970—and many new fortunes are yet to come.

So this book hasn't been written to scare you. To the contrary, its purpose is to show you how you can end your fears. This isn't a time to be afraid; it's a time to be prudent, to be ready, to meet the future and take advantage of it.

More than anything, I hope this book will relieve your anxieties and help you arrange your finances so you can relax. Then you can get on about your own business, ignore the scary news and rumors, and enjoy life—letting things unfold as they will.

As I said earlier, it all begins with an understanding of economics. There's nothing mysterious about what's happening today. Everything we see is the effect of prior causes, the consequences of the acts of the past several decades.

Economics and monetary theory are much easier to understand, and far more exciting, than politicians and college professors have let on. For economics is the science of allocating limited resources (time, energy, and money) in a way that will bring you the most of what you want.

It's really the art of making decisions—whether the scope of the decision is personal, social, national, or international.

Understanding the marketplace is an exciting adventure. I hope you enjoy it. And, above all, I hope you profit from it.

PART I Why There are Crises

2
Getting What You Want

WHAT YOU WANT in life is what *you* want—not what someone else thinks is best for you. If governments understood how persistently you continue to seek what you want, most of the economic crises of the world would be avoided.

You spend your entire life seeking to satisfy your desires and trying to eliminate undesirable elements from your life. *You* decide what you want and how you're going to get it. Laws and economic controls won't change that.

Despite the constant demands for "unselfishness," your preoccupation with getting what you want is neither immoral nor reprehensible; it's simply the natural state of a human being. You seek to arrange your life so that you experience as much mental well-being as possible—and as little discomfort as possible.

You work, you plan, you achieve, you exchange the fruits of your efforts with others. All these activities are aimed toward making your life what you want it to be.

The purpose of all production is consumption. You work in order to be able to have the things you enjoy. And what you enjoy will be different, in some ways, from that of any other human being.

Some work may be so enjoyable that you'd do it even if you received nothing in return for it. That only means that you get your enjoyment (consumption) immediately—through the doing of the work.

You only produce or exchange when you believe it will lead ultimately to something you want. And you do produce and exchange because, in the real world, there's no other way to get what you want. You can't consume what hasn't been produced.

Sometimes, however, your plans and work don't lead to valuable results. You may spend time working to earn something that doesn't satisfy you as much as you expected it would. Or you may look for a job that isn't available. Or you may create a business venture that doesn't succeed. Or you may build something for your home that doesn't work as intended.

So the amount of work you do (the amount you produce) doesn't necessarily indicate the ultimate reward to you. You have to produce something that's either useful to you or can be exchanged for something from someone to whom your production *is* useful.

In the same way, the Gross National Product might be measured by the number of things produced. But the wealth of a nation consists only of those things produced that satisfy the real needs and desires of consumers.

Real wealth consists of (1) what you have that you can use for a purpose enjoyable to you, and (2) what you have that you can exchange for something useful to you. Paper assets are meaningless; use value and exchange value are all-important.

Wealth can also include items that may be wasted eventually, but which you prefer to hold *in case* you decide to use them. In that case, the availability is a value. Wealth *doesn't* include items that are of no value to you and which can't be exchanged for something of value to you.

A *market* exists when you find someone who's willing to make an exchange with you. He wants what you offer more than he wants what you ask in return from him.

The exchange may consist of money in return for your labor, a product or service in exchange for your money, even his friendship in exchange for your friendship. In each of these cases, a market exists—an opportunity to exchange.

No market exists if you have something he doesn't want—or if you ask for more than he's willing to pay.

There are many, many markets in your life. You may be involved in numerous markets every day, as you go about the business of getting what you want from life.

RESOURCES AND DESIRES

Of course, you can imagine an infinite number of things that would make your life more enjoyable. They might include a more pleasant job, a better home, a higher quality of food, more leisure time, more friends, more romance. The possibilities are endless. In fact, you undoubtedly imagine many enjoyable things you have no hope of acquiring in your lifetime. Human desires are limitless.

But why shouldn't you be able to have *everything* you want? Because your resources (time, energy, and wealth) are limited. You have only so much time to live, only so much energy to expend. And while you may hope to increase your wealth in the future, at any given time your wealth is limited. Even if you acquire more in the future, that quantity will never be unlimited.

Because your resources are limited, you must make choices. You choose among the unlimited number of alternatives available to you—deciding how best to utilize your limited resources. You choose because you can have one thing only at the expense of several other things you might want.

So you decide whether there's more ultimate enjoyment (or less unpleasantness) to be had from a job that pays more or one that you enjoy more, from a new car or a new addition to the house, from an afternoon at the park or an afternoon on the couch.

In effect, you assign *values* to each possibility. All such values are relative; they have meaning only in relation to other possibilities. You can never forget that anything you do with your resources will involve foregoing something else. You can't have everything.

It isn't enough, then, to say that you want something. For

you want *many* things. The question must always be, "How *much* do you want it?"

If you answer such a question, "Very much," that tells nothing of the real value of the object to you—especially in comparison to the many other things you might want. But there *is* a way in which we can find out exactly *how much* you want it.

You reveal the value of something to you by how much you're willing to give in order to get it. Will you give $100? Twenty hours of labor? The time and energy required to make it yourself?

The value of what you want is expressed in the price you're willing to pay for it. You have an unlimited number of desires, but you can only satisfy some of them. Only by what you're willing to give up do you express precisely what something is worth to you.

Money provides a convenient means of comparing the prices of many different, apparently unrelated, things. You can translate your resources into money and then compare the many alternative ways of using those limited resources.

UNDERPRICING

Often, an object is available for less than you're willing to pay. And if you can obtain it for a given price, the fact that you'd be willing to pay more is apparently irrelevant and unnoticed.

For example, food is of obvious importance to you. You might be willing to pay $100 for a head of lettuce—if you were starving and you had the $100. As long as that isn't necessary, you won't be pressed to determine just how much you would pay to get a scarce head of lettuce.

But if food prices rise substantially, the higher value of food will come to light. Perhaps you'll eat less expensive foods, maybe even eat less overall, but you'll pay the higher prices to avoid going without something very important to you. You'll forego something else, instead.

For another possibility, suppose the price of food remains the same—but there's suddenly less food available. You might offer someone extra money for the food you want, rather than go without it. The price would go up, but *you* would have initiated the increase.

Food is obviously necessary for survival; so you might pay more for it than you would for almost anything else. But the same principle applies to everything else you might want.

Most of the things you buy are underpriced—in the same way that food is. You wouldn't purchase anything that required more than you're willing to pay. So everything you buy is priced either at the limit you're willing to pay or below that limit.

Underpricing exists because of competition among sellers. Every seller wants as much for his service as he can get. But if it's possible for him to sell profitably at a lower cost, he probably will—because other sellers will. And so the price gravitates downward to the lowest point where it's still profitable to market the item—as long as the product is readily available.

If that point is still higher than a sufficient number of consumers are willing to pay, the product is unmarketable. The seller must lower his price, take his losses, and look for something else to do—or else he should find a good book to read while he sits alone in his unpatronized store.

The market price is generally *lower* than you are willing to pay. And because of that, you have additional resources with which to buy other things—not everything, but many things.

So when shortages (or price increases) occur in some of the underpriced items, it won't necessarily stop you from getting them. You might expend extra time and effort in looking for them; or you might offer money or favors to someone to do the looking for you; or you might offer a seller extra money to put you at the head of the waiting list. You pay extra to avoid going without what you want. Then others, seeing that a higher price is necessary, agree to pay more, too.

Prices go down to their lowest profitable selling point as long as the product is readily available because the sellers compete with each other. Prices go up when a shortage develops because the buyers compete with each other.

Sellers make unusually high profits *only* when they've had the foresight to make available a supply of items that few others have to offer. Then the higher prices produce a higher profit—a reward for having the foresight to make available something that isn't available *at all* elsewhere. They've protected a source of supply for those consumers who want the item most (as expressed by what they're willing to pay).

DETERMINATION

Obstacles placed in your path won't destroy your desire to get what you want. The obstacles may alter the means by which you'll seek to satisfy your self-interest, but no problem, no governmental edict, no unusual marketplace phenomenon will overrule the natural, human desire to get as much as possible of what you want.

It is this self-interest that provides orderliness in the world and the marketplace. Self-interest makes the actions of individuals understandable; it's the unifying factor among the activities of billions of individuals with varying tastes and talents. Self-interest provides a direction and purpose to life and to the world. Without it, the world would seem chaotic, irrational, disorderly.

These principles may seem obvious, but they're vitally important. In fact, it's because governments ignore them that turmoil eventually occurs in the marketplace.

3
The Marketplace

YOU'RE INVOLVED in many, many markets every day—
and so is most everyone else. The total number of daily exchanges
in just your neighborhood probably runs into the thousands. Extend that to the state in which you live and the total is in the
millions.

Throughout the entire nation, there must be literally billions
of daily exchanges—billions of different markets that exist for a
moment or a whole day. We can call this vast totality of markets
the General Market.

The General Market is so big that it's beyond any individual
or agency to be able to keep track of it all. Even if you could
somehow comprehend all the desires and availabilities at this moment, your knowledge would be obsolete immediately. Markets
constantly change. The satisfaction of one desire leads to the
seeking of new things; producers change their activities to production they think more likely to please consumers; and new alternatives become available that change the buying habits of
consumers.

But general trends can be read, analyzed, and responded to.
This is done by observing *prices*. As we've seen, the prices people
pay tell us *how much* they want things.

SHIFTING RESOURCES

If the price of something goes up, it means the demand is now
greater than the supply. This could mean: (1) the item is actually

scarcer than it was before; (2) more people want it than was the case previously; or (3) people want it *more* than they did before (perhaps anticipating a possible shortage in the future).

Whichever the reason, it has become profitable to be a part of the industry that's experiencing the price increase. Human effort will produce a higher reward per hour expended there than before.

As a result, more businessmen will want to market that product. And those already producing it will want to produce greater quantities to take advantage of the higher price. So they gear up production to respond to the demand. They order new machinery that will produce more in less time; they run help-wanted ads to obtain the best available employees, offering them higher wages; they offer more money to suppliers to get deliveries faster—ahead of competition.

To obtain these limited resources, they must compete with every other producer in the marketplace, producers of *all* products and services.

And where will they be most likely to get these resources? Probably from industries that are *losing* consumer demand. For those industries now have less to spend since they're receiving less of the consumers' limited resources.

The declining industries find it difficult to get raw materials and supplies—since they're being outbid by more prosperous industries. To gain the resources, they'll have to pay more. To cover those costs, they may raise their prices—which might make their products unmarketable. They can profitably attract the needed resources only as long as their products are in the forefront of consumer demand.

The pricing mechanism causes workers, businessmen, and other resources to gravitate away from declining industries toward industries in increasing demand. The resources automatically go to the areas that consumers value most. Within each industry, the same mechanism is at work. Those who best satisfy the values of consumers are in greatest demand.

Competition exists between businesses offering similar products, as it does between all who offer anything in the marketplace.

But each business in any industry offers something different from its competitors. There's always a difference in product quality, styling, delivery time, personal service, credit arrangements, convenience of location, and other factors. No two businessmen offer exactly the same thing.

WELL ORGANIZED

The highest rewards will go to those who offer more of what consumers, in general, truly want. And the rewards will come through higher prices or larger sales volume. In either case, the successful businessmen will usually capitalize upon this good fortune by bidding for more resources to expand upon their successes. And they, in turn, bid resources away from their competitors who have been less effective in offering what consumers want most.

The productive resources of the General Market (workers, entrepreneurs, machinery, investment capital, raw materials, supplies, etc.) gravitate constantly toward production of those products and services most valued by consumers.

The General Market, powered by self-interest, is a self-regulating, self-correcting, self-perpetuating mechanism. It distributes limited resources so that they'll produce what consumers want most. No one person or agency could possibly manage the entire General Market, because no one could know all the real desires and needs of everyone else. Nor could he possibly keep up with the constant changes in those desires and needs.

Who knows what's needed most for a nation? Should its limited resources be used for better housing? A higher quality of food? Better automobiles? Less working time? More telephones? More friendships? How can such questions be answered?

Fortunately, the General Market answers such questions every day—automatically allocating the available resources to the needs and desires of the people in the marketplace. It appeals to self-interest by rewarding those who do the most for other people and penalizing those who do the least—including those who waste resources on projects not desired enough by consumers.

Since you can't consume what hasn't been produced, everything desirable that anyone can imagine has a cost in resources—a cost that can be paid only by foregoing something else. Who is the genius who can decide precisely how much people want some things and how much of other things they're willing to go without?

For example, product guarantees cost money; it would be nice if all products were guaranteed for one hundred years, but who would be willing to pay the cost of that? Who can decide just how long each product should be guaranteed, or whether fast delivery or product quality are more important, or how much personal service is worth?

Each individual businessman has to attempt to answer these questions—through his experience with his customers. He isn't infallible, of course. But if he's wrong, *he* will pay for his mistakes in lost business.

If someone says that a given industry "has failed to regulate itself properly," he must mean that the values of the consumers patronizing that industry are different from his own. He'd prefer that the industry provide its customers with less of what *they* want—merely to satisfy *his* values.

If he has perceived somehow that the customers aren't getting what they really want, the businessmen in that industry will go broke soon enough anyway. And there would be a tremendous opportunity for an outsider to enter the industry and give customers more of what they want. He'd earn a spectacular profit for himself because of his superior perception.

But the critic is rarely interested in putting his resources where his opinion is. The only valid judgments in business come from those who are willing to stake their resources on their judgments.

When someone says that consumers don't really know what they want, he really means that *he* doesn't understand what they want. They may not articulate their desires so that he can comprehend, but all he has to do is to view their *actions* as they bid for what they want, and then he'll know.

VARIETY

Another value of the marketplace is its ability to accommodate many differing tastes. Many different products are available to satisfy the same general desire. An individual who wants transportation can choose between new cars, used cars, buses, airplanes, trains, bicycles, etc. And many varieties of each product are available.

If the General Market consists of many millions of people, a taste held by even a small minority can be satisfied (as examples: kosher food, books that sell only ten thousand copies, art films, health foods, Mickey Mouse watches, orange Christmas trees, and opera). And if the General Market consists of the entire world, even greater choice is possible.

Anyone who tries to impose a single choice upon consumers only makes himself vulnerable to competitors who are willing to cater to the many varying desires that exist.

THE FUTURE

Because desires always exceed resources, the marketplace can't provide everything consumers might want.

However, as time passes, it becomes possible for people to satisfy more of their desires. Technological advances enable machines to produce more, so each unit of human energy and human time can produce more than before—and there's more to be consumed.

At any time, there are countless products or services that *could* be produced, things that consumers want, but the present cost of production requires more than consumers are willing to pay. You *could* have your own jet airplane or a butler to carry your cigarettes for you wherever you go or all the caviar and champagne you could ever want. But, needless to say, there are other things you want more. In addition, there are always many new ideas on the drawing board waiting for technology to reduce their costs and make them marketable.

There are only four ways such products can become marketable:

1. A technological breakthrough could lower the production cost of the product. Such was the case when Henry Ford found a way to mass-produce the automobile—a product already on the market but too expensive for most people.

2. Production might improve in *other* areas of the economy, giving those producers more profits to exchange in their roles as consumers. They might decide they can now afford the high price of the product in question. Or their technological advances might reduce *their* prices, leaving consumers more to spend on the high-priced item.

3. Necessity might force a higher value to be placed on the previously unmarketable product. For example, a crime wave might induce consumers to give up other things and pay the high price of a sophisticated burglar alarm system.

4. The government might force those who *don't* want the high-priced product to help pay for its cost. That way those who do want it could get it without having to pay so much. Examples are the government's subsidizing of art, sports, national parks, airlines, etc. Through government subsidy, the product becomes marketable; but the General Market is no better off. For those who want the product get it at the expense of those who don't want it. And the latter must now give up other things to help pay for what they don't want.

In the same way, people can be forced to pay for something they *do* want, but which they don't want as much as they want other things.

At any given time, the General Market is utilizing all the resources available to provide the distribution of the products and services that people want. Redistributing the resources won't *increase* them. Increases in consumption can take place only when technology provides ways to provide more return from each resource or when new resources are found and utilized.

Often a manufacturer will recognize a consumer desire, plan ahead, and invest a large sum of resources in preparation for the day when he can sell his new product only to find, when that day comes, that consumers don't want the product enough to pay the cost. He may hope to sell the product by spending great sums of money on advertising, but the money will be wasted if the advertising doesn't address an actual desire of a great many consumers.

In the process of discovering what consumers want, many plans and ventures fail. Fortunately, however, such failures are localized. Only a small portion of a nation's resources are lost through such experimentation—so long as no one individual in the marketplace has the power to commit resources other than his own.

THE NATURAL GOVERNMENT

This amazing mechanism called the General Market is the reason why each of us lives at a level far above mere subsistence. It provides a more efficient and fairer allocation of resources than any contrived institution could hope to accomplish.

It rewards those who give others what they want. And it penalizes those who try to get more for themselves than their services warrant. It discourages unrealistic uses of precious resources. It automatically adjusts to new possibilities, new alternatives, and new tastes and values.

It is what E. C. Riegel has called "the natural government of man."[1] It governs the affairs of men in precisely the way that most people hope for from man-made governments.

The General Market is the only democratic government pos-

[1] Riegel: *The New Approach to Freedom*, listed in the Recommended Reading.

sible, for it permits each person to decide for himself how he'll use his limited resources. And it allows people of different tastes, different resources, and different philosophies to live side by side. It doesn't require everyone to conform to one way.

Fortunately, this wondrous government doesn't have to be created; no constitution has to be written. The General Market *already* exists; it has *always* existed. It's merely hidden from view by the interventions of man-made governments.

The General Market's mechanisms are always operating—even when governments like to believe they've overruled it. For guns and bombs and red tape and regulations can only obstruct a consumer's quest for what he wants; they can never destroy his insatiable desire to improve his life and enjoy greater mental well-being.

The self-interest of each human being, his continual search for whatever he wants, is a natural law. Governments can make it difficult for him, but their roadblocks only cause him to seek other avenues in order to get what he wants.

As a result, the General Market will always triumph eventually whenever there's a conflict between consumer desires and government interference. And it's vitally important to understand this. For it's the reassertion of the market's sovereignty as the ruler of the world that's causing today's economic upheavals.

If you don't know what the market is and how it operates, you can't possibly understand what's happening today—nor could you hope to comprehend what lies ahead.

If more people understood the processes of the marketplace, it's just possible that there wouldn't be any depressions, lingering unemployment, "balance of payments" problems, food shortages, and the like.

And now we've reached the point where we must see why these things *do* happen.

4

The Government Intervenes

TODAY'S ECONOMIC PROBLEMS and monetary crises reflect the conflict between the marketplace (consumers and producers) and the governments who are trying to overrule the market. Very few people who analyze the international crises understand that. And so they attempt to explain events by referring to superficial trends and statistical studies.

As our study of the marketplace continues, it will become obvious why so many interpretations of the monetary crises miss the point.

INTERVENTION

The General Market allocates the available resources in ways that satisfy the most urgent demands of consumers.

But many people aren't satisfied with that. They want the advances of the future to be available *right now*—overlooking the fact that something will have to be foregone in order to accommodate their wishes.

The impatient individuals may want more for themselves than they've been able to earn in the marketplace. Or they may be concerned about those they feel don't have enough.

Whatever their motives, they must overrule the marketplace to achieve their objectives. As we saw in the previous chapter, there are only four possible ways a futuristic desire can become practical. Three of the ways involve increased technology or greater demand. But those who seek something for nothing can't be bothered with technology or attempts to reeducate consumers.

So they choose the fourth way—which involves asking the government to overrule the General Market. And since there's never any shortage of people asking, the government inevitably intervenes in the processes of the market.[1]

The idea that governments are responsible for the "general welfare" has become solidly implanted through hundreds of years of recorded history. By popular demand, the government poses as judge of the public welfare; it looks for injustices, imbalances, and unfulfilled needs in the marketplace and then sets about to correct them.

TYPES OF INTERVENTION

The forms of governmental intervention are limitless; but here are a few of the principal ways the government attempts to overrule the marketplace:

1. It tries to fulfill desires that haven't been fulfilled in the marketplace—overlooking the fact that other desires have been more urgent. It selects what *it* considers to be the most urgent needs and then forcibly allocates resources to satisfy those needs.

If the need is for "decent" housing, for example, it subsidizes the housing industry, guarantees repayment of loans at lower-than-market interest rates, and/or intervenes to prevent foreclosures when payments aren't made. It obtains the funds for these projects by coercively taking resources from people who wanted to use them for things they valued more.

2. In the name of "free enterprise," the government promises "fair competition" by penalizing those whose product quality and/or service so exceed that of its competition that it gains a

---

[1] From here on, the word "government" doesn't refer to Riegel's "natural government," but to the man-made central agencies of coercion usually referred by that name.

substantial share of the market for that product. When the government intervenes, the gainers are the company's competitors, who weren't able to acquire the business honestly in the unhampered marketplace. The losers are the company itself and all its customers who must now make do with poorer quality, lesser service, and/or higher prices.

3. Contrary to its commitment to "fair competition," the government grants monopoly powers to electricity and natural gas suppliers, taxicab companies, telephone companies, and other forms of business. Having excluded their competitors by force, the government feels it necessary to set "fair prices" for those so favored. Such prices, being man-made, can't possibly reflect accurately how much consumers want the services, the infinite varieties of services offered, or the constantly changing nature of the desires involved. And the fixed prices discourage the technological advances that would lower prices.

4. The government declares that everyone must be employed at a "decent" wage. To make this possible, it (a) subsidizes industries in hopes they'll employ more people; (b) enacts minimum-wage laws that make it impossible to employ less-productive people; and (c) uses its coercion to enable labor-union members to walk off their jobs without being fired.

5. To assure "full employment," the government prevents foreign products from competing with local ones. That, of course, denies the consumer access to all possible alternatives. Further, it encourages workers to remain in industries where they're not really needed when they could be working in other fields, extending the range of products available.

6. If the General Market determines that a desired service is economically impractical at this time, the government may go into the business of producing it. For example, the United States government builds electric power plants, operates printing plants, parks, insurance companies, and banking services, and in virtually hundreds of other ways is in marketplace businesses. It operates these enterprises at a loss, selling the services to consumers at artificially low prices, and makes up the differences with taxes taken away from people.

7. The government establishes minimum and maximum prices and other rules governing exchanges between individuals and companies. It attempts to dispense with the natural prices determined by the extent of consumer demand and the suppliers' abilities to produce.

In these and other ways, the government interferes with the General Market. The interventions are justified in the name of the "public interest." But who can really define the "public interest"?

There's only one way to know. The public expresses its interest through the General Market—and the market allocates the available resources accordingly. Anything the government does to change that must necessarily *reduce* the public welfare, not increase it.

HARM TO THE MARKET

The government subsidizes many industries—railroads, airlines, aerospace, the arts, universities, and housing to name just a few. When it subsidizes these industries, it hurts the public interest in two important ways.

The first way is obvious. The subsidies are paid with tax money. The taxpayers (consumers) have less money with which to buy the things they want more.

The second way is more subtle—but far more harmful to the economy. It involves the distortion of prices.

We've seen that the pricing mechanism is like a magnetic force—causing businessmen, workers, and materials to gravitate toward the industries in greater consumer favor. This mechanism makes it possible for resources to be spent as consumers want them to be spent.

When an industry is subsidized, the superficial appearance is similar to increased consumer demand. The industry now has increased strength with which to bid resources away from other industries. Workers are hired from other projects; raw materials are used; machinery is created specifically for that industry. Re-sources gravitate toward the subsidized industry. In other words, the resources are gravitating *away* from the areas of consumer favor toward projects already rejected by the marketplace.

Government regulation causes similar problems. By holding prices up in a given industry (supposedly to prevent "unfair competition"), the government encourages unneeded competitors to remain in that industry. Investments in resources are large—investments that consumers aren't willing to pay for.

GOODIES AND COSTS

In many ways, the government's promise to increase the general welfare always results in decreased welfare. There's no way the government can create something out of nothing any more than an individual can. There are only so many resources available at any given time; the government can't increase them by legislation.

The government's actions increase the wealth of *some* people at the expense of others. By using the government's coercion to force others to support them, some can thereby achieve prosperity they wouldn't achieve in the marketplace. And that, of course, can't be labeled "general welfare."

Of course, the government's activities are so extensive that virtually everyone receives *some* subsidies from the government. And those freebies may make him feel he's benefiting from the arrangement.

But the great majority of people, even those receiving subsidies, pay far more in taxes than they receive in subsidies. The difference pays for the huge, expensive machinery of government. If the consumers could have their taxes back, they could easily purchase any desired service the government had provided—and have a great deal of money left over with which to buy other things.

In addition, they lose more than they'll ever know when the

government prevents them from utilizing attractive alternatives the marketplace could have offered—lower prices, non-monopoly choices, foreign products, etc.

Every dollar spent by the government lowers by at least one dollar the general standard of living of the people in the market where the government operates. That dollar is now unavailable to satisfy a true consumer demand.

LONG-TERM INJURIES

If that were the only problem, it would be bad enough—but it wouldn't be disastrous. It's the government's effect upon investments and productive energy that cause the catastrophes we call depressions.

In an unhampered market, investments and productivity are naturally drawn to the projects that best serve consumers. When the government intervenes, investments of time, energy, and money are diverted to areas other than those that best satisfy consumers' wishes.

But consumers won't be denied that easily. They continue to seek what they want. And producers continually look for ways to exchange with them—with or without government intervention.

This natural law of self-interest creates a moving force that works against the government's programs. And so the programs never achieve their stated objectives.

When rents are controlled in price, housing shortages develop. When new industries have been "stimulated," they fall apart after the subsidies stop. These reactions are simply the marketplace fighting to continue down the path of consumer self-interest. Everything the government does is aimed *against* the market and the self-interest of consumers—whether or not so intended.

The government's actions bend the market out of shape. And the market seeks inexorably to bend itself back into shape.

The two great powers are like the irresistible force and the immovable object. But when they clash, something must give. And eventually something does.[2]

[2] A more detailed analysis of government is given in my book, *How I Found Freedom in an Unfree World*.

5

The Market Responds

LAWS DON'T SOLVE ECONOMIC PROBLEMS; they only alter the ways in which the problems are manifested.

Governments can coercively regulate exchange between individuals, create new industries, and put industries out of business. But no government can regulate the minds of consumers. Governments can obstruct self-interest—but never repeal it.

The General Market, the sum total of the interests of consumers, is impersonal. Consumers (in the aggregate) don't buy to support businesses; they buy in order to satisfy their most urgent needs.

The market rewards those who produce what consumers want and punishes those who invest in, and produce, the wrong things.

At the time of a purchase, a consumer doesn't care whether a product has been subsidized or regulated. He merely evaluates the prices of the various alternatives and buys in a way he believes will maximize his self-interest.

So if a price is high because the government is trying to prevent "unfair competition," that won't make the consumer want the product more. Or if an industry has recently lost its subsidy and must raise its prices, the consumer won't sympathize and go without something else to pay the higher price. So government stimulants can aid an industry only temporarily. If a company survives artificially through subsidies, it's highly probable that it will fail when the subsidies end. And this failure is much different from a simple mistaken investment. For the subsidy has had far-reaching effects.

Suppliers have geared up to the demands of the subsidized industry. They've rejected other work in favor of the high prices paid by the subsidized company. Workers have invested time in training for that industry. Machinery has been created for the purpose of producing goods at a faster rate than consumers would have asked for at true market prices.

All these investments will be affected by the fall of the subsidized company.

If only one company, or one small industry, has been subsidized, its failure will cause a localized recession. There will be layoffs, suppliers going out of business, machinery liquidated, and a sag in local retail business.

NEW PROSPERITY

But the problems don't have to last forever. The people affected will look for new opportunities. And when they find them, they'll be engaged in productive activities realistically geared to the market.

In effect, the recession is a cleanser. It washes out misguided projects and frees the individuals involved for more productive work.

If the government's subsidies are confined to one small industry, there's probably no reason for the subsidy to end. The government could afford to keep that industry going indefinitely —preventing the ultimate market reaction or recession.

But such is never the case. If one industry is benefited, others will clamor for equal treatment. Any industry can create a superficially imposing brief to demonstrate that it's necessary for the "general welfare." Once the concept that governments must promote the general welfare is accepted, there's no end to the areas that will be proposed for attention.

It's important to realize, however, that all governments' resources are limited, just as everyone else's are. They can only tax so much. Although they've discovered some pretty ingenious ways of increasing revenues, they can't confiscate more resources than those that exist. Even a total communist state can't keep a whole economy of losing businesses going indefinitely.

Most likely, the government will engage in a juggling act—trying to keep as many activities going as it can, but constantly shifting them in an attempt to please everyone.

If one government subsidy comes to an end, the result is a localized recession. If the intervention is more widespread, the principles at work are the same—and the result is a larger recession.

Whenever the government lets up for a moment, the market quickly reasserts itself. It seeks to bend itself back into shape. There are strong pressures to begin the cleansing process—to liquidate the unsound investments, to encourage workers to retrain for more valuable jobs, to pull resources toward the activities that will satisfy real consumer demand.

A recession is nothing more than the General Market working itself into proper shape in preparation for a period of greater prosperity.

During government intervention, consumers are forced to accept less than present technology could provide for them. The recession is an attempt to end that period and reallocate the resources to more valuable uses.

RENEWED INTERVENTION

But, of course, the government won't give up easily. It taxes more heavily in order to continue the subsidies. And since the subsidies are supporting inefficient uses of resources, it's not likely that the managers of those industries will be terribly prudent with the money. After all, they believe they've been guaranteed against failure. So it usually requires larger and larger subsidies to keep the unsound enterprises going.

Whenever a recession appears likely, the government pumps

more money into ailing industries—thus delaying the inevitable cleansing. If the government were willing to stop and accept the inevitable consequences, the cleansing process would be fairly short-lived, with a minimum of discomfort to most people.

The biggest losers would be businessmen who have invested too much in unmarketable projects. And many workers would have to accept the need to retrain for more productive jobs.

The biggest readjustment problem in an unhampered market is getting businessmen and workers relocated to areas where they're in actual demand. And today, mobility and communications are so advanced that anyone, anywhere in the country, could be made aware of the needs of others.

The process of readjustment could be brief—if no one tries to direct it and if the General Market is left alone to reallocate resources.

No matter how little money is in circulation, no matter how many losses have occurred, the principles of human action are still the same: desires far outrun resources, everyone has unsatisfied needs, there are markets for many things, and people can exchange on some basis.

Unfortunately, no government will let the market alone. When threatened by recession it responds eagerly to demands that it alleviate unemployment (which need be only *changing* employment) and end business failures.

The cleansing process is delayed by further government intervention. It tries to perpetuate the losing enterprises and activities. But it costs more and more as the cycle progresses.

And so the conflict continues between the government (attempting to rule the marketplace) and the General Market (trying to reassert itself to satisfy consumer desires).

Since the government is fighting a losing battle, it needs to raise more and more resources to keep up the fight. And it can tax only so much. Perhaps it can point to high employment and prosperity in key industries that are used for statistical indexes. But even this justification isn't enough to permit it to tax to extremes. So it must find a more subtle way of taxing—to be able to continue to point to its "triumphs" without the costs being so obvious.

And such a way is available. It's called *inflation*.

That brings us to the question of what money is.

6
Money

FOR MANY YEARS, the cry was heard around the world, "The U.S. dollar is as good as gold." Now opinions are changing rapidly and many people are turning to other currencies they feel are more useful as money. But much of the discussion of currencies overlooks the basic meaning and function of money; so it's important to review here what money is, and then we can see how it may be distorted. Later, we can determine where one can still find real money.

An understanding of money must begin by repeating the self-evident principle that you only produce or exchange if you believe it will lead ultimately to something you want. The word "ultimately" is important, because there may be several intermediate steps between your production and the eventual enjoyment of whatever you've been working for.

It's impractical to barter your services or your wealth directly for the things you want; so you almost always use an intermediary medium of exchange—what is generally called *money*. Money is a commodity that you accept in exchange but which you intend to eventually trade again for something else.

You'll accept something as money only if you have confidence in its future value. You won't exchange the products of your efforts for something that may soon be valueless. You don't work merely to pass time; you work in order to obtain values you can trade for the things you want.

Thousands of years and countless individual exchanges have led to *gold* being considered the safest medium of exchange. It

41

isn't valued because of an "irrational attachment to a yellow metal," or because of government edict.

Gold is valued because it's durable, easily divisible, compact in weight, convenient to handle, consistent in quality, and because it is highly valued apart from its use as money. Gold has unique qualities that make it valuable for jewelry, dental work, durable art objects, machine tools, and in many other areas where its qualities are irreplaceable.

If gold suddenly became unfashionable as money, you could still exchange it for something of value with anyone who needed it for its productive or enjoyment values.

Its scarcity is also important. Despite the high value placed on it, less than 100,000 tons of it are known to have been produced in all of history.

So gold is money. For thousands of years, individuals have eagerly accepted it in exchange for their services—because they knew it could always buy something of value for them.

Gold dust, chips, and bars aren't very convenient, however, for the millions of small exchanges that take place daily. Gold's value is always measured by the ounce or the gram; and so the gold would have to be weighed prior to every transaction.

Out of necessity, gold coins came into circulation. Each coin contained a given weight of gold that was clearly indicated on the coin. The receiver of the coin could count on that gold content if he trusted the agency that minted the coin.

But gold coins also have drawbacks for small exchanges. Even the smallest coins have more gold than is appropriate for many daily exchanges. So *money substitutes* were introduced. A money substitute is a paper receipt for gold that's in storage in a warehouse. Since the paper receipt's value comes from the metal it represents, the receipt can retain its value only if the gold *is* in storage and can be obtained at any time by turning in the receipt.

Money substitutes, money receipts, paper money, and currencies are all names for the same thing—paper receipts that are used as a medium of exchange in place of gold (or any other commodity respected as money).

GOVERNMENT MONEY

Most governments have made the use of gold as money a legal matter. But it's important to realize that money systems are *not* invented; they *evolve*. No government has decreed that gold should be valuable as money. Governments have only accepted what has already been determined by the General Market.

When governments issue gold-backed currencies, they do so because they know that's the only way their currencies will be accepted and have value in the marketplace.

Whenever governments have tried to dethrone gold, their currencies have eventually collapsed. They can legislate legal-tender laws, they can issue all sorts of coercive commands to make their paper, gold-less currencies valuable—but *they can't make people produce or exchange in ways those people know won't lead to something of value.*[1]

---

[1] Fuller explanations of gold, paper money, and inflation are given in *How You Can Profit from the Coming Devaluation,* listed in the Recommended Reading.

7

Inflation

WHEN GOVERNMENTS OPERATE the gold warehouses, they invariably issue more paper money than is warranted by the gold in storage.

We saw in Chapter 5 that the government might face resistance if it tried to tax the people directly for every expenditure it wants to make. If the citizens knew that 30–50% of their productive efforts were being expropriated by the government, public hostility might be enough to cause changes.

So the government favors so-called "hidden taxes" (import duties, corporation taxes, license fees, etc.) because consumers aren't aware, in most cases, that they're paying them. But the government's ultimate weapon is an invisible way of extracting resources from the General Market; it's called *inflation*.

Inflation is the issuance of paper currency for which there's no gold (or other commodity) in storage. Since currencies are originally intended to be receipts for actual gold, inflation is nothing more than the counterfeiting of paper money.

WHY INFLATION?

If you want to acquire $50,000, there are three basic methods by which you can obtain it:

1. You can find people who will pay you that much in ex-

44

change for your services (productive effort, the use of your money, etc.).

2. You can find a gun and use it to rob people.

3. You can find a printing press and print the currency.

For the government, method 1 is out, of course. The government's only purpose in the market is coercion. It isn't created to make exchanges with individuals on a voluntary basis. People appeal to the government only when voluntary methods have failed—when they want someone to be forced to do something.

Method 2 is, of course, the basic revenue-raising activity of the government. Although the tax collector doesn't appear at your door with a gun in his hand, his effectiveness stems from the people behind him with guns and jails.

A company such as General Motors doesn't *tax* you; it offers a product which you can choose to buy or not. But the only alternatives to paying taxes are going to jail or having your property confiscated.[1]

The government can also borrow the money it wants. If it refuses to repay it, it's using method 2 again—this time against the lenders. If it *does* repay the money, it must resort to method 2 to raise the funds from the taxpayers.

In addition, if the money is borrowed, it will lower by an equal amount the money available to be used in private investment. The money is clearly removed from productive use, so a more invisible method is required.

The government resorts to method 3 to augment its tax revenues. In effect, it prints more paper money receipts than it has gold in storage to back them. This is inflation.

In modern times, the government doesn't inflate by using the printing press in such an obvious way. Instead, it sells its bonds to the central bank (the Federal Reserve System in the United States) which creates a fictitious checking account deposit in payment. The government then writes checks as if they were backed by real money. The effect is exactly the same as if paper currency had been printed. In the same way, banks contribute

---

[1] There are many ways to *evade* taxes, of course; but the basic principle remains the same.

to the inflation by lending out the funds in checking accounts (demand deposits), even though the depositor may also be writing checks on those same funds.

PRICES GO UP

When the government spends that new paper money, it creates artificial demands for whatever resources it purchases. It bids up the prices of those resources—just as an increase in true market demand would bid up the prices of highly valued items.

Without inflation, these price increases would have to be accompanied by decreases in price for other things. But *with* inflation, there's still as much paper money available to bid for other resources. So the price of one item can go up without any other prices going down.

As a result, the *general price level* (an average of all prices) will go up. Everything will cost more than it would have without the inflation.

Inflation makes it easier for the government to carry out its programs. No immediately visible reactions take place in other industries—since prices don't fall there. Taxes don't go up, so it's as if the government program hasn't cost anyone anything.

HOW INFLATION TAXES

But of course it *must* cost someone something. Someone has to pay for whatever the government does. How is the cost paid?

It's easier to see the answer if you remember that at any given time there are only a limited number of resources available. We can't consume more than those resources (raw materials, machinery, knowledge, and human effort) can produce.

The government's inflation can't add to the resources available; it can only rearrange them. But a consumer with more paper money in his pocket can believe that more resources are now available to *him*. So he will increase his purchases, bidding against other consumers in the process.

The other consumers will want to continue their normal purchases, and so they'll bid back—if they, too, have added paper money. If their money supplies haven't been increased, they'll have to go without something they've been able to buy before.

In either case, prices will go up. In the end, the prices of everything will be bid up to a point commensurate with the new total of paper money in circulation. There will be higher prices, but no greater quantity of goods to consume.

However, the process will serve to *rearrange* the resources. Production projects aided by government funds will obtain resources formerly used by other producers. And the owners and employees of the government-aided projects will get to spend their new paper money *before* inflation has pushed prices up very far. So they'll obtain consumption items that will eventually be too expensive for those who used to purchase them normally.

LOSERS AND WINNERS

If wealth could be measured in paper dollars, no one would lose from inflation. Some people would have more paper dollars than before, while others would have at least as much as they had before.

But paper dollars aren't wealth. Wealth is what you have that you can enjoy and/or what you have that you can exchange for something you'd enjoy. If prices go up, the paper dollars you hold will purchase less for you than they would have before.

So there will be losers—many of them. Anyone holding paper dollars, at home or in the bank, will lose purchasing power as the inflation proceeds. Anyone who has been promised a given number of dollars in the future (through loans, annuities, pensions, etc.) will lose. Anyone in an industry that has lost valuable resources to subsidized industries will lose. And any employee who receives the new paper money *after* prices have gone up will lose.

And as mentioned before, all consumers lose to the extent that the products they want can't be produced as easily since resources have been diverted—resulting in shortages and/or higher *real* prices.

In this way, the government programs are paid for. The government has extracted the resources from the economy and diverted them to its own use, but through a method so invisible that few people realize that the government has financed its programs at their expense.

The gains and losses can't be measured statistically because there's no way one can account for all the costs and gains in the marketplace. Neither can you measure the value of *all* the products and services available. Such things as reciprocal favors with friends, mowing your own lawn, do-it-yourself projects, etc. are just as productive as the manufacture of an automobile. In fact, they can be of *more real value* to the consumer than many of the more noticeable kinds of productive activity.

The government, however, conveniently creates a Consumer Price Index, based upon *some* of the prices in the marketplace. And it gathers statistics that total a Gross National Product. Since it can't possibly compute all the value produced, it uses certain key industries (including many of the ones it subsidizes, needless to say) and guesses the rest.

Not surprisingly, considering the data used, the government can compare the Consumer Price Index with the Gross National Product and say, in effect, "Yes prices *are* going up; but in terms of 'real dollars,' the Gross National Product is larger than ever"— meaning that we all have more than we would have had without inflation.

Perhaps this is why even the critics of inflation are compelled to say that inflation's harm comes only in the long term. They concede the current prosperity but claim that the costs of inflation will be too great in the long run.

But there's no way inflation can increase the general living standards of the nation—even in the short term. How can printing-press money increase the resources available?

It can't. It can only redistribute the resources to the areas that the government and economists measure prosperity by. They don't see the incalculable costs being incurred in the present by those who must go without what they could have had without inflation.

You can't judge the value of inflation by comparing today's standards of living with those of thirty years ago. Inflation existed then, too. Since inflation has been a way of life in the U.S. for two centuries, you can only compare the possibilities on a theoretical basis. If inflation is used to divert resources away from the production of items valued most by consumers, the result *has* to be that the consuming public winds up with less.

Increases in living standards *have* occurred during the inflationary period, of course. But that's only because technology constantly advances. Our progress to date is the result of modern technological knowledge *less* governmental interference. Without the government's intervention, we would have much more to enjoy. For one obvious example, research might be devoted to lowering food production costs instead of placing a man on the moon.

If you believe that space projects cost nothing in resources, no argument will be valid to you. But if you understand the simple reality that space programs use scientists and construction people and machinery and fuel and raw materials, perhaps it will be obvious that those same resources could have been devoted to increasing actual living standards.

We can only imagine what our living standards would be today if the government had stayed out of the economy. The more I think about it, the more awed I am by the tremendous advances that might have taken place—if the market were free to respond to real consumer demands.

PLACING THE BLAME

Inflation causes both visible and invisible problems. The most visible one is the constantly increasing price level.

In fact, an "increase in the general price level" is the common definition of inflation. But in every economy in the modern world, artificial expansion of the money supply is the primary cause of rising price levels. Other causes that occasionally occur have no long-term economic significance. So it's much more to the point to define inflation as an increase in the paper money supply that isn't backed by gold in storage. And that, in turn, causes price levels to rise.

But an increasing price level is no concern of the government—at least not for a while. For price increases can be blamed easily enough on businessmen who are said to be taking advantage of the public.

Perhaps some people will get the idea that businessmen are only passing on the increased costs caused by labor unions. But even with all their government-backed coercive powers, labor unions can't charge more than the market will bear. When a wage increase exceeds both increased production and increased inflation, the employer will be priced out of the market when he tries to pass the costs onto his customers.

Price increases are stimulated ultimately by consumers. And if they hold additional paper money in their hands, they'll inevitably bid up the prices of products, which in turn will permit the wage increases.

Some politicians and economists, seeing the relationship between demand and price, have suggested that consumers stop inflation by buying less. How ridiculous! If that *would* have an effect, prices would be lower only until consumers resumed their spending habits.

But it won't work even for a day. For what will be done with the unspent money? Largely, it will go into savings and investments which in turn will be used for (1) loans enabling *other* consumers to spend the money, or (2) investments that will bid up the prices of workers and other resources. Money is never inactive for long; someone will always be using it to bid up prices somewhere.

The cause of the constantly increasing price level is the government's issuance of paper money backed by nothing. Attempts to divert the blame to businessmen, labor unions, or consumers won't solve the problem.

Eventually, the rising price levels do become a government problem. For you can expect that, sooner or later, the "public" will demand that the government "do something" about inflation. Since wage and price controls are the only solution consistent with placing the blame on businessmen and labor unions, nothing practical happens. But the public pressure puts the government in the uneasy position of having to concoct a panacea that won't actually interfere with its inflation.

THE CONFLICT CONTINUES

Inflation is another battleground in the war between the government and the marketplace. To see how this war is fought, let's follow the paper money through the economy.

The increases in the money supply are fed into the economy largely through government spending programs. This provides increased purchasing power for the workers in the favored industries. In terms of wages paid for actual productive effort, the government and government contractors are traditionally high-paying employers. Companies in these industries constantly increase wages to attract new workers.

These employees have more paper money to spend than they would have had without the inflation. They buy products and services they couldn't have afforded otherwise. This generates increased demand (and higher prices) in the areas they favor.

This temporary stimulant in those areas draws resources away from production in other areas. But the market will attempt to return ultimately to an allocation of resources more in keeping with the total desires of the marketplace.

This happens even while the subsidy programs are still operative. For the subsidized worker falls victim to inflation, too. He expands his purchasing power only until the new paper money has gone through the economy and forced *all* prices up. That makes his "high" wages less valuable than they were originally. He then must cut back some purchases from his new routine, lessening the demand for some of the products that had recently enjoyed a boom period.

His purchases had been bidding resources away from products formerly in consumer demand. So, meanwhile, other people have been going without some of their favored products—because the inflation has made them too expensive. But as the paper money flows through the economy, it will eventually increase *their* wages, too. Then they can put new demands upon their favorite products, drawing resources back in their direction again.

This shifting of resources to their more natural position is precisely what the government was trying to overrule in the first place. So it will increase its expenditures, increase the inflation, and draw the resources back to *its* favored areas again.

This creates a chaotic situation. In an unobstructed market, there would be conflicts of demands, but the resources would gravitate toward the predominant demands. With government intervention, however, there's a constant pulling back and forth of the resources as one group and then the other predominates. The results are confusion and chaos.

A boom-and-bust pattern is always most pronounced in government-connected industries. There, millions of workers will make large amounts of money while the government contract is operative. But then they face unemployment when their otherwise-unmarketable services are no longer needed. Their security would be much greater if they had to respond only to the understandable and somewhat consistent demands of consumers, rather than be subject to the whims of politicians spending money they haven't earned.

THE ENLARGED CONFLICT

If governments couldn't inflate the currency, they would still cause economic problems. But the principles of governmental intervention discussed in Chapter 4 would result only in relatively minor recessions. The government wouldn't have the resources to intervene on a large scale because public hostility would minimize taxes.

With inflation, however, the government is free to enter the economy on a much broader scale. Thus it makes possible gigantic mistakes in investment and purchasing patterns. So when the market moves to reassert its natural state, the changes are enormous. And the result is more than a small recession; it becomes what we think of as a full-blown depression.

Since the government relies so heavily upon inflation, observing the amount of inflation is a short-cut method to determine how large the problems have become. And inflation has reached critical levels today.

In 1928, the paper money supply in the United States was backed 11% by gold—meaning there were approximately nine times as many paper money receipts in circulation as there was gold in storage to cover them.

As recently as 1957, the paper money supply was backed 16% by gold. But since then the government has repealed all legislation requiring minimum gold reserves. At the end of 1972, the gold backing for the currency was only 3%. There were 1,121 paper dollars in circulation for every ounce of gold in storage—while the government maintains that each dollar is equal to $\frac{1}{42}$ ounce of gold (official gold price = $42.22 per ounce).[2]

Obviously, the extent of the inflation and governmental intervention is enormous. The General Market has been grossly deformed thereby. But it will always work to twist itself back into

[2] Gold and silver are always measured in troy ounces, and so all references to *ounces* in this book mean *troy ounces*.

shape. And it will take an enormous number of changes for the market to reach a natural state that can be the foundation for a realistic prosperity.

MONEY

Paper isn't money. As far as I know, no civilization has ever used the commodity *paper* as money. But many governments have issued paper money receipts for gold, then withdrawn the gold out from under the paper, leaving the paper with no inherent value.

In all such cases I've been able to discover, either the paper currency became totally worthless or gold was reintroduced eventually to back it—but not before there were very bad consequences.

Paper isn't money. As a substitute, U.S. paper money was once "as good as gold." But when you can no longer exchange it for gold, you can't expect it to retain its value.

It may continue to be accepted in exchange years after the gold backing has been removed, because a sufficient momentum has been established. But it's only a matter of time until people start fleeing from the currency—trading it for gold, silver, or stronger currencies.

And when that flight begins, you can be sure that the weak currency is in its terminal stage.

8
Falling Currencies

INFLATION HAS MANY SIDE EFFECTS, one of which is its effect upon international trade.

The consumers in the U.S. market rely heavily upon products produced in other nations. They couldn't have very high living standards if they could choose only among materials and manufactured products from within the United States.

This can be seen more easily if you imagine a family of six people who refused to exchange with anyone outside the family. How well could they live if they relied upon only those resources extracted from their own property?

In the same way, international trade is necessary to expand the alternatives available to consumers in each country. And because currencies are the normal medium of exchange, internationally as well as domestically, the debasement of a nation's currency can profoundly affect the ability of its consumers to take advantage of foreign products.

INTERNATIONAL EXCHANGE

In daily trade, Americans think in terms of *dollars;* Englishmen think in terms of *pounds;* Mexicans think in terms of *pesos.* Each of these people knows approximately how much he can buy with his own currency, so he translates every purchasing medium or opportunity to trade into units of his own currency.

As a result, there are foreign exchange markets that exist to exchange one currency for another. Each currency has a price in terms of all other currencies. With one dollar you can buy a given number of German marks or Italian lira, for example.

How are the various currency prices established? In the same way that all prices are established—by comparison of supply and demand.

Currencies usually begin as paper substitutes for gold (or silver). For example, currency A might be issued at an official rate of six units for every ounce of gold in storage. If currency B is issued as three units for each ounce of gold in storage, the two currencies can be compared—since each is a substitute for the same thing, gold.

In that case, each currency A unit would be worth ⅙ of an ounce of gold, and each currency B unit would be twice as valuable per unit as currency A. So two units of A would be equal in value to one unit of B.

Since all governments inflate their currencies, the actual gold values of the currencies are constantly changing. The more inflated currencies will be dropping in gold value compared to the less inflated currencies.

This creates problems for importers and exporters who must buy and sell in foreign currencies that are constantly changing. It also displays the flaws of the weaker currencies rather openly. So it's not surprising that the major governments of the Western world met at the end of World War II to create a method of preventing currencies from changing in value—a method called "fixed exchange rates." [1]

Although inflation has devoured all the countries involved in the agreement, some currencies have inflated more than others. And the United States will serve as an example of the international effects of inflation.

If it weren't for fixed exchange rates, the price of the dollar versus stronger currencies would have gone down some time ago. In that case, foreign companies would have had no special advantages in the American market. Higher U.S. prices would seem

[1] I'll explain the method in Chapter 15.

to be an inducement for foreigners to sell here. But when the large quantities of dollars they received were exchanged for their own currencies, the prices would no longer seem high because it would take more dollars to purchase each unit of their own currencies.

But *with* fixed exchange rates, another picture emerges. As prices go up in the United States, it's an opportunity for foreign companies to sell at lower prices than their U.S. competitors. For they can exchange the dollars for their own currencies at the same rate that prevailed before the latest U.S. inflation began. It's a typical example of a windfall profit created by governmental intervention.

However, it initiates a chain of consequences that comes back to the government doing the inflating. The foreign company exchanges the dollars for its own currency. The dollars make their way through foreign exchange dealers and banks until they arrive at the central bank of the foreign country. The central bank is a government-created bank that supervises the commercial banks of the country and issues the nation's currency.

The foreign central bank presents the dollars to the U.S. Treasury in exchange for any of its currency held here. If the United States has had more inflation than the other country, the exchange of currencies will probably leave an excess of dollars in the hands of the foreign central bank.

The central bank then presents those dollars to the U.S. Treasury for gold at the official gold redemption rate established by the U.S. Treasury (until 1971, 35 dollars per ounce of gold).

This creates serious problems for the U.S. Treasury. It has, of course, issued far more than 35 dollars for each ounce of gold it possesses. It's true that only a portion of the dollars find their way to foreign central banks to be presented for gold, but that doesn't solve the problem.

For example, suppose the U.S. government had 1,000 ounces of gold. That would warrant issuing 35,000 dollars. But suppose also that it has actually issued 350,000 dollars. If only 70,000 of those dollars have gone overseas, it's a large problem. For if only half the foreigners holding dollars asked for gold, the

35,000 dollars presented would use up the entire gold reserve.

In 1933, the U.S. government tried to alleviate the problem by refusing gold to all U.S. citizens, continuing to redeem gold to foreign central banks. By the late 1960s, its gold stock had dwindled to the point where it couldn't begin to honor all the claims in the hands of foreigners.

This is the famous "balance of payments" problem—a problem that wouldn't exist without inflation. For if the government issued only the currency for which there was gold backing, it could redeem every unit of currency that was turned in for gold.

But because the government *has* inflated the dollar it has to try to keep dollars from going overseas. It may impose controls on the exporting of dollars; it may brand those who spend money overseas as "unpatriotic." But, sooner or later, it has to face the problem as it is.

And then it devalues its currency. A devaluation is the government's way of going into bankruptcy. It has issued money receipts on the basis that 35 receipts are worth one ounce of gold. But then it changes the rules in midstream and says that it will take 38 receipts to claim one ounce of gold—or 42 receipts. This devaluation creates a new fixed exchange rate with other currencies, and the game begins all over again.

Some governments devalue continually. But their currencies have poor reputations throughout the world; anyone receiving such currency immediately discounts the value of it—knowing a devaluation can't be far away. To avoid that fate, other governments resist devaluing as long as possible.

But once a government is in trouble from its inflation, it must either devalue or *deflate* the currency. Deflation means that the government withdraws the excess currency from circulation. It does this by spending less than it receives in taxes, retiring from circulation some of the currency it receives in taxes.

However, deflation will make it easier for the General Market to reassert natural conditions, bringing to light many mistaken investments. Deflation will also end "booms" in the stock market and land investments that have been financed with inflationary paper money. That means financial crashes and panics.

So even though the government may resist devaluing its currency, deflation is an even worse alternative. But one or both of these alternatives will be the inevitable consequence of inflation.

UNFIXED CURRENCIES

If foreign exchange rates *aren't* fixed, the inflated currency will simply drop in value compared to other currencies. It will be harder for foreign companies to sell in the inflated country, because what they receive in payment will buy very little of their own currencies.

Once the government inflates, there's no way to avoid the final retribution—no matter what tactics are used.

And since the United States has suffered a severe inflation for forty years, there are some awesome consequences yet to come. We've already seen higher import prices, causing less purchasing power for consumers.

But there are more consequences to come, which will be identified as we proceed. Once you know what must happen, it will be much easier to know what you must do to protect yourself.

9

Depression

THE SEEDS OF A DEPRESSION are planted with a government's first step into the economy. But without inflation, there would be little chance for the interferences to accumulate to the point where the General Market would require a massive readjustment process.

With inflation, however, the government can appear to be able to expand its economic programs almost without limit. This means that misinvestments can be greater and can be maintained much longer before the General Market gains the upper hand again. But when that time does come, the readjustment process is much more severe than it would have been without inflation.

That readjustment is what we call a *depression*.

A depression is normally understood to be a period of high unemployment, business failures, lack of purchasing power, deflated investments, shortages, and bank failures. That's true, but these are only symptoms of the basic element of a depression—which is really the General Market's attempt to establish a foundation for a new, more realistic prosperity.

A depression is a period in which the General Market attempts to cleanse itself of the misguided uses of resources that have been encouraged by government intervention, and to redirect its resources to productive activity more desired by consumers.

The keynote of a depression is the *need for change*—changes in business/industrial investments, changes of employment, changes in the use of raw materials. The General Market is straining to put resources to more efficient use.

It tries to do this in the following ways:

1. Misdirected investments must be terminated so that the salvageable resources can be put to better use.

2. Many workers must *change* employment so that they produce more actual value to consumers.

3. Inflationary paper money must be cleared out of the economy so that prices can return to levels where the value of one thing can be realistically compared with the value of others.

4. Insolvent banks must fail so that they can no longer foster inflation or perpetuate the mistakes caused by inflation.

These are the more obvious ways by which the market tries to resume its natural functions, so that genuine prosperity can begin.

SHORT DEPRESSIONS

It's common to think of depressions as long, miserable ordeals. And rightly so, for past experience has taught us that. But depressions don't *have* to be so.

If the paper money supply is deflated, people can still exchange with each other; goods and services will simply cost fewer dollars apiece.

And no one needs to be unemployed indefinitely. There's never any shortage of demand. All people have limitless numbers of desires that would enhance their lives. So no individual has to be unemployed very long—if he's willing to explore all the opportunities that exist.

The key factor is his willingness to *change employment*. If a man has studied to be, and worked as, an engineer for an aerospace company, he may one day discover that he has been living off an artificial market. He's then faced with the choice of stoically maintaining that he's an aerospace engineer (albeit unemployed) or finding a new occupation.

If a new job is the only means of earning food and other necessities, he'll probably choose to change his occupation. And the economy will benefit by his transition to valuable labor.

Because desires are unlimited, there's always a market for something. So unemployment is prolonged only when one of two conditions exist: (1) an individual refuses to work at anything except an unmarketable occupation, or (2) the government interferes with market employment by subsidizing the unemployed or by pricing workers out of the market through minimum-wage laws.

Even with the gigantic misinvestments that must have occurred during the past thirty years of inflation, I still don't see how the next depression could last for more than a year or two—provided the General Market is unobstructed in its efforts to provide recovery.

With modern communications and mobility, there should be no difficulty making consumer demands known and locating workers to produce the goods that consumers really want.

UNFORTUNATELY . . .

Alas, however, all that is a pipe dream. For the government is certain to interfere on a grand scale with the recovery process.

A "benevolent" government won't allow the nation to suffer through an entire year of misery. So it will act to alleviate suffering—and thereby cause ten years of misery.

The history of depressions is the history of governmental attempts to be the salvation of economies, and the resulting extension of the agony. That's why the word *depression* creates such frightening images for us.

Traditionally, governments have consistently reacted to depressions in the following ways:

1. They encourage workers to remain in their old occupations and industries, subsidizing them (through "unemployment in-

surance") as long as they can't be reemployed in their old jobs. Naturally, the subsidies are paid by individuals who *are* working in marketable occupations.

2. Prices and wages are held up by edict. For some strange reason, high wages and prices are considered to be a sign of prosperity. If deflation has occurred, it becomes impossible to trade at the required price levels since there isn't enough paper money in circulation to support those high levels. Hence, trading and employment come to a standstill.

3. Those who have saved or lent their money are often denied repayment because the government doesn't want debtors to lose anything they've bought on credit.

4. The government tries to continue subsidizing unneeded companies and industries—at great expense to those who are working and are taxed. This prevents the latter people from raising their living standards.

5. And by subsidizing the misguided businesses, the government prevents the needed resources from shifting to where they'd serve a more useful purpose. This creates shortages of the things consumers really want.

6. People who have protected their savings are forced to subsidize insolvent banks and depositors. This might be done in two ways: (a) to stop runs on insolvent banks, the government closes *all* banks, and (b) the government may lend taxpayer money to insolvent banks to meet their liabilities.

All these things interfere with the General Market's ability to bring about recovery. A readjustment process that might have taken only a year or two is transformed into a seemingly interminable nightmare.

The length of the depression will depend primarily upon the amount of power the government has. And the history of the United States is one of constantly increasing governmental power and constantly worse depressions—culminating in the catastrophe of 1929–45. By that time, the government had enough power to bring the economy to a virtual standstill until production geared up for war (which is hardly a satisfaction of consumer desires).

THE NEXT DEPRESSION

Since governmental powers have expanded tremendously since the 1930s, the next depression should be *by far* the worst in the history of the United States.

Wage and price controls have already been imposed; subsidy programs have no apparent limits; welfare programs—including Social Security, unemployment insurance, and job training programs—are far beyond anything that existed forty years ago.

Even more important, the point has been reached where "national emergencies" could be considered justification for *anything* the president might deem necessary. Could anyone believe the president wouldn't use every legal power at his disposal (and more) in the "national emergency" of a major depression?

You can't hope to foresee today all the controls that might be invoked tomorrow in a misguided attempt to save the economy. Since price controls are the current governmental answers to inflation, I shudder to think what the answers will be for problems yet to come.

It isn't that politicians are necessarily determined to wreck the economy. It's just that they're as opposed as anyone else is to changing employment—*their* employment. And pressure from academic and governmental economists is universally in favor of greater governmental intervention. Anyone concerned about his job is bound to bow to such pressure.

But the greatest danger of all is that the government will rely upon inflation as a tool of salvation. With only 3% gold backing now, it's unlikely that it would take much more inflation to bring about *runaway inflation.*

And that's the worst kind of depression that can happen.

10

Runaway Inflation

INFLATION AFFECTS THE GOVERNMENT, just as it affects consumers. For the government is the largest single purchaser of products and services in the nation. As inflation pushes the general price levels higher and higher, the government has to pay more for what it buys than it had budgeted.

One of the reasons why federal deficits usually turn out to be bigger than predicted is that the government has budgeted on the basis of prices at the beginning of the fiscal year. By the time the year ends, prices are a good deal higher—causing the government to go further into the red to cover the costs.

And, of course, the added deficit is financed by inflation. So the government is much like a cat chasing its tail: it inflates, suffers high prices because of the inflation, and so must inflate further, but then suffers even higher prices, requiring even more inflation, etc.

For a long time, the effect upon the government may be small. But the compounding of inflation must reach substantial proportions eventually.

When the cycle reaches the point that there's general public concern over rising prices, you can be sure that it's created problems for the government, too.

The government may then take positive steps to slow the rate of inflation. But, as we've seen, this allows the General Market to reassert itself—creating the appearance of a recession. The government's only alternative (it believes) is to resume the inflation in earnest in order to keep the the economy going in the direction it desires.

It's common to hear public officials stating that a little inflation is necessary for economic growth, or that the economy can be "fine-tuned" (to prevent both a recession and too much inflation). But once inflation has begun, the pressure will be on the government to continually increase it.

And, sooner or later, it must reach crisis proportions.

THE SEQUENCE

I believe we can create a scenario to show the development of inflation over the length of its cycle. The scenario encompasses the histories of many past inflations, along with some speculation concerning what might happen if inflation is continued to its ultimate conclusion in the United States.

1. Over a period of years, retail prices go up only gradually— if the government hasn't been too ambitious in its programs. During that time, price increases are small enough that they're noticeable on an annual basis only.

2. However, the inevitable compounding of inflation (described on page 65) leads to a point where consumers become concerned about constantly rising prices. In addition, the gold supply may be jeopardized by foreign claims (as described in Chapter 8).

3. If the government respects these market reactions, it will show some frugality, cut its spending, and diminish the inflation. This will result in a recession. If the government fails to heed the market signals and tries to avoid the recession, inflation will continue in earnest.

4. If the cycle is allowed to continue, there will be a period, perhaps of several years, during which inflation will be a national concern. Prices will be rising steadily and substantially; there will be concern about the losses suffered by people on fixed incomes. But nothing will be done to halt the inflation.

5. Eventually inflation will be noticeable on a monthly basis, instead of just annually. A consumer may notice that an item he buys regularly has gone up in price several times during a few months. If that happens with a number of things he buys, inflation has reached an advanced stage.

6. If the government heeds this belated warning, it will finally capitulate to the General Market and stop the inflation. This, of course, will initiate a full-scale depression.

ACCELERATION OF THE CYCLE

7. If the government is *unwilling* to allow that to happen, it will continue the inflation despite the warnings from the market. Then the flight from paper money takes place in earnest. Many individuals will rush to get rid of their dollars before they depreciate further—exchanging them for gold, silver, gold-backed foreign currencies, or commodities usable to the buyer in the future.

8. The original compounding effect at the governmental level now reaches crisis proportions. Government employees won't settle for the same old wages, even with a nominal "cost-of-living" increase built in. And inflation has reached the point where prices of the supplies the government needs have reached extraordinary levels. So the government must pay higher wages and prices—immediately. It can do this only by inflating the currency at a faster rate.

9. Naturally, the new inflation makes everything even worse. Prices rush upward. Weekly price changes become the rule at the retail level. Soon, products formerly costing a few dollars are priced in the hundreds of dollars.

10. The government is caught on a merry-go-round it can't stop. Tax-collectors, policemen, and bureaucrats who once received $15,000 per year, for example, are now paid $500 per day. But even *that* isn't enough for them to keep up with skyrocketing prices. Most of them could do something else for $1,000 per day

—even without special skills. To keep them, and to purchase supplies, the government must offer market prices and wages. If it doesn't, the government itself will collapse—for lack of tax-collectors and policemen.

11. Soon, prices increase every day. And the prices of the simplest items are measured in thousands and millions of dollars. Again, the government must step up its inflation in order to hold onto its employees.

12. Eventually, prices change by the hour. Workers demand to be paid twice-daily or more often, in order to rush out to spend the paper money before it depreciates further. The government, still caught in a dilemma of its own making, must print the money even faster—or go under. Million-dollar bills come off the presses in the quantities that one-dollar bills were printed a year earlier. And the bills may be printed on only one side—to save time and ink.[1]

13. Even though the government wouldn't stop the inflation earlier because it wanted to avoid a depression, there *is* a depression—along with runaway inflation. For "business as usual" can't be carried on during a runaway inflation. It's too difficult to trade and produce. Factories close from inability to keep up with the inflation.

14. By this time, the government is clearly licked. It must halt the printing press orgy and return to sanity. There's only one way this can be done. It has to introduce a new currency that's backed by gold or silver and can be converted into gold or silver by anyone. Nothing less would give the new money any stability. And, of course, the old currency would be totally worthless. This isn't a new problem to savers; they will have lost the value of their savings long before.

If the government introduces a new gold-backed currency, the economy can begin the long road back to normality. There will be gigantic losses to be liquidated, plants to be reopened, jobs to be found. And all that must be done with less efficient

---

[1] One could almost say that the money finally has intrinsic value. For the first time, the paper and ink in the currency are worth approximately what the paper will buy.

communications and mobility than would have been available had the government surrendered to the market earlier.

THE ULTIMATE DISASTER

15. But what if the government has no gold or silver with which to back a new currency? What if it has long since squandered all its *real* wealth? And what if there's no foreign government or others who will lend it the gold necessary? Clearly, saving the dollar will no longer be in the interest of any foreign government at that point.

In that case, the monetary system will collapse entirely. There will be no way that individuals can use billions of dollars, depreciating hourly, to trade and exchange for necessities. The currency will be totally worthless because no one will be willing to accept it.

The currency will fail and, with it, the government. For the government will have no resources with which to pay for what it needs to survive.

Throughout the marketplace, normal exchange will come to a halt. Chaos will reign as all the normal trappings of civilization as we know it disappear. There will be no law, no order, no communications other than verbal, no companies to turn to for help.

16. Exchanges can occur then only on a barter basis, such as trading a loaf of bread for a gallon of gas. But precious little bartering can take place. For it's practically impossible for a large company to employ thousands of workers on a barter basis. So who will produce the loaf of bread or the gallon of gas? After current supplies have been exhausted, only what's been hoarded in advance can be bartered.

Individuals in rural areas will have a very difficult time living at subsistence levels. They'll need to have marketable commodities stored with which to barter for surplus food with those who are growing it. Individuals living in cities may not survive at all.

17. When the worst of the aftermath of runaway inflation has passed, barter may evolve to the point where exchanges become more frequent and more extended, covering longer distances and bigger trades.

Commodities in especially high demand (such as food, cigarettes, liquor) may be used as money. An individual would accept them in exchange even if he doesn't intend to use them himself. He'll know that he can always trade them to someone else for something he wants. They will have accepted value and be widely needed. This, of course, is the same way that money came into existence originally.

18. Eventually, however, a more useful trading medium will probably assert itself—most likely coins of real silver or gold. As the coins feed through the community, a semblance of order will return. A durable money commodity is the lifeblood of civilization—making possible the specialization of labor, the ability of one person to employ another, the opportunity to accumulate long-term savings.

And so, from the ashes of a dead civilization, a new one arises —painfully, slowly, and probably fully prepared to make the same mistakes that eventually killed the old one.

Once step 5 has been reached, the economy is in for rough going—no matter which choices the government makes thereafter.[2] But if step 15 is reached, in which no valuable currency can replace the old one, the doom of the country is sealed.

THE END OF A CIVILIZATION

Perhaps this sequential summary of a runaway inflation has demonstrated how easy it is for such things to happen. When hearing of runaway inflations of the past, many people are prompted to wonder why the governments didn't stop the inflating when disaster was imminent. But, obviously, they *can't*

[2] I believe that's where we were in late 1973.

stop it; to do so will make the governments powerless to purchase in the marketplace.

Historically, most runaway inflations *have* ended short of the ultimate disaster. Either the government has held back a small supply of gold or it has been able to borrow gold from other governments or individuals.[3]

Because the end of inflation automatically triggers an immediate depression, there's always pressure on politicians to inflate too far. Since no one can identify the point of no return precisely, it's easy enough for those in power to convince themselves that the next dose of inflation won't be too much.

But the depression is never avoided. For runaway inflation is a depression itself. There are shortages, difficulties in trading, massive employment problems, business failures on a widespread scale—all the characteristics of a normal depression. And the aftermath of a runaway inflation is far worse than any normal depression.

For then it's too late for the General Market to reassert itself easily. Communications, mobility, exchange—all the prerequisites of recovery—have been disabled. Resources that once could have been used to rebuild will have become largely worthless.

Mostly, only modern knowledge remains as a tool to be used in the long, slow process of rebuilding what will have become a primitive civilization.

As always, the General Market will have won its war with the government; but only at a terrible price.

This is the ultimate denouement of the government's attempts to promote the general welfare. This is what a "harmless amount of inflation" can lead to.

---

[3] Several books detailing runaway inflations of the past are listed in the Recommended Reading.

11
Price Controls

BY THE FALL OF 1973, people in the United States had
been given ample opportunity to see that price controls aren't the
panacea they're touted to be. Controls *must* lead to shortages.

Even the argument of shortages versus high prices isn't valid.
Price controls create shortages *without* eliminating high prices.
Those who can circumvent the shortages do so by paying black-
market prices. And for those who are denied access to products,
who cares how low or high the price is supposed to be?

This is illustrated by the story of a woman who walks into a
butcher shop to buy pork chops. She's shocked to find the chops
with a price-tag of $3 per pound. She indignantly asks the butcher,
"How dare you charge so much? Pork chops are two dollars a
pound at the meat market across the street."

"Then why don't you buy them there?" asks the butcher.

"Because they don't have any," she replies.

"Oh. Well, when I didn't have any, they were two dollars a
pound, too."

HOW PRICES RISE

General price increases aren't caused by businessmen, labor
unions, or greedy consumers. They're caused by the government
printing too many paper dollars.

If the money supply is inflated, prices *must* go up. Inflation won't be stopped by imposing legal limits on prices; that will only cause additional problems. There's no way that controls can cover every price. (If your neighbor pays a local boy a dollar over the legal limit to mow his lawn, will you report him? Or will you also pay the higher price?)

All money that hasn't been burned or buried in the backyard will be used—in one way or another. If it's put in a bank, it will be lent to someone else who will spend it. And as long as the money supply is inflated, prices will be bid upward. The General Market will continue to operate on its normal principles.

If a manufacturer or retailer can't legally raise his prices, he'll be unable to bid for the resources he needs—because someone else will be bidding those prices upward. That someone else will be a manufacturer or retailer who isn't legally price controlled or who can easily circumvent the controls.

Thus, resources will gravitate to those enterprises that aren't hampered by the price controls. And shortages will develop in the areas that *are* hamstrung by the controls.

Unfortunately, the government often limits price controls to "essential" products and services—food, medical care and supplies, rents, etc. So the government is causing shortages in what it considers to be the most critical needs of consumers.

As the price controls create shortages in these areas, consumers become desperate. They induce sellers to raise prices—as the consumers would rather pay higher prices than go without the products.

The price increases are handled covertly in order to circumvent the law. Thus, you have a *black market*—which is nothing more than a free market operating outside of legal sanction. Black markets evolve and prosper wherever laws create shortages; they come into existence for the same reason normal markets do—because of consumer demand.

Black market prices are higher than normal prices, however, because the seller has to circumvent the law to please his customers. As a result, many important products are priced out of reach of many consumers who have neither the money nor the knowledge to buy in the black market.

"CHEATING"

There are numerous ways to circumvent price controls. Here are a few of the traditional methods:

1. "New" products are offered that differ only slightly from their price-controlled predecessors.

2. Discounts are eliminated—or higher volume minimums are required to earn the discounts.

3. Quality is cut.

4. Producers divert their resources to products within their fields that aren't controlled.

5. Pay-offs are taken under the table for putting an eager customer at the front of the waiting line.

6. Exemptions are gained by doing favors for those in the government.

7. Producers barter products and services with each other so that monetary prices aren't involved.

8. Package deals are created. The buyer gets the product he wants at the controlled price, but the deal also includes his buying something he doesn't want—at an unrealistically high price.

In his book, *The Vampire Economy*, Guenter Reimann offered many examples of the problems that plagued Nazi Germany under price controls. As an example of number 8, he told the story of a peasant who sold pigs to private buyers. He'd always sell the pig at the legal price, but the buyer was led to understand that he couldn't buy a pig without also buying the peasant's dog. They would negotiate the price of the dog, and ultimately the buyer would pay an outrageous price for the dog. The buyer would leave with the pig and the dog; but a mile down the road he'd release the unwanted dog who would then run back to his master—who sold him over and over again.[1]

Wage controls bring about the same need for circumvention that price controls do. An employer has to offer his employees

[1] Reimann: *The Vampire Economy*, page 68 (listed in the Recommended Reading).

more to keep them from looking for unregulated jobs. Among the typical methods of circumvention are:

1. Employers provide unrecorded fringe benefits to better workers—company cars, better offices, more impressive titles, etc.

2. Employees are given more time off, so that they make more per hour while the weekly wage remains the same.

3. New job titles are created, with higher wages, so that a simple wage increase appears to be a promotion. (A small plant may wind up with ten foremen out of twelve employees.)

4. When new employees are hired, they start at higher positions with higher wages. They usually replace previous employees who've left to get the same deal elsewhere.

If employees can't hope for wage increases during an inflationary period, they either look for work at higher wages elsewhere or they lose the incentive to perform well at their present jobs. If they remain, the quality of workmanship must suffer. In either case, the employer of a price-controlled company isn't going to be able to offer good value or good availability to his customers.

Another problem of price controls is that they ignore the differences between sellers of the same product. With price controls and inflation existing simultaneously, all prices within a market will inevitably rise to the maximum legal price. That means the General Market can no longer reward individual sellers for their distinctions: personal service, better quality, prompt delivery, extras, etc. There is no encouragement to the better sellers, and so no gravitation of the resources to those who better serve consumer desires.

OPPORTUNITIES

Since price controls never achieve the desired objectives, they're usually temporary—although history records some examples of extended controls.

Once the controls are lifted, prices will move drastically in the direction opposite to the control. The General Market has been hindered from moving naturally, and now it will have to make up for lost time. Prices will move much faster than would have been necessary if there had been no controls in the interim.

This is an important point. *Once controls are lifted, extreme price movements take place.* And there are three important investments, necessary for protection from monetary crises, that have been released recently from long periods of price controls. They are gold, silver, and a group of strong foreign currencies. We'll look at each of these in Part V.

COMPOUNDING PROBLEMS

It's obvious that price controls won't stop inflation. They compound the problems of inflation by creating new obstacles for the General Market.

No one will produce or exchange unless he believes it will lead ultimately to something he wants. Price controls, like all legislated economic programs, are attempts to make people act against their own self-interests. They are a continuing part of the conflict between the government and the interests of consumers. As a result, controls never achieve their objectives. Instead, they produce shortages, black markets, and higher real prices for everything the consumer wants.

I don't expect the government to realize this, however, no matter how much history is available as evidence. The false assurances created by wage and price controls can encourage the government to believe it can inflate without bad consequences —increasing the possibility of runaway inflation.

But if *you* understand the effects of controls, you won't be convinced that they've solved the problems. And you'll take steps to be sure you're protected, no matter what the government does. You can even use the effects of controls as a vehicle for personal profit.

12
The General Welfare

APPARENTLY, MANY PEOPLE believe that inflation is a justifiable cost that must be paid to enable the government to promote the general welfare.

From our coverage of the consequences of inflation in previous chapters, it's hard to see how the general welfare has been promoted by the government's activities.

If the general welfare is served by using the nation's resources in ways chosen by the people, the General Market does that already. Any interference by the government will result in less general welfare, not more. There's no way the government can give the people more of what they want.

Some say that people don't know what's best for themselves. If you believe that people are too evil or too stupid to govern their own lives, then you must also believe that they're too evil or too stupid to govern the lives of others.

No matter how the question is approached, I can find no way to justify the government's interference with the General Market. It always results in a net loss to consumers.

It's often argued that the General Market benefits the rich or the more talented. That's true. But it also benefits the poor and the less talented.

In the General Market, the rich get richer only if they provide services to others that those others are willing to pay for. All examples I've heard of graft or corruption by entrepreneurs include one or both of two vital factors: (1) the entrepreneur went broke trying to cheat the public, or (2) he achieved and maintained his success by enlisting the aid of the government.

In a government-controlled economy, the rich get richer by buying government favors. They then receive money from others without providing the best service in return.

Government subsidies are paid mostly to the rich, not to the poor or the disadvantaged. Housing subsidies go to big home builders; food subsidies go mostly to farmers with large acreage and effective advocates; school subsidies go to contractors.

Some subsidies go directly to consumers—such things as food stamps, welfare, unemployment insurance, Social Security, etc. But the costs of those programs are paid as much by the poor as by the rich.

Income taxes, in general, don't "soak the rich." The rich find ways of getting around them. Instead of paying large income taxes, they pay fees to attorneys, accountants, and bureaucrats. Most income taxes come from "middle-class" and "lower-class" income groups—from people who don't realize it's worth the trouble to look for loopholes.[1]

The rest of the government's tax revenues come from sales taxes, excise taxes, property taxes, import duties, and similar revenues that discourage commerce, increase costs, and hurt all groups somewhat equally.

And, of course, the government relies heavily upon inflation (borrowing fictitious money) to pay its bills. Inflation hurts high-income groups least, as they can finance hedges against dollar depreciation and utilize black markets much more easily.

Government programs divert resources from programs desired by consumers—making it more difficult, more costly for them to get what they want. When shortages occur, the poorer, less talented people are the ones who are hurt the most.

And governmental minimum-wage laws make it difficult for unskilled workers to be employed. Without such laws, employers could afford to train them and utilize their services.

[1] The Canadian Revenue Department reported that, for 1971, there were 8 Canadians with income aggregating $2,012,000 who paid no income tax at all. Altogether, there were 204 Canadians who had incomes of $25,000 or more who paid no taxes. Meanwhile, 265,408 old-age pensioners had average incomes of $4,385 apiece and paid an average of $415 each in taxes. (The Toronto Star, August 22, 1973.)

You can, if you choose, waste a great deal of your time trying to devise a governmental system that's "fairer." But such a quest is hopeless. Governments *can't* improve upon the General Market. The only improvement now would be to let the General Market alone so it can do its job.

It's important to realize that governments haven't created prosperity; it's happened in spite of them. You have no duty to protect and support the government's interests. There's no reason to respond to patriotic calls to help the government save the dollar or restrain prices. Any such cooperation you give will be futile, and will be at your expense, not the government's.

Instead, the principal task at hand right now is to find ways to protect and support yourself. There are difficult times ahead; your resources and talents are needed for the all-important job of seeing to it that you survive the crises and prosper.

The crises will be interpreted in many ways in the newspapers. But 99% of those interpretations will be wrong. The crises are merely symptoms of the unrelenting war between the governments of the world and the consumers of the world, represented by the General Market. The General Market will win ultimately, it always does, but not before the consumers suffer heavy losses.

Whether or not you'll share in the losses depends upon what you do now.

13
A Visit to Rhinegold

ONCE, IN A FANTASY, I had the opportunity to visit the mythical nation of Rhinegold. I was doing research for this book, and I'd heard there was a strange money system in Rhinegold—so I thought I should investigate.

Rhinegold is a very small country (about the size of Luxembourg—around 1,000 square miles) situated on the river Rhine in a little nook at the corner where France, Germany, and Switzerland would otherwise meet. There are about 160,000 inhabitants, all of whom speak the ancient tongue of Cash (at least that's the only language they understand).

When I went there, I figured the best way to learn about the monetary system was to head for the capital city and speak to someone at the central bank. But no one I asked had ever heard of a central bank. In fact, no one even knew what the capital city was—an ignorance I was to come to understand only later.

So instead, I went to the city of Glitter, where I was able to make friends with a businessman named Brian Sell. Seeing my interest in finances, he arranged a luncheon meeting comprised of a leading banker (I. M. Solvent), a renowned economist (G. N. Product), Mr. Sell, and myself.

After the amenities had been completed, we began discussing the economy of Rhinegold.

It seems that the monetary unit there is the gram. Having written in the past about francs, Swiss francs, Belgian francs, Japanese yen, and even Qatar/Dubai riyals, I saw nothing strange about a government naming its currency the gram.

So I asked my first question: "What is the gram backed by?"

"Backed by?" replied Mr. Sell, rather quizzically. "What do you mean 'backed by'?"

"I mean what is your monetary reserve—silver, U.S. dollars, SDRs, what?"

"But, Mr. Browne, the gram is not backed by anything."

"Not backed by anything? Well, it must be a very inflationary currency then. Many currencies are backed by gold, for instance."

"No, Mr. Browne, you do not understand. The gram is not backed by gold. It *is* gold. What do you think a gram is? The gram is a weight of gold—equal to .03215 ounces, consisting of one hundred centigrams or one thousand milligrams. Have you never heard of a gram?"

"Yes," I said. "But gold isn't money; it's only a backing for money."

"Maybe where you live, but not here. We would not dream of considering anything but gold as money."

"But you don't actually exchange gold in daily trade, do you?"

"Of course we do. I cannot imagine anyone accepting anything else in payment."

"But isn't that rather cumbersome?" I asked.

"Not at all," Mr. Sell replied. He reached into his pocket and extracted an assortment of things. "Here is a 100-gram bar of gold, for example. I would not ordinarily have this size bar with me; in fact, I was going to take it over to the warehouse of Mr. Solvent after lunch."

I turned to Mr. Solvent and said: "But I thought you were a banker."

"You may call me anything you choose," he said, shrugging. "A bank is merely a warehouse for gold."

Mr. Sell handed the gold bar to me, and I must admit I was impressed—holding gold in my hand for the first time in my life. It was a wafer-thin little bar, about two inches long and an inch wide. I looked at the inscription on it. It said, "Alberich's Mint. 100 grams, .9999 fine. Assayed by I. M. Solvent." It turned out that Mr. Solvent's warehouse included an assay office. He was highly respected in the country, as were his father and grandfather before him.

"How much is the gold bar worth?" I asked.

"It is worth what 100 grams will buy in the marketplace," said Mr. Sell. "For example, I could buy a nice color television set, a bedroom suite, many things."

"But what is the price of a nice color television set?" I asked.

And with a straight face he replied, "The price is 100 grams."

"But how much is 100 grams?"

He became a little annoyed and said: "My dear sir, 100 grams is 100 grams. Are you trying to make fun of me?"

At that, Mr. Product, the economist, intervened. "I think what Mr. Browne wants to know is what 100 grams are worth in American paper currency. With U.S. dollars selling for about $\frac{1}{3}$ of a gram or $\frac{1}{100}$ of an ounce each, you could buy about 300 U.S. dollars with that gold bar—if you *wanted* to."

"Don't you mean that gold is selling for about $100 an ounce?"

"My friend, you do not *buy* gold, you spend it. Gold is money. You might buy dollars (they are not money) if you had some reason for wanting them; but, off hand, I cannot think of any reason. You Americans have everything upside down."

Satisfied that my questions were prompted by ignorance, not malevolence, Mr. Sell continued showing me his money.

He displayed various coins—several more from Alberich's Mint and a few from Miser's Mint. They were denominated in 30 grams, 20 grams, 10 grams, 5 grams, and 1 gram.

I quickly tried to compute the value of each in the only terms I knew—U.S. dollars. It appeared that the 1-gram coin was worth about $3.00. It was a tiny thing, about half the size of an American dime.

He noticed my consternation at the small size of the 1-gram coin, and said, "Yes, it is a rather inconvenient coin—too easily lost. So we also have a 1-gram token; here is one of them."

I looked at the "token." It was a typical copper–nickel coin (as I had always thought of the word "coin"), about the size of an American silver dollar. I noticed that the inscription on it said,

"Good for one gold gram at Rhinemaiden Safekeeping Company, 'Guardians of the Rhinegold.'"

"That is my warehouse," said Mr. Solvent. "Anyone can redeem that token for a gram of gold at any time."

Mr. Sell showed me some other tokens. They bore labels of 50 centigrams, 25 centigrams, 10 centigrams, 5 centigrams, 2½ centigrams, 1 centigram, and ½ centigram. The first four had the same look of nickel about them that the 1-gram token had, decreasing in size along with the value. But the 2½, 1, and ½ centigram tokens were plain copper, brown like American pennies; and so were a little larger since they were easily distinguishable from the more valuable tokens.

Thinking I was one up on them, I said, "I'm surprised at you folks. With your apparent fetish for intrinsic value, why don't you have silver coins?"

They each looked surprised, but then Mr. Solvent came to the rescue. "I think I understand your question. But I do not think you understand that tokens are not money. They should not have intrinsic value as gold coins do. A token is a money substitute, something you exchange for gold when you want to—just as your paper currency was once redeemable in gold.

"You would not think of printing money receipts on some special paper that was worth more than the money it represents. That would be a waste. The same thing is true for tokens. A one-gram token contains about one centigram's worth of copper in it. It is merely a substitute. If we put silver in the token, the value of the silver might be greater than the amount of gold it is meant to represent."

"But *we* once had silver in our coins in America."

"Ah yes," Mr. Product broke in. "I have read about that. And that is precisely why you continually had so-called 'coinage problems.' The silver in the 'coin' as you call it, was often worth more than the so-called 'money' it was supposed to represent. And when it was, people would not use them; they would hoard them. As more were minted, they would disappear from circulation immediately."

"But the coins had intrinsic value."

"Yes, that was their problem. You cannot have two kinds of money circulating, gold and silver; one will always be worth more proportionately than the other and so will not circulate. Your government would try to force people to accept them at the same value; how silly."

"What is a 'government'?" Mr. Sell asked, but Mr. Product went on with what he was saying.

"If you offered me some silver, I would accept it—because silver is very valuable. But I would be calculating in my mind how much the silver is worth in terms of gold."

Seeing his question wasn't going to be answered, Mr. Sell shrugged and brought the rest of his money out of his pocket. In his hand was a wad of currency.

"And here we have money receipts. They are like tokens, exchangeable for gold but more convenient to handle in larger amounts."

He showed me the receipts. Many of them were from Mr. Solvent's warehouse. They were somewhat similar to U.S. bills—finely engraved (probably to discourage counterfeiting), had denominations on them from 100 grams to 1 gram, and also had pictures of men and women.

I leafed through them, looking at the unfamiliar faces—probably the former presidents of Rhinegold, I thought—until I came across the face of *John D. Rockefeller!* And there was one of Andrew Carnegie.

"Yes, Mr. Browne," said Mr. Solvent. "I grace my money receipts with honored men to lend a sense of prestige to my warehouse. People in Rhinegold are very grateful to John D. Rockefeller for what he did to make gasoline inexpensive for our motor cars."

At my request, he explained the warehouse business. He stored gold, gold coins, and money receipts for people. He offered demand deposits—a pure storage function—for which customers paid a small fee. And he also borrowed gold from people by setting up time deposits—whereby customers left gold with him for specific lengths of time, for which he paid *them* a fee. He, in turn, lent the gold to others for larger fees. As he put it, he was a loan broker.

He also offered a foreign trade department—which I later realized was similar to a foreign exchange business. Mr. Sell imported products to be sold in his stores and he handled the transactions through Mr. Solvent.

If Mr. Sell wanted to buy products from Germany, for example, he would get a price in German marks. But he kept no supply of German marks, so Mr. Solvent would check their value by determining the exchange rate between Swiss francs and German marks, and by getting a commitment from someone in Zurich to buy gold from Solvent's warehouse. That way, he could tell Mr. Sell exactly how much gold was required to buy the products. He would then handle the exchange transactions for Mr. Sell.

"As an exchange broker, I guess you stock various currencies, too."

"Very little," replied Mr. Solvent. "We have some business selling currencies to Rhinegolders who intend to travel to other countries, but I just keep a small inventory. I would never want to have a large supply of this strange paper that fluctuates in value."

Then I remembered that gold had gone up in value recently —rising from $35 per ounce to $100 per ounce in just the past three years. When I mentioned this, Mr. Product replied, "Yes, you people have had some strange ideas about gold. Your authorities kept dumping it on the market for years—trying to make your paper currencies more valuable. How ridiculous.

"But we knew you couldn't do it indefinitely. And so most Rhinegolders restricted their purchases over the past few years, knowing things would change, holding onto as much gold as possible.

"We buy many things from other countries. You see, we do not produce many things here—some dairy products, a few cereals, potash, some agricultural products, a rather inferior quality of wine, and, of course, we have the power plant. So as long as you people had such contempt for gold, we would not buy very much from other countries. But *now,* now every gram of gold will buy about three times as much in foreign products. We are all far wealthier than we were three years ago; we are importing luxury cars, excellent French wines, and all sorts of other things we have always wanted."

"But if you're importing so much, business must be terrible here."

"Oh no. I suppose most people are taking it a little easy for a while. And why not? They are enjoying the fruits of past labor. But no one expects to live the rest of his life off your follies. Meanwhile, we are buying many things we have always wanted."

"But what about your balance of payments?" I asked. "It must be in terrible shape."

"What is balance of payments?" Mr. Sell and Mr. Solvent asked in unison.

"You don't know what balance of payments is? That's the comparison between your imports and exports. Right now, you're running at a deficit; it could ruin your money system."

"I do not understand," said Mr. Sell. "How could we run at a deficit? Our imports and exports are always equal; how can they be otherwise? No one is willing to give us anything without getting something in return. I do not understand what you mean by a deficit."

"I would look at it another way," said Mr. Solvent. "You could say that we always import more than we export. After all, an individual only exchanges when he gets back something of greater value than he gives up; otherwise he would not bother making the exchange. So, taking all our people as an aggregate, we always import things of greater value to us than we export. But then so do people of every other country. Is that what you mean?"

"No, that is not what he means," interrupted Mr. Product, the economist. "I've read about this balance of payments matter. It is really very simple. What they do in the United States is to buy on credit, in effect. They import products but do not pay for them with gold. Instead they give IOUs that are supposedly payable in gold—something like our money substitutes. But they issue far more IOUs than they actually have gold for.

"And so they are constantly besieged by creditors demanding payment in gold for the IOUs. As a result, they always hope they will export more food and cars and other things in exchange for other people's IOUs (or to get their own IOUs back), thus keeping foreigners from asking for the gold that is not there.

"We do not have that problem here, because we do not deal in that kind of credit. Everything we buy is paid for with something immediately—potash, cheese, any of our other products, or gold. So every import is simultaneously an export, too.

"Occasionally, someone pays for an import with one of Mr. Solvent's warehouse receipts—sort of the way you pay with 'dollars' (a strange term that denotes nothing specific). But any foreigner can exchange the receipts for gold in storage at the warehouse anytime he wants. And there is always gold there for every receipt; Mr. Solvent can prove it.

"So if everyone holding a receipt wanted to exchange it for gold at the same time, all the receipts would be redeemed. No one would be left out. The only problem might be that Mr. Solvent would have to hire a couple of extra clerks to handle the increased business that day."

"Ah, that would be no problem," said Mr. Solvent. "And if everyone took the gold they have stored with me, I would be able to take that vacation I have been putting off."

"But that's not true," I said. "You couldn't satisfy all the demands for gold. You've already told me that you've lent out some of the gold."

"Not *that* gold," he said. "I cannot lend gold that is covered by a receipt; that is dishonest. Two different people would be trying to spend the same money at the same time. The gold I lend is gold that is *lent* to me, not stored with me. No one who has lent gold to me has a claim upon it until the due date of the note I gave him. And before then, I will be paid back the gold by the person I lent it to. I could not possibly lend gold unless I have the exclusive right to it for a given period of time."

"That sounds like a very restrictive credit system to me. How can you stimulate business that way?"

"I do not understand. How would we have any more resources or workers by doubling the money substitutes? That is what would happen if I lent gold that someone else was spending with his receipts.

"All that is rather academic right now, anyway," he added. "No one has borrowed much gold the past few years. Everyone in Rhinegold knew the world's respect for gold would be increasing. As long as gold was being dumped on the market by your authorities, gold was buying artificially small amounts of things temporarily. So our friends have been waiting, saving as much gold as they could, waiting until it would buy much more. No one wanted to borrow money and spend it at relatively high prices and then pay it back when prices would be much lower. In fact, the price for borrowing money has been around one percent a year for several years now."

"You mean prices are dropping?"

"Of course, *you* price U.S. goods in dollars. Well, until recently an ounce of gold would only buy about 35 'dollar's worth' of U.S. products. Now an ounce of gold will buy 100 'dollar's worth' of U.S. goods. Three years ago, it would have cost Mr. Sell 300 grams to buy that American color TV set; now it only cost 100 grams. And that, of course, has also forced local prices to go down, too, because foreign products can be bought so cheaply now.

"In fact, to facilitate the lower prices, I have recently started issuing a 2½-milligram token. There are now some things that cost less than ½ centigram."

That sounded ominous to me. "Then you must be suffering a depression—if prices have dropped to one-third of what they were."

"What is a depression?" asked Mr. Sell.

Calling upon my vast knowledge of economics, I said, "A depression is when you have to reduce your standard of living because of bad times."

"Oh yes, we had one of those," replied Mr. Sell. "During that ridiculous war you people had back in the 1940s. Most of the borders to other countries were closed and it seemed like nobody in any other country was producing anything of value. We could not buy automobiles from any other countries, for example; and we had to go without a lot of other things for several years. So we ate a lot of cheese and waited it out. Is that what you mean by a depression?"

"Well, sort of, I guess. I'm not really sure. Wars are supposed to be good for business. At least that's what my economics text-book said. But I mean a real depression—like we had in the 1930s."

"I know what you mean," said Mr. Product. "We had something like that just after the war. When the war ended, Rhinegold was overrun with tourists from the United States. They wanted to buy all sorts of things—potash, cheese, sight-seeing, even our cheap wine since the French had been producing very little for several years.

"You see, we were so glad to see people from the outside world again, we did not ask many questions. And they had stacks of money substitutes—your 'dollars'—which they said were 'good as gold.' So we took their word for it and accepted the dollars.

"When people took the money receipts to Mr. Solvent, he checked them out and found out that they *were not* as good as gold—not hardly. The people who had printed the receipts would not give you any gold for them; you had to get in a waiting line.

"So there we had given up a great deal of our production for something of much less value. We all suffered a bit from that—our standards of living went down for a while. It was like having worked for four years for nothing. That was our real depression."

"But wait a minute," interrupted Mr. Solvent. "We had another depression right after that, remember? When the people in Glitter City realized that the money substitutes were not ex-changeable for real money, they had a big bonfire in the city square and burned all these phony receipts. The fire spread and a third of Glitter was destroyed by fire. It took some time to get back to normal living standards after that. So we have had two depressions—thanks to this funny money of yours."

Anxious to change the subject, I turned the conversation back to the war. "How in heaven's name did you manage to stay out of World War Two? Here you are right between Germany and France. Didn't the Nazis occupy Rhinegold while they were overrunning France?"

"They tried to," said Mr. Product. "A large band of soldiers in tanks moved in and said that Glitter City was now under Nazi occupation. That is, they tried to say it, but they could not find anyone to listen to them. They posted signs on the buildings and went looking for something called the 'City Hall' to take over the government."

"Then what happened?"

"You see, we do not *have* a government. No one here respects *any* authority except his own self-interest and the self-interest of any person with whom he might have some intercourse."

"By the way, what *is* a government?" asked Mr. Sell.

Ignoring him, Mr. Product went on with his story. "So that meant *they* would have to set up a government. They sent home for more troops; but since no one here had any concept of what a 'government' is, it meant they could control us only if they had one policeman for every Rhinegolder. At first, they tried stationing a soldier on every corner with a tommy gun—but people just went on about their own business.

"Finally, they realized they would have to have 160,000 soldiers here to guard 160,000 Rhinegolders. And for what? Just to say they had conquered a little country of 1,000 square miles. That did not make sense—even to them. So they stole some cheese and went on to France."

"That's very inter—"

"Wait, that's not all. In 1945, it happened again—sort of. Then the American soldiers came. They had even *more* tanks and soldiers than the Germans had. They rode into town and a man in uniform with some artificial silver stars on his shoulder stopped me on the street and said, 'Take me to your leader.' So I took him home and introduced him to my wife.

"Well, either I had misunderstood or *he* misunderstood, because he threatened to shave my head and denounce me as a collaborator. Fortunately, he changed his mind—but I do not think he ever really comprehended our way of life here, and I certainly do not understand his.

"So after a couple of days, they stole some cheese and headed into Germany."

This was all a little too much for me to grasp. "But you *must* have a government. Who decides when prices get too high or how much is a fair profit?"

"What *is* a government?" insisted Mr. Sell.

"We all decide such things," said Mr. Product.

"Oh," I said. "You mean you vote on such questions."

"I guess you could say that. I vote when I buy something. I am telling the seller that his price and profit are not prohibitive. If enough other people also vote for the product in that way, the seller keeps offering it. If not, he is voted into changing his prices or doing something else for a living. Is that what you mean?"

"No, but we'll set that aside. Even if you don't want a government to control your economy, you *have* to have one for national defense. If nothing else, that's a necessity."

"I disagree with you. In fact, I see it to be exactly the reverse. If we had a government running our economy, we would survive. We would have to put up with the recurring price distortions of inflation and the inevitable depressions that you people take for granted. Our standard of living would go down considerably with such a government running our lives, but—as I said—we would still survive somehow.

"But the one thing we could not tolerate would be a government responsible for our defense. Depressions are bad enough—but *wars!* Wars that send our people off to fight the personal battles of some stupid politician; large shares of our production taken away from us to buy guns and fortifications; bombs raining on our cities. I am surprised that you imagine that we would want that."

"But how do you defend yourselves?"

"By minding our own business. Oh, we have had other people wanting to conquer us a few times. But a nation is conquered only when the government surrenders; then the people surrender. A people who do not respect any authority but themselves have no one to surrender for them. That means they would each individually have to surrender. No conqueror has the resources to waste trying to conquer 160,000 different and individual enemies.

"Each time the foreigners have come to make war, they have left soon enough. And yes it is true that they killed a dozen people or so before they left. And we *all* mourned—because I doubt that there is a single person in Rhinegold who does not consider such deaths to be senseless.

"But fortunately we did not have a government. If we had, the 'great' ruler would have called for blood and vengeance 'on behalf of an injured nation.' He would have drafted half the population and sent *thousands* off to die. If a dozen people killed is such a tragedy, then why bring on the even greater tragedy of thousands killed?

"No thank you, Mr. Browne, no national defense for us. It is too dangerous."

I could see it was time to change the subject again. "Tell me about your industry. I notice you have a pretty impressive power plant on the river. If you have no government, how was it built?"

Mr. Sell handled that one. "By production, of course. Some people worked, saved their money, and invested it in the building of the power plant—hoping enough people would want the electricity to make the investment pay off."

"But such things as power plants are too expensive to be built with private money. That's why governments always have to put up the money."

"I do not know what is this thing you keep calling a 'government,' but I know one thing: If the people of Rhinegold are not rich enough to have the money, starting a government is not going to make them any richer."

"Well then, let's talk about your other industry. I've seen some large farms. Who owns them?"

"Some of them are owned by local residents. And a few of them are owned by Germans. They do very well with them, too. I understand Herr Dorado made quite a profit last year."

"Doesn't that bother you—Germans coming in here, buying up valuable property, making money on it, and taking the profits out of the country?"

"I do not understand; why *should* it? Evidently, the local people do not consider the property as valuable as the Germans do or they would offer prices that would buy them out. As for 'taking profits out of the country,' how can that hurt us? They only make their profits by offering something in return. They get the gold; we get the food we want. And when *we* sell something we produce, we get gold in return—or we don't do business. What is the problem?"

"No problems, I guess. Well, I see the time is getting late. So we'd better break up this very informative meeting so you can get back to your businesses. I appreciate your taking the time to tell me about your rather strange money system. It's really quite quaint, though a bit primitive."

"What is primitive about it?" asked Mr. Product. "We have no shooting wars, no trade wars, no balance of payments problem, no inflation, no depressions of the kind you take for granted, no borders really (just the borders of other countries), no one to prevent us from buying what we want from whomever we want at whatever price we can agree upon, no one to tell us what we can produce, what we can own, whom we can deal with. If that is primitive, I would rather be primitive than have to face the problems inherent in your contrived, 'sophisticated' controlled economy."

I had been clearly outflanked and out-argued. They'd pushed me into an intellectual and ideological corner. It meant that I had to bring up the one thing that, out of courtesy, I'd wanted to avoid. *I* didn't want to bring it up, but they'd forced the issue. I *had* to raise the ultimate argument—my *coup de grace.*

"All right, you've just made the most telling point about your system. Everything you think is so good about your system has to do with money. *Money!* That seems to be all you ever think about, all you can talk about. You're so preoccupied with money, where's the aesthetic interest, the spiritual concerns, the higher order of things that you have no time for because of your preoccupation with money? This is the most materialistic society I've ever seen."

They all looked surprised; clearly I'd gotten to them. Then Mr. Product spoke.

"Money? You think we are preoccupied with money. You invite us to lunch and ask one question after another about money—and then think that *we* are preoccupied with money. How very funny.

"We talk about money because you insist upon it. *You* have taken us away from our pleasures, our aesthetic enjoyments, and —yes—our businesses, because *you,* my friend, are the one who is totally absorbed in the subject.

"Why are you writing a book about money? Only because your own money system is in such terrible straits. If it worked right, you would be writing about something else. Our money system works precisely because no one ever sat down and invented it. It simply evolved over hundreds of years as thousands of individuals just did what was in the self-interest of each.

"We never became so preoccupied with money that we tried to invent it out of paper in a vain attempt to have more than we have earned.

"As a result, we *understand* money. We know what it is and we know what it is not. It is simply some commodity of such accepted value in the community that an individual is willing to hold it while he waits to purchase something else with it.

"And because we understand money and earn a lot of it, we are rich. And do you know what that means? It means we do not have to be preoccupied with it. We are free to enjoy many things in life that you cannot enjoy because you are too absorbed trying to figure your way out of the dilemmas *your* primitive money system has caused.

"We live fruitful lives here because we are not so pompous as to believe we know what is best for other people. So we do not take the earnings of one person to give to another we 'judge' to be more deserving.

"Mr. Solvent here gave up the matinee at the opera this afternoon to indulge your preoccupation with money. And Mr. Solvent regrets that—not because opera is culture but because opera is enjoyment.

"You talk of materialism as 'opposed' to spiritual and aesthetic values. But there is no opposition between them. What I have just said about money and the lack of the need to be preoccupied with it was not meant to disparage money. Quite the contrary.

"There are people here who go to church quite often. But I doubt that anyone of them thinks that Bibles are printed on paper by prayer. Nor do men like Mr. Solvent believe that operas are reproduced on gramophone records by aesthetic meditation. Those things are accomplished by effort, by productivity, by a sound understanding of what money is—so that one's limited resources are not used up chasing after pieces of paper that have no durable value.

"When your country learns what money is, your people will be able to produce so well that the aesthetic and spiritual endeavors of your country will no longer be so expensive that you cannot afford them.

"I advise you to become so preoccupied with money that you learn to understand it, and to earn it, so that you can finally become preoccupied with something else."

When he finished, I said, "Well, I respect your position. Of course, I don't have to accept it. Especially since my president said last week that everything will be much better next year—after the new controls have had a chance to work.

"And gentlemen, I appreciate your taking this time to talk with me." As I shook hands with each of them, I said, "Thank you, Mr. Brian Sell; thank you, Mr. I. M. Solvent; thank you Mr. G. N. Product. Oh, one other thing, Mr. Product; do you mind my asking what the initials G. N. stand for?"

He looked at me a bit surprised and said, "Why no; they stand for Gerald Nathan. Why do you ask?"

"Oh, no special reason. Thank you very much."

And so I left Rhinegold and headed back to the warm, reassuring, comforting homeland where I could deal with things I understood—strikes, food shortages, exchange controls, etc.

When I arrived, the customs official asked me, "Do you have anything to declare? Any money over $5,000? Any gold? Anything else?"

I thought of the 10-gram gold coin I'd bought on my way out of Rhinegold, which was now hidden in my shoe; I cleared my throat and said, "Er, no, not a thing. Uh, that is, except for some cheese."

PART II *The Nature of the Crises*

14

The Past Leads to the Present

THE PROBLEMS WE FACE TODAY are the natural, inevitable conclusion of a trend that started two hundred years ago.

The economy of the United States has never been free of governmental intervention—no matter how much some people may romanticize, or criticize, the *laissez faire* conditions that supposedly existed during the nineteenth century. The history of the United States is the history of a "limited government" continually expanding its limits.

THE BEGINNING

It all began with the American Revolution.

Since the revolution was supposed to be a war against taxation, the Continental Congress decided that it wouldn't be prudent to tax Americans to finance the war. Instead, in August 1775, the Continental currency was issued. It was in the form of notes (IOUs), to be repaid in eight to thirteen years in gold and silver. There was nothing immediately available backing the currency.

The disastrous consequences of the fiat money [1] were similar to those experienced from the inflationary currency issued during the French Revolution shortly afterward. In fact, there are many parallels between the two revolutions.

[1] Paper money that can't be exchanged for gold—which, by governmental fiat, must be accepted in trade.

Coercion was necessary to force acceptance of the Continentals at face value, because within a little over a year they had lost 50% of their value. Each state had a "Council of Safety," which is a euphemism that refers only to the safety of the state, not the individual.

The Councils and the Congress decreed price controls with severe jail sentences and confiscation of goods for anyone who acted as if the Continentals had depreciated. Hoarding of goods was also a punishable offense.

The controls created shortages of salt, grain, and other necessities of life. By March 1779, there was general starvation in Boston; commerce had been reduced to a barter basis. There was no blockade against the colonies at the time. Food could have been imported easily, and the nearby wilderness provided an abundance. But the government managed to squeeze the life out of a formerly thriving city through inflation and price controls.

The government's response to such problems as grain shortages was to make it a crime to use grain to distill liquor.

Soldiers were paid at rates that ignored the inflation, so it was hard to recruit anyone to fight; only one man of every eight who were qualified would serve in the army. Wage controls were introduced to alleviate the problem, but that led to people working for offshore privateers who weren't bothered by the controls.

The Continental dollar was issued in August 1775. By the end of 1776, it was worth only 50¢. By April 1779, it had depreciated to 5¢. Its value continued falling until the Continental Congress declared bankruptcy—at which time the Continentals were trading for silver dollars at the rate of 500 to 1. The Congress then issued new paper money, exchangeable at the rate of one new dollar for twenty old dollars. But the new currency lost 50% of its value within a few months.

It's interesting that Americana eulogizes the heroism of the starving colonists—at Valley Forge and throughout the colonies —without investigating the source of the problem. "War is hell" is the sum of the explanation. But if war is hell, inflation is something even worse.

Facing the disastrous consequences of inflation, it's unlikely that the colonists would have won the war had they been fighting a country adjacent to its borders. In all probability, only the great distance between England and the colonies made "independence" possible.

During the runaway inflation, a great deal of silver and gold was hoarded because it was against the law to use it. But when the Continental failed, Congress repealed most of the price controls and prohibitions, and the hard money came out of hiding. In addition, British and French troops in the colonies had hard money and that found its way into circulation too.[2]

In 1792, after the Articles of Confederation had failed and the new Constitution had created a new Congress, a sound money was introduced. The currency was backed by silver, with allowance for a gold coin to be minted which would also be legal tender. It's important to realize that nothing had prevented the Congress from doing the same thing at the beginning of the revolution.

Although it's little recognized, the American Revolution was a war between two governments. On the one hand was the British government which enjoyed monopoly trade privileges with the colonies, imposed duties and tariffs on all items entering the colonies, and extracted what little it could enforce in taxes.

On the other hand was the Continental Congress, a group of men who wanted the monopoly trade privileges and tariffs for themselves. They called for an end to duties and trading with England, somehow won the war, and then imposed duties and tariffs, and resumed the trade with England.

After the revolution, the American government imposed taxes and restrictions far greater than those the British could have enforced.

The new government simply followed tradition. Controls and intervention were nothing new. It had always been the common practice throughout the colonies to regulate by law:

[2] Most of the foregoing story can be found in William Graham Sumner's *The Financier and the Finances of the American Revolution* listed, along with other histories of the period, in the Recommended Reading.

the price and quality of commodities like bread, meat, bricks, fire-wood, and leather; fares charged by public conveyances, storage and wharfage rates, and fees for such public services as corn-grinding and slaughtering; licences, fees, and wages of millers, carmen, porters, draymen, and smiths; prices of food, drink, and lodging in taverns, and market practices in general.[3]

So the new government imposed the normal import and export taxes, port regulations, embargoes, bounties, monopoly privileges, and subsidies. Intervention into private affairs was assumed to be a necessary function of a benevolent government.

Needless to say, however, no one produced or exchanged in any way that wouldn't lead to something he wanted. Most people managed to circumvent the interference, even if they generally supported the government. And, of course, as each regulation produced unexpected consequences, it was replaced or amended in a way that provided for *more* governmental control over the economy.

And so the seed was sown. The institution of government was firmly established, and it grew and grew—slowly at first, but picking up speed ever so steadily.

EXPANSION

As the years went by, governmental policies produced the inevitable consequences. Economic tinkering led to panics and depressions. Enforced trade policies led to wars. And each time a government policy caused a bad consequence, the proposed solution was a bigger government program.

Occasionally, special disasters provided opportunities to speed up the government's growth rate. The Civil War allowed Abraham Lincoln to command extraordinary powers over the lives of U.S. citizens, and permitted two landmarks in the history of monetary blunders.

One was the National Banking Act, which gave the government power to control banks throughout the country. Heretofore,

[3] Clinton Rossiter: *The Seedtime of the Republic,* page 62.

many local banks had issued inflationary banknotes and caused localized bank failures and recessions. Hereafter, inflation could be produced on a nationwide scale, enlarging the bad consequences.

The other policy was the issuance of United States Notes in April 1862. They were just like the Continentals; in fact, this point was raised in Congressional debates on the subject. But the majority of Congress was sure that the government could control the situation and prevent a repetition of the Continental debacle.

One argument against the note issue was that it would open the door to more such issues until the nation was drowned in paper money. The proponents argued that necessity required the one issue, and that it would never be repeated.

The second issue came four months later.

By 1863, the U.S. notes had driven other forms of money into hoarded hiding. Gold and silver stopped circulating; people spent the U.S. notes instead because they were rapidly depreciating. Within four years, retail prices had doubled and the price of gold had risen 185%.

It's amazing that some people are claiming today that the government should be issuing similar notes—in order to avoid paying interest on the national debt.

The notorious "Greenbacks" led to the depression of 1873, the worst in American history up to that time. It dragged on until 1879 as the government tried to bring about recovery. Surprisingly, it was only the veto of Ulysses S. Grant that prevented Congress from issuing more inflationary currency to get the country out of the depression.

THE PACE ACCELERATES

By the latter part of the nineteenth century, the governmental growth rate was curving upward at a sharper angle. It was assumed by then that almost any social problem should be solved by the government.

For example, many businessmen had tried to create voluntary price-fixing arrangements between themselves. But as is inevitably the case, the arrangements lasted only until they could get back to their offices to instruct their salesmen to cut prices and undersell the competition.

Finally, the businessmen turned to the government to enforce their high prices and end "cut-throat" competition. This was done through the passage of antitrust laws and the establishment of various regulatory commissions. Contrary to present-day opinion, these things *weren't* done to enforce low prices for consumers. Quite the opposite; they were designed to protect big business from competition.[4]

The early part of the twentieth century included the Income Tax amendment and further efforts to break up the large companies that were best satisfying consumers.

It also included the passage of the Federal Reserve Act in 1913. It was designed to end the banking panics caused by the National Banking Act. It provided for a uniform system of bank inflation throughout the country.

By then, the U.S. government resembled the typical old-world governments, and was anxious to take its place as a "world power." This was facilitated by entry into the European "World War."[5]

Again, the cost of the war was financed largely by inflating the currency. In 1921, when the Federal Reserve System attempted to withdraw some of the excess currency, a recession ensued. Having learned its lesson, the FRS inflated the dollar with a vengeance through the bulk of the 1920s.

By 1928, the inflation was causing a run on the government's gold supply, so the money managers felt compelled to deflate. The deflation started at the end of 1928, the General Market began to reassert itself, and resources were shifting during 1929.

[4] This period is well documented in two books by Gabriel Kolko: *The Triumph of Conservatism* and *Railroads & Regulation*.

[5] For one interesting example of how U.S. citizens were misled into thinking they were attacked, read how the sinking of the *Lusitania* was arranged in Colin Simpson's book, *The Lusitania*.

The stock market crash in October merely confirmed what was already visible: A depression was in progress.

By 1921, the government's powers had been greater than ever. The period of the 1920s had seen more government involvement in the economy than ever before. It felt it could keep an inflationary boom going indefinitely—"fine-tuning" the economy with public works programs, farm subsidies, hundreds of other federal spending projects, and monetary management.[6]

Thus, when the crash came in 1929, it was a gigantic crash. The Federal Reserve Act had been hailed as a way to end such depressions, but it merely helped make them larger.

RECOVERY OBSTRUCTED

The General Market had a great deal to do to recover. But, of course, the government was determined not to give it a chance. A larger depression, in turn, called for "bolder" action by the government—which meant even *more* of more of the same.

President Hoover used the opportunity to initiate many of the powers he'd been calling for during his political career. He was anything but the "do-nothing" president that history has labeled him.

Franklin Roosevelt berated him for creating a swollen bureaucracy; he promised to cut the federal payroll and taxes by 25% each. Of course, he did just the opposite once he was elected. He launched expensive and expansive programs, and experimented with every kind of dictatorial control over the economy that his advisers could think of.

American citizens were prohibited from owning gold, the dollar was devalued, subsidies abounded, and inflation resumed. As a result, the depression dragged on through the 1930s.

[6] For a detailed survey of governmental economic intervention during the 1920s, read Murray Rothbard's *America's Great Depression*, listed in the Recommended Reading.

Many people think the depression ended in 1933, but the unemployment total was still over nine million in 1938. Others think the depression ended at the beginning of World War II. But there were only two groups of people during the war. One group was living in foxholes—which are certainly depressed areas. The other group was at home, possibly making more paper money than ever before. But there was nothing to buy with the money. You couldn't get new tires for your car—or even a new car. You couldn't get much meat, sugar, gasoline, cigarettes, or any of the other things we take for granted as necessities of life.

Those who were piling up paper dollars during the war expected to have great wealth when the war ended. But by the time production of consumer goods had resumed, the dollar had lost 40% of its prewar value. Once again the government had financed a war with inflation.

TECHNOLOGY VS. GOVERNMENT

As wartime controls were lifted, a new boom period started. Technology was somewhat free to cater to consumer demands—though still hampered by governmental programs. American standards of living resumed their upward curves.

Since the Industrial Revolution, technology has expanded at a rapid rate. This growing technology, the ability to have machines perform the greater part of a man's work, has expanded the productive capacity of the nation by geometric proportions.

One could almost tolerate the government's attempts to divert some of that capacity to wasteful programs. But no government will be contained; it always breaks through its bonds to expand its sphere. After World War II, the U.S. government enlarged its interest to promote the "general welfare" of the entire world. Great amounts of American resources were shipped out of the country.

No nation can tolerate that kind of waste; the losses are

irreplaceable. The gold supply was drained and the economy became more and more dependent upon government subsidies at home.

Most of the spectacular "recoveries" of the Western European economies resulted from never-to-be-paid-back investments by the U.S. government. The actual spending of the money was directed by the governments of the nations involved. And so those economies are built upon sand—just as the U.S. economy is now—and the consequences there may be even more tragic.

TREND UNBROKEN

Throughout American history, each president has played his role predictably, without interrupting the overall trend. Public attitudes about history tend to be cloudy and misconceived. For example, John Kennedy is remembered for his "bold" new plans, even though Dwight Eisenhower did as much as he to increase the size of government. *Every* president has felt it to be his duty to enlarge his government.

There are those who feel that America would be quite different today if it weren't for Roosevelt, but they just don't see the irresistible trend. There's absolutely no reason to believe that things would have been much different had Hoover been reelected. The man in office at the time simply jumped aboard a bandwagon that was moving at top speed.

The history of U.S. governmental intervention was once one of turning local problems into national problems. Now even those have become international as the governments of the Western world have banded together, hoping to overcome their mutual weaknesses.

But through it all, no human being produces or exchanges unless he believes it will lead to something he wants—despite the laws, the regulations, the mutual assistance pacts. And the intelligent people all over the world are rushing to get rid of dollars and other weak currencies. They grab gold, silver, diamonds, less weak currencies—anything they believe may give them a chance to preserve what they've worked for.

The General Market is energetically reasserting itself. And governments are running out of the steam necessary to fight it. More and more, their weapons are reduced to pronouncements, empty threats, and new agreements between governments.

THE PRESENT

Today, the U.S. government is running out of time. The inflationary cycle has reached the point where it doesn't respond to fine tuning anymore. The elaborate structures the government is trying to protect are becoming more and more vulnerable to the slightest mistakes.

Much has been said about how close the United States came to a banking panic and a stock market crash in 1970.[7] These incidents have often been cited as proof that the crashes and panics can be avoided. To me, they're proof that the system is so shaky that it was saved in each case only by the best luck imaginable. I don't wish to be dependent upon such a vulnerable system.

We're obviously getting very close to the depression that's been in the works for thirty years now. When it will begin, if it hasn't already, no one can say. But the drop of the dollar, the flights to gold and silver, disasters like Penn Central, Lockheed, the credit crunches of 1970 and 1973 indicate that it can't be far off.

In addition, the government is flirting dangerously with runaway inflation. The built-in spending programs of the government mean that there's practically no chance of budget reductions, deflation, or even a let up in the constant expansion of inflation.

[7] For chronologies of these events, see Adam Smith's *Supermoney* and Charles Ellis' *The Second Crash*.

Further, the U.S. dollar is no longer backed by any precious metal. The government refuses to pay out gold to *anyone* in exchange for dollars. Of course, if it did it would quickly lose its small hoard of $10.4 billion—since there's at least eight times that much in dollar claims against the gold held by nervous central bankers throughout the world.

What we have seen in recent years is just the beginning. There are millions of economic mistakes the market must liquidate. The dollar has a long way to go downward before it reaches a realistic level relative to its gold content.

If the mistakes accumulated so far weren't bad enough, consider the fact that the government is doing nothing to change all this. Quite the contrary, it is talking about "free" medical care for everyone, guaranteed annual incomes, more aid to underdeveloped nations.

Things aren't getting any better; they're continuing to get worse—even before the crash comes.

15

The International Monetary System

PRICE CONTROLS HAVE BEEN applied internationally, as the governments of the Western world have tried to keep their currencies from fluctuating against each other. As with any price control, the ending of it signals a long movement away from the direction of the controls. So an understanding of the currency price controls is necessary to understand the movements of the dollar today.

As explained in Chapter 8, the prices of currencies in exchange with each other are based upon their official gold contents. Thus, the Swiss franc (which officially contains .006996 ounces of gold) is officially priced at 3.3855 francs per U.S. dollar (which officially contains .023685 ounces of gold).

There are two ways to express a currency exchange rate; it depends which currency is used to express the price. For example, the official exchange rate between Swiss francs and dollars is 3.3855 francs to the dollar. But this can be stated also as $.2954 (29.54¢) to the franc. These are two ways of saying the same thing.

Throughout this book, I'll cite all exchange rates using the second way—expressing the price of a foreign currency using U.S. dollars. To translate any of my figures to the other way, simply divide my figures into $1 ($1 ÷ .2954 = 3.3855).

The official exchange rates are based upon the official gold contents. But as governments inflate, the *actual* gold contents of their currencies change. And inflation creates side effects—balance of payments deficits, the possibility of an impending devaluation, etc. And so supply and demand considerations create pressure on the currency prices to change in one direction or the other.

THE SYSTEM

At the end of World War II, the governments of the Western world agreed to a system of fixed exchange rates. They decided it would be better if there were no extreme fluctuations between currencies. Such fluctuations would be limited to 1% in either direction.

That means, for example, that the Swiss franc, officially pegged at that time at 22.9¢, would be allowed to go up only as far as 23.1¢ or down as far as 22.7¢.

But how would they keep the prices within these limits? Laws couldn't prevent international speculators or concerned savers from exchanging in a black market. Another method was required.

The arrangement worked this way: If the price of the Swiss franc reached 23.1¢ (the upper limit), the Swiss government was required by the agreement to enter the exchange market and buy as many dollars as necessary to keep the price from going higher. They would sell as many francs as demanded at 23.1¢—to keep anyone from selling them at a higher price.

If the price moved in the other direction, approaching the lower limit of 22.7¢, the U.S. government was obligated to enter the market and purchase as many Swiss francs as necessary to keep the price from going lower.

The actual buying operations were conducted by the central banks of each country.

Naturally, the system encouraged governments to inflate, since their currencies couldn't fall more than 1% below their official rates. But it was expected that any currency that was inflated more than other currencies would be devalued by its government. This would create a new, lower official gold content and create a new exchange rate with other currencies. The new rate would be protected by the system.

The system seemed to work well for many years. There were recurring devaluations by some nations, but that simply made it easier for other nations to support their currencies at the lower rates.

If a government waited too long to devalue its weak currency, other governments would accumulate large quantities of it. They would present the currency to the issuing government and demand gold in exchange for it—at the prevailing gold content rate. This was an incentive to any weak nation to devalue, because if it waited too long it would lose too much of its gold reserves.

It seemed to be an air-tight system—a showcase example of governments' ability to rule the market and the world.

THE DOLLAR'S ROLE

At the end of World War II, the U.S. dollar was the strongest, most respected currency in the world. In 1949, the government had gold reserves of 701 million ounces.

Because the dollar seemed truly "as good as gold," a number of smaller nations used dollars for their monetary reserves, rather than gold. And it became accepted practice among even major nations to count U.S. dollars among their monetary reserves, along with their gold supplies.

In international exchange, it was easier to refer to things in dollar figures than in ounces of gold. The dollar had attained a truly supreme position in world finance.

PROBLEMS DEVELOP

However, the American rulers seemed more intent upon making America the benevolent patron of the world than upon maintaining the integrity of their currency. Inflation at home was compounded by irresponsible distributions of dollars abroad. The U.S. government was subsidizing almost every other government in the world—including its avowed enemies, the communist countries.

The heavy U.S. inflation, at home and abroad, put pressure on the dollar in international exchange. Central banks had to buy large quantities of the dollar to keep it within the allowable fluctuation limits.

Not surprisingly, many central banks turned in their dollars for gold, and before long the U.S. gold reserve started to disappear. From its high in 1949, the reserve dropped to 651 million ounces in 1950, to 509 million ounces in 1960, and to 394 million ounces in 1965.

By 1960, the dollar was clearly overpriced. Perhaps any other nation would have devalued at that point, but the U.S. government was determined not to do so. It counted on its huge gold reserve to meet all claims. It didn't even curtail its massive "foreign aid" programs. So dollars continued to pile up in foreign treasuries.

The diminishing gold reserve created additional problems. By law, U.S. currency in circulation was to be backed one-fourth by gold; and commercial bank deposits at the Federal Reserve banks were also to be backed one-fourth by gold.

These two requirements left little gold with which to honor foreign claims. So the government simply repealed the two laws —removing the only legal limits on inflation in the United States.

Although these moves were designed to reassure foreign governments that there would always be plenty of gold to pay them, the reassurance fell on deaf ears. The run on the gold supply continued unabated. By 1968, the gold stock had dwindled to 296 million ounces ($10.37 billion worth at $35 per ounce).

At that point, the government decided that the gold stock would be reduced no further. Foreign governments with dollar claims had to wait in line until the U.S. acquired new gold to pay out.

EXPORTING INFLATION

All this created terrible problems for the foreign governments —as long as the fixed exchange rate system continued.

The central banks could only support the dollar by *buying* dollars in the exchange market. And with what did they purchase dollars? With their own currencies, of course. And, since none of the governments could tax its own citizens for such a program, the dollars were bought with new issues of the local currency. The new currency was paid to buyers in the exchange market who preferred that currency to the dollar. And, of course, they didn't bury the currency in the ground; they used it.

The currency eventually found its way back to the country of origin, either through investments or deposits in that country's banks. And it had the same inflationary effects upon the country as if the government had simply inflated the currency at home.

In other words, the cost of supporting the dollar was domestic inflation for the foreign government.

If the dollars accumulating in the central banks could have been exchanged for gold, the increased gold reserves would have justified the new currency issues. But once the U.S. government restricted gold payments, the foreign governments were in trouble. They had inflation at home—and increasing sums of depreciating dollars in their treasuries.

This is the origin of the expression "the U.S. is exporting inflation to Europe."

TO SOLVE THE PROBLEM

The various governments were faced with real problems and no apparent solutions. The obvious remedy was for the U.S. to devalue the dollar and resume full gold payments at the new rate of exchange.[1]

---

[1] The late economist F. A. Harper pointed out that, as recently as 1970, the U.S. government could have *doubled* its gold stock simply by using less than half of its annual budget deficit to purchase gold in the free market.

But the U.S. government was determined not to devalue the dollar. Since the various American rulers of the past several decades have shown absolutely no interest in fiscal responsibility, I have no guess why the government was so reluctant to devalue and cheat its creditors.

The government was clearly violating the fixed exchange agreements by refusing to devalue, so it's a wonder the foreign governments continued to play the game as long as they did.

Finally, on September 26, 1969, the German government withdrew temporarily from the agreement, allowing the dollar to drop against the German mark. During the next month, the dollar plunged downward by about 10%—a very significant change in foreign exchange markets where fluctuations were usually 1–2%.

When the dollar appeared to stabilize at a new lower level, the German government declared an *up*valuation of 9.2896%. This means the Germans *increased* the gold content of the mark by 9%—requiring fewer marks to redeem an ounce of gold. This is the opposite of a *devaluation*.

The upvaluation made the official exchange rate between the mark and the dollar the same rate the free market had arrived at. With the new, apparently more realistic rate, the German government resumed its agreement to support the dollar.

Why the Germans were so anxious to get back into the system, I can't say. They had to upvalue to do so (since the U.S. wouldn't devalue), as the old rate clearly invited a run from dollars to marks.

But by increasing the gold content of the mark, the German government increased the amount of gold it owed for *its* currency. The cost of the upvaluation was at least three billion marks (equivalent to nearly a billion dollars).

The German upvaluation was the first break in the dam that had been erected to withstand the inexorable flood of currency changes.

On June 1, 1970, Canada [2] (which had only joined the fixed

[2] All references to nations mean the governments or central banks of those nations, of course. And all references to Germany mean West Germany.

exchange system in 1962) dropped out, announcing that the Canadian dollar would now *float*. A float is simply the absence of a fixed exchange rate; the currency price is determined by supply and demand in the marketplace. The nation still redeems its currency with gold, but no longer supports the currency of any other government.

Canada actually floated its dollar for only a couple of months. Once the Canadian dollar reached approximate par with the American dollar (C. $1.00 = U.S. $1.00), the Canadian central bank intervened from time to time to keep the rate generally at par. However, it continues to refer to its currency as floating— even though it buys and sells U.S. dollars to keep the exchange rate where it wants it.

This is what's called a "dirty float"—an official float muddied by occasional central bank purchases and sales of a foreign currency.

MORE UPVALUATIONS

In the spring of 1971, after a few calm months, the run from the U.S. dollar accelerated again. In early May, the pressure became so great that several European governments closed their foreign exchange markets to halt the onslaught of dollars.

Over the weekend of May 8, 1971, several governments took further action. Germany, Belgium, and the Netherlands decided to let their currencies float. Switzerland upvalued by 7.06937% and Austria by 5.05%.

On August 15, 1971, the United States announced that it would "temporarily" stop paying out gold to foreign governments for dollars. Since the U.S. government had in fact been paying out very little gold in the two years prior to that, the suspension merely meant that foreign governments shouldn't bother standing in line anymore.

The runs against the dollar continued through 1971 until, finally, the U.S. agreed to a devaluation on December 18. The devaluation was only 7.89%, however, which promised little to alleviate the currency problems—despite President Nixon's belief that it was the greatest monetary agreement in history.

Concurrently, other currencies were upvalued; among them the German mark by 4.61%, the Austrian schilling by 5.05%, the Netherlands guilder and the Belgian franc by 2.76% each. All the nations rejoined the fixed exchange system.

At the same time, it was agreed that currencies could now fluctuate by 2¼ % in either direction—a total range of 4½ %.

Despite the reassurances of the money managers, the dollar problems were far from settled. Dollars continued to pour into European countries to be converted to foreign currencies. In June 1972, the Swiss government imposed limitations upon interest rates that could be paid to foreigners holding Swiss franc accounts in Swiss banks.[3] Other governments soon followed suit.

During January 1973, another major run from the dollar developed. At that point, the Swiss government finally threw in the towel; the General Market had won again. The Swiss withdrew from the fixed exchange rate system, and all other major governments withdrew shortly afterward.

The float so far has not been entirely a clean one. But most major currencies are moving in realistic directions, and the stronger currencies have increased substantially in price.

On February 13, 1973, the U.S. government devalued again —for what reason it's impossible to guess. Since the government hasn't been paying out gold since 1971, its two devaluations mean only that the U.S. government has raised the price at which it will *not* sell gold from $35 to $38 to $42.22!

With all major currencies floating, the latest devaluation had no effect upon currency rates.

Any future U.S. devaluations will be similarly insignificant until one of the following things happens: (1) fixed exchange rates are reimposed; (2) the dollar is made convertible again (meaning the U.S. will redeem dollars with gold); or (3) the devaluation is large enough to meet the free market price of gold.

For the indefinite future, then, free market currency prices and free market gold prices are far more important than any U.S. devaluations.

[3] These limitations will be explained in Chapter 23.

VALUE OF FLOATS

Many people believe that fixed exchange rates are a more orderly system, and hope for an early return to them. I don't agree. The floating system is realistic, and eliminates many inequities and distortions that occur with the fixed system.

It's said that importers and exporters are hurt by the uncertainty of floating rates. This is no problem, however. Suppose a U.S. businessman is exporting to France and expects to receive 300,000 French francs a year from now. He doesn't know what the francs will be worth in U.S. dollars a year hence. But he can eliminate the uncertainty by buying a futures contract for 300,000 francs—at a price determined today in U.S. dollars.

If the price now is 25¢ per franc, for example, he can make a deal today to sell the francs a year from now for, say, 25.5¢. He may be required to put up a small deposit as a guarantee that he'll deliver the francs.

Whether the price of the franc goes up or down during the year, when he receives his 300,000 francs he'll deliver them for $76,500 to the person with whom he made the contract. As far as *he's* concerned, the exchange rate *is* fixed.

If he has to pay a small cost for the protection (which isn't always necessary), it's an incidental cost of doing business. That's far better than if all taxpayers had to support his business through the inflation caused by fixed exchange rates.

Another objection leveled at floating currencies is that the exchange rates become the prey of speculators who supposedly cause wide price fluctuations.

Just the opposite is true. It's far easier to speculate in currencies when the rates are fixed. With the dollar basically weak, you simply wait until a temporary fluctuation takes the Swiss franc to its lower level and then buy. You know the franc can't go any lower but it can increase by 4%. And with only a 4% deposit required on a futures contract, the 4% rise produces a 100% return on your investment.

Now, however, if the Swiss franc is floating around 35¢, you have no way of knowing how far downward an interim fluctuation might take it. A drop of 1.5¢ is sufficient to wipe out a 4% investment. It was much safer and easier to speculate when the rates were fixed.

It's important to realize, too, that speculators don't create chaos in the market, they stabilize it. Using the exporter example from page 118, suppose there were no speculators in the current market. On the day he needed to make a contract, what if there were no businessmen with opposite needs willing to buy his francs? Instead of getting a price of 25.5¢ for them, he might have to take 22¢ in order to encourage someone to make a deal with him.

But with speculators in the market, there's always someone to deal with. The larger (and freer) a market is, the more stable it will be. Speculators increase the size of a market—providing more alternatives and liquidity. They perform a service by watching out for bargains and grabbing them before the price goes too far in one direction. The more speculators in the market, the more competition, the more differences of opinion, the more likely that someone will be available to take the other side of a contract.

The large movements in currency prices today result from the dollar being overpriced for so long. When the dollar finally reaches its proper level, speculators will keep the price from moving too fast in any one direction at any given time (unless there's a good reason for it to do so).

THE GNOMES OF ZURICH

Another popular fallacy concerns the famous (or infamous) "Gnomes of Zurich" who presumably manipulate the world's currency and gold markets. The Gnomes, supposedly, are certain Swiss bankers who rule the financial world.

Rumors abound concerning the actions of the Gnomes at any given time. It's assumed that the Gnomes are carrying out their nefarious schemes by some action in the market—and a smart operator will do whatever they're doing.

Swiss bankers have a well-deserved reputation for prudence, discretion, honesty, and objectivity. They're generally astute money managers who have learned to ignore the statements of governments and look at balance sheets instead.

But they aren't infallible. I've had a good many differences of opinion with them over economics, monetary theory, and coming events. And so far, I've found it better to trust my own opinion.

Swiss bankers don't make things happen in the markets. They try to be alert enough to be on the right side when things do happen.

The largest part of the money invested by Swiss bankers belongs to their customers, invested on instructions from the customers. If a client wants the banker to buy gold for him, the banker buys gold. So if the rumor is that "Swiss banks are buying gold right now," it means partly that, on balance, the *customers* of the Swiss banks (from all over the world) are net buyers of gold.

Many of the banks' customers have "trust" accounts—which authorize the bank to make the decisions for the customer. But often one bank will choose to buy what another bank is selling.

The monetary crises of the world aren't caused by the Gnomes of Zurich. In fact, the upvaluation of the Swiss franc in 1971 reportedly cost the Swiss banks over one billion francs, because of the foreign currencies they were holding at the time.

The same accusations of market manipulation are sometimes charged against the London gold bullion dealers. A handful of men get together everyday at noon to set the price of gold for the day. This has led some people to believe the dealers can establish any price they choose—making the price go up or down to their own profit. But the real world doesn't work that way. The dealers set a price they *hope* will protect them from undue losses. They set two prices—a buying price and a selling price— a few cents apart.

If they set the prices too high, they'll be overwhelmed with customers wanting to sell, and they'll be required to buy a lot of overpriced gold. If they set the prices too low, they'll have to sell a lot of underpriced gold, and then replenish their stocks with purchases at higher prices. If they set the prices too far apart, they invite competition from other markets where the prices are closer together.

Bullion dealers are simply businessmen hoping to make a profit. They usually do make a profit—because they *understand* the market, not because they control it.

The same principles apply to the South African government, which is the major seller of gold in the world. It can hold back its gold, waiting for higher prices; but what if the price doesn't go up? If demand diminishes while it's waiting, the gold will eventually be sold at a lower price.

Even if, by refusing to sell, it could cause the price to go up, the price would start down again the minute South Africa began to sell.

Monetary crises aren't caused by conspiratorial individuals or groups who hope to profit from them. The crises are the result of the General Market's attempt to reassert a natural position consistent with consumer demands. Speculators can't make a crisis; they can only seek profit or protection when they think one is coming.

When it becomes obvious that a crisis is impending, many people will rush to be on the right side when the crisis hits. This leads others to believe that those who rushed caused the crisis. They didn't; they were only fortunate enough to see it coming.

No one rules the General Market. Those who make big profits are the ones who *understand* the market.

PROMOTING EXPORTS

Another argument today is that a government *should* support the weaker currencies of nations to which its own citizens export products. If the exporting nation's currency is too highly priced, it will discourage exports and encourage imports. Thus, to protect its balance of payments, the government should prevent its own currency from rising too far in price. So goes the argument.

As we've already seen, the balance of payments issue is solely the result of inflation. If a government didn't inflate its currency, it wouldn't be concerned with its balance of payments. Any currency spent outside its borders could be redeemed for gold with no threat to the government; there would be no more currency outstanding than there was gold in reserve.

But suppose the government *has* inflated. Should it protect its exporters by supporting weaker currencies? Why bother? If its currency rises, greater imports will follow. Its balance of payments may show a deficit, but floating exchange rates would then cause its currency to go back down in price, once again stimulating exports. With floating rates, the market is self-correcting. It's only with fixed rates that a government has to be concerned with international balances.

The issue isn't really that simple. But those who argue for fixed rates make it appear to be that simple. And the conclusions I've reached stem from their own simple premises.

In addition, any government that supports weaker currencies does so at the expense of its own citizens. Through inflation or taxation, the consumers will pay for what amounts to a subsidy to the exporters.

Also, the discouraging of imports deprives the consumers of many better alternatives—penalizing them to benefit the exporters.

There are many reasons why supporting weaker currencies isn't in the best interests of a nation. Perhaps the most telling evidence is the state of the U.S. dollar today after years of supporting other governments.

However, none of this means that some of the stronger governments won't try to support the dollar in the future, thinking it's in their own interests to do so. Such a policy on their part may be in *your* best interest, though, because it will tend to delay the ultimate conclusion—giving you time to make your own investments before the dollar drops too far.

WORLD CURRENCY

One other matter should be examined before we leave this subject.

The nations of the world, apparently believing the age-old fallacy that "in union there is strength" have tried many schemes to protect each other's currencies. The last attempt was the creation of a world reserve currency called Special Drawing Rights—SDRs. Presumably, they're intended to replace both the dollar and gold as reserves for the currencies of nations.

It's interesting to note, however, that within a few years of the SDRs inception, nations and the International Monetary Fund (which issues the SDRs) were requesting gold (not SDRs) in payment of obligations. The SDR system has never really begun to work—and probably never will.

A world currency might have been imposed upon the market twenty years ago—before the problems started. Now it could only survive with the support of the stronger currencies. And those governments appear to be awakening at last to the hard fact that their own survivals are more important.

World currencies, present or future, won't prevent you from keeping your assets in a safe medium and in a safe place.

There is no strength in union, only greater weakness as the weak pull down the strong. Other nations have pulled down the U.S., and now the U.S. has been pulling down the few remaining strong nations that are left.

As a result, there are no strong currencies today (except for a few minor ones that don't offer any advantages to a protection-minded investor). Fortunately, however, some currencies are considerably less weak than the dollar.

And since their governments appear to be detaching themselves from the problems of the dollar, there are still havens of safety to be found.

16
When Will the Crises End?

DURING AUGUST 1973, I received a number of calls from investment clients and readers of the *Devaluation* book—wanting to know if I thought the monetary crises were over. The dollar had risen 13% against European currencies and gold had dropped from its July high of $127 to around $100.

There will undoubtedly be many lulls in the middle of the storms. There will be short-term tranquilities created by governmental pronouncements and superficial events—such as the increase in U.S. interest rates or short-term government interventions in the currency.

And most important, the U.S. government will undoubtedly seek to stem the crises by measures *that will only make matters worse in the long term.* For example, if the government sells gold in the free market, it may temporarily depress the price for a few days or even a few weeks. But that will make the eventual price of gold just that much higher. For the less gold the government has, the more likely that there will be a runaway inflation.

There will be many false settlements. The crises won't end as a result of new laws, new international agreements, the borrowing of gold or foreign currencies, new controls, statements of reassurance, or apparent reversals in market speculation.

There are several specific events that must occur before the crises can be considered over. Until those things happen, you can be sure there's more to come. Here are the minimum requirements:

1. *Devaluation and convertibility*: The dollar will have to be devalued by at least 75%—creating a gold redemption price of $160 or more. This would increase the dollar value of the gold reserve to $42 billion which would cover around half the short-term claims against the gold presently held by foreign central banks.

With a price of $160, the government could resume convertibility of the dollar—paying out gold on demand to other central banks. Without that convertibility, there will be continual downward pressure on the dollar.

However, the longer the government waits to do this, the higher the necessary gold figure. Whenever the government devalues, the gold figure will have to be at least as high as the free market gold price, and it must make the gold reserve worth at least half the short-term dollar claims.

A $300 figure would be even firmer. A devaluation is an admission of bankruptcy; but it's only an admission—the bankruptcy has already occurred.

2. *Float*: For the various currencies to find realistic levels relative to each other, the floating of currencies must continue. Fixed exchange rates would disguise weaknesses, preserve unrealistic rates, and allow currencies to be inflated without short-term consequences.

3. *Depression*: A depression is 100% inevitable because of what's already happened. How bad the depression will be is totally dependent upon what the government does. You can assume it will be prolonged and agonizing if the government doesn't cut its budget and allow the General Market to bring about recovery and prosperity.

4. *Shortages*: The shortages will get worse if all controls enacted from 1971 until now aren't removed.

5. *Runaway inflation*: If the paper money supply continues to increase, the chances are very slim that a runaway inflation will be avoided.

The crises will terminate if there's a massive devaluation, restoration of convertibility for foreigners, floating currencies, federal budget cuts, removal of recent controls, and a stabilization of the paper money supply. If those things haven't happened, don't consider the crises at an end.

But that would only bring tranquility to the general situation. It wouldn't lay the foundation for a new prosperity.

LONG-TERM REQUIREMENTS

And so you can expect the worst from the next depression unless the following measures are taken:

1. *Devaluation and convertibility*: The dollar must be devalued by a minimum of 90%—to a gold price of $400 or more. This would make it possible for U.S. citizens to exchange dollars for gold at the U.S. Treasury.

Only when full convertibility is restored can the dollar be considered stable and the government restrained. Constitutions, elections, and "informed citizenries" have proven to be abject failures in controlling governmental expansion. Only unlimited convertibility of gold can keep a government in line.

The $400 gold price would be a good beginning. It would simply be a realistic confirmation of the dollar depreciation of the past forty years. And it would be enough to prevent a run on gold after convertibility is resumed. (As of December 1972, there were 1,121 dollars in circulation for every ounce of gold in reserve.)

2. *Withdrawal of government from the General Market*: To provide a sound basis for a new prosperity, the government would have to terminate all its subsidy programs, foreign aid, welfare programs, grants, insurance companies, factories, retail outlets, the Post Office, etc. Those that have any value to the marketplace can be sold to private companies who would operate them competitively. Then the General Market can determine which are useful and which aren't. The funds currently tied up in these programs could then be diverted by consumer demand to more valuable enterprises.

3. *Termination of economic controls*: To allow full freedom

for the General Market to allocate resources realistically, there would have to be an end to all governmental regulation. That would include import duties, export controls, antitrust laws, monopoly grants, minimum-wage laws, labor laws, investment controls, foreign exchange controls, gold restrictions, etc. Each of these controls interferes with the consumer's ability to get what he wants.

(If the last two measures were enacted, probably less than 5% of the U.S. citizens would suffer a net loss. The rest would gain far more than they'd lose by missing their subsidies or special privileges. And the measures would unleash an unprecedented prosperity that would benefit everyone.)

4. *Deflation*: With the government out of economic activities, the reduction in federal budgets would allow government debts to be retired and currency to be withdrawn from circulation. Eventually, the deflation should reach a point where currency and gold were on a one-to-one basis. Future budgets would have to be financed completely by taxes—to prevent reopening the door to inflation.

5. *Liquidation of the Federal Reserve System*: This is actually part of items 2 and 3, but it's important enough to warrant a separate listing. All regulation of the banking system should end. If a clearing system or other inter-bank service is necessary, the General Market can provide it—paid for by those who actually want the services.

Private banks could then compete with each other to determine the kinds of reserve requirements that their customers want. Some banks would undoubtedly store gold or money substitutes on a one-for-one basis with no inflation; anyone who wanted such stable money could have it, unlike in the present system in which stable money is outlawed.

These five requirements may seem quite radical, but the United States has reached the point where anything less may not be enough to restore a thriving economy. All previous inflation/depression cycles were short enough that the economy could recover eventually without optimum conditions.

Now, however, the government has developed techniques

that have been used to prolong the current cycle for around
forty years. It has encouraged such massive misinvestments that
the market will require a great deal of freedom and mobility
to be able to readjust itself.

In my opinion, anything less than the five requirements will
cause the depression to drag on interminably. It could conceiv-
ably last the rest of our lifetimes.

All indications point in that direction, unfortunately. If anything, the government will expand its participation in the marketplace. So I'm not very optimistic about the future of the American economy.

"Grin and Bear It" by George Lichty, Courtesy of Publishers-Hall Syndicate

© Field Enterprises, Inc., 1971

"I believe that inflation will be beat, I believe that
wages and prices will stabilize, I believe the war will
end, and I believe in magic!"

17
The Future

NO ONE CAN PREDICT the timing and specific nature of future events. The specifics depend too much upon the individual judgments of too many different people. No one could hope to have all the detailed information necessary to predict those judgments and pinpoint the specific times that future events will occur.

However, it *is* possible to utilize the economic principles of the marketplace to determine that certain events are inevitable, or highly likely, even if the timing can't be predicted. We know that no one will suddenly disregard his own self-interest; and that means that large groups of people will turn to other alternatives when their normal methods become unprofitable.

The renowned Gresham's Law is an example of this. It says, in effect, that when two types of money with equal purchasing power become unequal in intrinsic value, most people will spend the money of lesser value and hold onto the money of greater value (or "Bad money drives good money out of circulation"). This is simply a recognition that each individual can be expected to act in his own self-interest.

From the principles reviewed in the first part of this book, we can draw certain general conclusions regarding the future. And while that future may seem complicated and abundant with possibilities, we can bring some order to it by reducing everything to three neat categories: (1) the dollar drop; (2) the next depression; and (3) runaway inflation. Any realistic investment program will consider the basic characteristics of these three phenomena.

129

THE DOLLAR DROP

For many years, American citizens were told that a dollar devaluation would have little effect upon them. But the significance of the dollar's decline in international exchange is already quite visible.

Because of a combination of U.S. inflation and fixed exchange rates, it was possible for many years for foreign companies to undersell American companies. Americans have come to depend upon the prices charged by foreign companies in many product areas—radios, stereo equipment, business machines, other electronic products, watches, automobiles, wines, clothes, etc. Now they must pay higher U.S. prices for these things, whether purchased from foreign or domestic companies.

In addition, there are numerous raw materials or largely unprocessed products that aren't produced in the United States—including natural rubber, industrial diamonds, bananas, cocoa, coffee, tea, etc. And there are others that have very little U.S. production—manganese, bauxite, and other aluminum ores. Plus the many commodities that have current consumption levels far beyond U.S. production—oil, silver, cheese, some textiles, etc.

Prices of all these commodities, and the products made from them, have gone up over the past three years.

And there's an additional price factor involved. There are many commodities produced in the United States that can be sold overseas. If the dollar drops by 20%, such a commodity can be sold for the same number of dollars, but it will cost the foreign importer 20% less than before in his own currency. In that situation, the American producer can even *raise* his dollar price by 10%, and still provide a 10% *reduction* in the foreign currency.

This means that many American products, formerly sold mostly in the U.S., can now be sold more profitably overseas. The result is that American consumers will have to bid higher if they want to continue buying the products. By this process, U.S.

prices of many commodities have gone up—wheat, wool, cattle, corn, copper, and many more—resulting in substantially higher retail prices for clothes, beef, other foods, hard goods, etc.

These upward price trends will continue as the dollar drops further. Even without runaway inflation, it's entirely possible that we could see, within the next year or two, a price of $1 or more for a loaf of bread, $3,500 for the least expensive Volkswagen, and proportionately higher prices for other products. You can also expect some shortages—partly caused by the dollar's depreciation in international exchange.[1]

Investment returns such as interest and dividends can't possibly keep up with the higher living costs. Even normal capital profits from *successful* investments may fall behind. So it's extremely important that you have your assets in investments that will go up at least as fast as U.S. prices increase.

Fortunately, the lengthy price controls on gold, silver, and foreign currencies have created opportunities for much greater than normal growth over the next few years. In fact, the growth should far exceed the purchasing power decreases for the next several years.

When watching the dollar decline, don't look only at official U.S. devaluations. For the most part, they aren't significant.

The devaluation effects foreseen three years ago have come to pass, but they've occurred through devaluations, upvaluations, and floating currencies. While U.S. devaluations have amounted to only 17%, the dollar has actually dropped 30% against the Swiss franc and 30% against the German mark. Expressed in a different way, the Swiss franc *rose* 42% and the German mark rose 42%. So an individual who transferred his savings to a Swiss bank in 1970, to be kept in Swiss francs or German marks, now has 42% more purchasing power than anyone who left his money in dollars. This has been more than enough to cope with rising prices. And there's more to come.

Any assets you hold in dollars will be vulnerable to the sinking dollar. These include U.S. savings accounts, bonds (gov-

[1] The potential lows for the dollar versus other currencies are stated in Chapter 24.

ernment or corporate), mortgages, other debts owed to you, cash
value life insurance policies, pensions, and retirement plans of
any kind.

There are excellent alternatives available to these depreciating investments. There are even ways to maintain the purchasing
power of a mandatory pension or retirement fund as the dollar
drops. These alternatives will be covered in Part V.

THE DOLLAR DROP CONTINUES

If at any time you wonder if the dollar has dropped to its
ultimate market price, review the items listed in Chapter 16 and
the potential currency rates in Chapter 24. If the dollar still
seems to have a long way to go downward, wait before recon-
verting to dollar assets.

And don't be swayed by news of a rising dollar. There are
bound to be interim fluctuations in both directions that have
nothing to do with the long-term trend. They are only lulls in the
middle of the storms.

During August 1973, the dollar rose significantly. This rise
was generally attributed to higher U.S. interest rates—attracting
capital to the U.S. to get the higher return. That could have been
the cause, but it would have no long-term significance.

Mexican interest rates have been abnormally high for many
years, but the Mexican peso dropped 20% against the major
European currencies between 1970 and 1973. High interest rates
won't support a currency's value for any length of time.

And certainly, high interest rates won't continue very long
in the United States (if they haven't already dropped by the
time you read this). For the political pressure is all directed
toward low interest rates. Allowing them to remain high indefinitely would be likely to trigger a recession or depression.
And the only remedy for high interest rates will be heavy inflation.

As it turned out, however, the dollar's rise during August
1973, was engineered by the U.S. Federal Reserve System and

the German central bank. On September 6, 1973, Charles A. Coombs, senior vice-president of the New York Federal Reserve Bank, revealed that the FRS had borrowed $273 million worth of foreign currencies (called "swaps") which it used to purchase dollars in the currency exchange markets in August. In addition, the German central bank purchased $300 million in the market ("dirty float").[2]

These purchases of dollars pushed the dollar upward. But eventually, the swaps will have to be repaid with foreign currencies, so the dollar will go back downward again. All such remedies are short-term in effect, and merely serve to weaken the dollar further.

It's important to realize, too, that dollar increases don't proceed in the same fashion as dollar declines. When the dollar rose in price during the summer of 1973, the increase was very orderly. The increase was substantial—about 13% over a period of a month—but still very orderly. No one panicked to get *into* dollars.

But when the dollar *drops*, the bottom can fall out. Investors, foreign bankers, and speculators rush to get out of dollars while they can *because they don't know how far it can drop.*

The same has been true of gold price changes. Even the 25% drop in price during August 1973, involved no panic. You could buy or sell on any given day without difficulty. But when the dollar looks shaky, the price of gold shoots upward.

The conclusion to be drawn from these trends is that you can't wait until the timing seems right to purchase foreign currencies or gold. You have to invest too soon—perhaps even on a downturn. Only then can you be sure that you'll be covered when a panic drives their prices upward.

THE DEPRESSION

The most important factor to consider regarding the next depression is the inability to determine in advance *what kind*

[2] *Herald Tribune,* Paris edition, September 7, 1973.

of depression it will be. There are two possibilities: (1) an orthodox depression, brought about by deflation of the currency, including the traditional stock market crash, price plunges in real estate and other typical investments, and the increased purchasing power of cash and bonds; or (2) a depression that occurs in the middle of a continuing inflation, which would eliminate the aforementioned traditional characteristics of a depression.

The 1929 depression was triggered by various pressures placed upon the Federal Reserve System to halt the inflation of the 1920s. A deflation was undertaken and that made it impossible to support the high speculative prices in the stock market and real estate.

Now, however, the government appears to believe that it has eliminated the traditional pressures that necessitate an end to an inflationary period. They haven't eliminated the consequences of inflation, though, and so the depression will come anyway— but it may not be triggered by a deflation. If that happens, the characteristics of the depression may be quite different in many ways. And since I've never felt confident that I could outguess bureaucrats or politicians, I believe it's necessary to be ready for both kinds of depression.

TRADITIONAL DEPRESSION

If the depression is a traditional one, it will be easier to recognize, to understand, and to deal with. It could be signaled by a stock market crash, in which case you'd know it would be too late to liquidate dangerous investments such as stocks, mutual funds, and real estate.

Cash might be considerably more valuable, but it may be a string of bank failures that will touch off the depression—in which case it would be too late to withdraw your savings after the need to do so became apparent.

Bonds might be more valuable as a result of a severe drop in prices. But you can't be sure that the issuer of the bonds will survive the crash—whether the bonds be corporate or governmental.

In the same way, debts owed to you might increase in purchasing power theoretically, but you have no guarantee that the debtor will be able to repay you. Your "right" to repayment might be impotent against bankruptcies or governmental intervention.

Various factors *might* make it possible for a specific investment to profit from the situation. But there's no way you can foretell those factors with assurance, so you're better off getting out of all traditional investments now—before it's too late.

INFLATIONARY DEPRESSION

If the depression is an inflationary one, the situation will be considerably different. There will be many problems, but they'll be harder to see and to analyze.

There could still be a stock market crash, but it's less likely. It would have to be precipitated by large brokerage houses failing or a credit-banking crisis, rather than from an orthodox deflation. More likely, there will be some relatively panicky periods, some long downward slides (similar to 1969–1970), and periods of heavy mutual fund selling. But nothing similar to 1929—which was comparable to what a 120-point Dow Jones Industrial Average loss in one day would be now.

There should be a continual upward pressure on the prices of *all* things, accelerating as time goes on, and possibly leading into runaway inflation. As a result, cash, bonds, and other fixed-dollar investments will be constantly losing value.

The principal problem of such a depression would be the inability to see things clearly. Inflation is a relatively invisible phenomenon. You could be holding stocks that are rising in price fairly steadily, and you might not realize that they're constantly losing purchasing power.

This can be illustrated most easily by the chart on page 136.

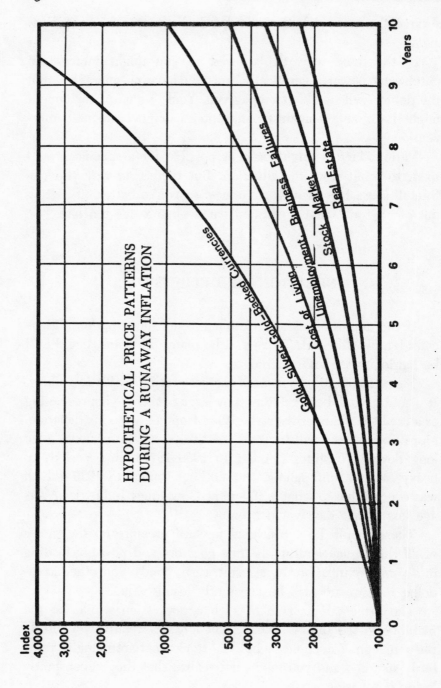

HYPOTHETICAL PRICE PATTERNS
DURING A RUNAWAY INFLATION

The graph isn't meant to represent exact relationships between investments or exact potentials. It's merely an abstraction designed to illustrate a situation in which all things are moving upward in price, but in which *some are moving much faster than others.*

Since no one can measure the cost of living precisely, you can be deceived easily by government figures indicating that your investments are climbing faster than the cost of living. But that may not be the truth, and you'll realize it eventually when you can no longer maintain your previous standard of living.

Another problem involved is that the increasing paper profits in your investments will increase your income taxes, even moving you into higher and higher tax brackets. And so more of your income and profits will be diverted to taxes, even while your purchasing power is dropping. The added taxes will further aggravate the problem.

Thus, you'll need investments that run far ahead of these problems—and you may be inclined, also, to take up tax avoidance as a hobby.

It will be considerably more difficult to pick the right times to buy and sell in these investments. Normally, you would think of a buying signal as being the time when a stock had dropped as far as was practical for its potential or its price-to-earnings ratio.

During such an inflation, you would have to look for a time when the stock had fallen behind the general price pattern. But how *far* behind? You'll have to develop new techniques for determining the value of the stock—and you'll have to consider new factors, such as the company's ability to cope with the problems of such an inflation.

It will be much easier to know where you stand if your assets are in investments that are measured in non-dollar prices and can, in turn, be measured against purchasing power and other values.

The uniqueness and difficulties of an inflationary depression will be a profitable opportunity for those who accept the challenge and devise methods for perceiving reality through the inflationary blur. But for most people, the problems are far too great to cope with. Unless you intend to become a specialist in this new field, I strongly recommend that you stay completely out of all traditional investments—stocks, mutual funds, bonds, real estate, normal commodities.

EITHER KIND

There are also guidelines that apply to either kind of depression. Whichever way it comes, we can be relatively certain that the government will increase its intervention in the marketplace. Just as no one could imagine in 1928 the incredible regulations of 1933, it's difficult today to know what the rules of the game might be in the next few years.

There are a few strong possibilities: rationing, "excess profits" taxes, investment controls, suspension of debt repayments, regulations requiring that "need" be demonstrated to withdraw bank deposits, controls that prohibit the sending of money out of the country, prohibitions on foreign bank accounts, prohibitions on ownership of gold coins, prohibitions on many things we take for granted now.

More than anything else, *liquidity* and *flexibility* are the cornerstones of any preparation for the next depression. Have your money in media that can be used profitably *whichever* way things develop. Don't lock your funds in investments that take forever to sell—like real estate or business enterprises—or in investments that must be watched carefully and perceptively— like the stock market.

Don't be caught in investments that may be destroyed by sudden totalitarian economic controls. Assume that the government will try every fantastic scheme proposed to reduce suffering. Assume that the government will have no regard for the property of anyone who owns anything valuable. Anticipate that normal, legal activities of today will be blamed for the crises and will be prohibited.

Don't have your money in anything you can't move out of

quickly and easily if the situation calls for it. Be in a position to be able to act upon any development.

The investments recommended in Part V—principally gold, silver, and foreign currencies—fit these qualifications. They're investments you can forget about until the depression is a stark reality. Then, you can choose whether or not to act upon apparent bargains, and you'll be invulnerable to new government controls.

RUNAWAY INFLATION

A depression is a period of low living standards while the economy rebuilds within the existing economic structure. Runaway inflation, however, damages the structure itself, and may even destroy it entirely.

Runaway inflation makes it very difficult to conduct normal exchanges; it diverts numerous resources into the otherwise simple task of handling money and spending it. And if it isn't stopped in time, it destroys completely the basic functions of the marketplace—exchange, employment, investment—because there's no currency to facilitate those functions.

The extent to which a runaway inflation would damage the U.S. economy would depend, more than anything else, upon what the government does with the 246 million ounces of gold it apparently possesses now. If the government retains the gold, it may be able to halt a runaway inflation before it goes too far. But if it squanders the gold, it will have nothing with which to issue a new gold-backed currency that can retain value.

The possibility of a runaway inflation becomes greater every day. The federal budget has a multitude of built-in spending programs that are renewed and enlarged upon automatically every year. Even a truly frugal Congress would be hard pressed to find anywhere to cut. And the possibility of a truly frugal Congress seems even more remote.

Any politician seems to know that a depression is sure to follow an end to subsidies and inflation. And that threat is worse than any other he can imagine. A depression is bad for business—the government business—and his job would be in jeopardy.

As of 1973, I see runaway inflation as a 75% probability within the next five years. That means the dollar depreciating to the point where daily purchases will be measured in the thousands, millions, or billions of dollars.

Some of the startling price increases of 1973 were caused by the increasing prices of foreign currencies, as explained in the first part of this chapter. But the overall picture is more suggestive of the early stages of runaway inflation.

It's important to understand that the normally used cost-of-living and dollar depreciation figures tell very little of the story. They come from the U.S. government, which must be considered a biased source. If it were truly possible to measure the prices of all products and services, you might find that the general price level had gone up 20% in a given year when the index shows only 6%.

A more reliable indicator is the Dow Jones Spot Commodity Index, which measures the prices of commodities at the producer level. The index was set at 100 for the years 1924–1926. *It took 48 years to increase by 50%*. During 1972 it started climbing in earnest. On August 28, 1972, the index reached 166.97. One year later, on August 27, 1973, *the index was at 322.54*. After taking 48 years to increase by 50%, it doubled in one year. *That* is an acute change in the trend.

It takes a few months for such price increases to reach the retail level. But I would guess that the retail price explosion will occur within a month either way of the time this book reaches the bookstores. If it hasn't happened by the time you read this, look out!

The price explosion should cause the dollar to nosedive in international exchange, and the price of gold and silver to shoot upward in dollars. So if the price explosion hasn't happened already, it would be prudent to exchange as many dollars as possible into Swiss francs, gold, or silver before the dollar plunges.

That price eruption could well be the beginning of a pro-longed runaway inflation. If an immediate runaway inflation is avoided somehow, it will still be an ever-present possibility for several years to come. You can't consider the threat to have been eliminated until there's been large-scale deflation. And that, as we've seen, is highly unlikely.

The next important question is: If there's a runaway inflation, will it stop in time? Will a new currency be introduced in time to preserve the economy's structure before it collapses totally from lack of an exchange medium?

I see that as a 50/50 question. When the damage becomes more obvious, the government may act to save itself and the nation, but I can't count on it. It seems by far the smarter move to be prepared for a total collapse—and then be relieved if it doesn't happen.

RUNAWAY INFLATION PROTECTION

This means, in effect, two types of preparation. The first part is protection against runaway inflation; the second part is protection against the aftermath if the inflation leads to a total collapse.

For the first part, the advice offered as protection against a dollar drop earlier in this chapter applies equally to runaway inflation. Don't hold assets that are convertible to dollars at a fixed rate—savings accounts, mortgages, debts owed to you, etc. Even if some arrangement is made to adjust repayments to a depreciating dollar (a "cost-of-living" bonus), it's unlikely that the system will work well when inflation accelerates.

The stock market is a bit of a mystery regarding runaway inflation. During the famous German inflation of 1918–1924, the stock exchange went through differing periods—very bad and very good. During 1918, stock prices dropped 50% in terms of purchasing power; during 1919, they dropped by 80%. They lost another 50% during 1920–1922. But during 1923, they increased by 600% in terms of real purchasing power.[3] Again, for the specialist, the volatility represents a challenge and an opportunity. But for the protection-minded investor, the dangers are far too great.

Again, too, you can expect the government to declare "a national emergency," condemn speculators, impose unrealistic price controls, establish rationing, and, in general, do its benevolent best to make matters worse.

The basic protections against a runaway inflation will be—as has always been the case historically—gold, silver, and foreign currencies that aren't afflicted with similar runaway inflations.

For the second part—the possibility of a total collapse—the same investments are warranted. The use of them during such a period will be discussed in Chapter 34. In addition, however, the chaos that would accompany the collapse calls for some additional provisions:

1. A safe place to go and a way to get there.[4]

2. The ability to survive there for an extended period of time —at least one to five years. That means stored food and the ability to grow more, plus anything else you consider necessary to good living.

3. Additional commodities (food, cigarettes, liquor, medicines) that you can trade to others for things you'll want later.

4. Silver coins, and possibly gold coins, to use as money after some order is reestablished, but before a new purchasing medium is available.

5. A safe medium and a safe place to store all excess wealth (not needed for interim survival) so that you can have a large headstart when normality returns.

Ideas like these aren't the stuff of which sophisticated investment books are made. They have an air of paranoia and cultism about them. But unfortunately, the events of the past forty years have brought us to the point where one can't rest

---

[3] Detailed price records in many categories are given in Costantino Bresciani-Turroni's *The Economics of Inflation;* and useful summaries of the price changes are given in the Axe–Houghton study, *Inflation and the Investor* (both listed in the Recommended Reading).

[4] This will be described more fully in Chapter 28.

easily until he *has* faced these possibilities and protected himself.

I assure you that I'm not a pessimist. I enjoy life, and I'm not given to whispered stories about conspiracies. But part of the reason I enjoy life is that I *have* recognized where the events of the past and present are taking us, and I've made provisions so that I no longer have to worry about it.

THE FUTURE

It's obvious that we're entering a new and uncertain era. The timing of future events can't be predicted with precision. And as the future unfolds, there will be many surprises—even for those who have prepared for it.

But that doesn't mean there's nothing you can do to protect yourself. You can eliminate at least 80% of the potential danger for yourself by following a few simple guidelines.

First, stay out of fixed-dollar investments entirely.

Second, stay away from the stock market, mutual funds, and real estate—unless you're prepared to speculate at great risk.

Third, convert as much of your resources as possible to gold, silver, and those foreign currencies that appear most able to avoid runaway inflation.

And lastly, in case the currency is destroyed entirely, create an emergency plan by which you can escape the worst of the aftermath of runaway inflation.

When would be the most profitable time to convert your investments to these forms? If you had done this anytime between 1968 and 1970, you might have felt for a while that you had acted too soon. But when the dam started cracking in the spring of 1971, you would have been well ahead of those who were just waking up. And as the crises began breaking in rapid succession, only those who had been ready too soon were spared the frustration of being too late.

Now we've reached a point where you could be considered

too soon only if you convert just before a minor stock market rally or just before a temporary firming of the dollar. If that happens, you might be in a small loss position for a few months before the market turns your way. But any temporary losses you experience will be more than offset by the profit you'll receive in peace of mind—the knowledge that, whatever happens, you're ready.

The war between the General Market and the governments of the world is reaching an intense stage. Those who bet on the government to win will suffer heavy casualties.

Those who know the General Market must ultimately win will place their bets accordingly. And then they'll be free to relax, to enjoy the present, to be unafraid of the future. They can let the future unfold as it will, because they've insulated themselves from the damage that will afflict so many.[5]

---

[5] The "energy crisis" occurred after this book went to press. For the long term, it will alter nothing said in this book. For the short term, it has created a few bargain prices for some of the investments recommended in Part V.

PART III *A Short Course in Investing*

18

Investment Principles

PEOPLE WHO CONSISTENTLY MAKE MONEY in their investments succeed because of their *understanding*—more than because of information. They apply basic principles of the real world to their investments, rather than allowing specific information to direct them.

While some of those basic principles seem obvious, I've found that few people apply them consistently to their investments. And today they're especially valuable because the stakes are so high.

I've identified seven principles as invaluable to investment success. They can be labeled as seven character traits: humility, moderation, restraint, sanity, direction, courage, and individuality.

HUMILITY

The first principle is: *Don't act as if you know everything.* You *can't* know everything—about the entire world or even about any single investment.

The final outcome of any given investment will depend upon the actions (or non-actions) of literally millions of people. They'll affect the market for whatever you may want to exchange—a stock, gold, real estate, paper money, anything. They'll follow the universal principles of self-interest, but they'll each decide individually how they'll pursue their own self-interests.

You can't possibly know the motivations of all those people; nor can you know *when* they'll decide it's time to act upon a given motivation. You can't know what new technological developments will alter the supply or demand factors for an investment in which you have an interest.

In short, you can't know everything you need to know to act with 100% assurance of success. And neither can anyone else. Don't be swayed by people who seem to have all the answers. No matter how right they seem to have been in the past, they can make mistakes in the future.

There are many things you *can* know, however, and you should examine closely the investments you're considering. You can be aware of basic trends, of economic rules that must prevail, of cause-and-effect relationships that appear to govern the situation.

With understanding and knowledge, you can make investments that have a high probability of success. Act upon what you think best; do it deliberately and with conviction. But always recognize the possibility that some of the hundreds of unknown factors may work against you.

Humility is simply the recognition that you don't know everything. You always allow for the possibility of loss, and you determine in advance how you'll handle that loss if unknown factors work to your disfavor.

MODERATION

Moderation in this case means: *Don't try to buy at the absolute bottom or sell at the absolute top.*

The scenario of a successful investment is supposed to go something like this: You buy on a hot tip, just before the market rushes upward, watch the price go up, and then sell out just before it starts to plunge. Such dreams are exciting but they are, in fact, only dreams.

In the real world, the investors who succeed never expect to buy at the bottom and sell at the top. They know that the bottom of a market is only obvious *in retrospect*—long after the bottom has passed. Only then can one look at the record and know exactly where the bottom was.

When the price of silver was around $1.70 per ounce early in 1971, I talked with a fellow who kept detailed charts of the silver price movements. I told him I thought that silver could drop to $1.50 or so before going up further. He disagreed, saying he was sure it would drop to $1.29 and then start a long climb upward. I didn't see how he could be right. But sure enough, silver *did* drop to exactly $1.29 and then started a long movement upward. He'd been absolutely right; I was impressed, to say the least.

It was several months before I bumped into him again. When I finally saw him, I said, "Boy, you were right. You must have made a bundle when silver hit $1.29 and then went up. You knew exactly what was going to happen; you must have been prepared to buy a ton of silver when the price hit $1.29."

He looked at me rather self-consciously and said, "No, as a matter of fact, I didn't make any money on it."

"Why not? You knew what was coming—you couldn't miss."

"Well," he said, "I watched and waited as the price dropped. And when it finally hit $1.29, I said to myself, 'I wonder if it will keep going to $1.15.' I was afraid to act before it hit the absolute bottom. When it went up a little, I thought that might be only a technical correction. But pretty soon it was up over $1.40 and I decided it was too late to fool with—so I said 'to hell with it.'"

At the time we talked, silver was back up to $1.60. He'd been so angry with himself for losing the 11¢ profit to $1.40 that he'd missed out on the 20¢ profit beyond that. Now he's out looking for another bottom.

Meanwhile, many other people who bought at the "wrong time"—when the price was $1.70 or even $2.00—are enjoying their profits with the price at $2.50–$3.00.

You may run into many people who chart markets and will tell you how well they've done. I've met many such people, but there appears to be a natural law working against me. For no matter how perfect a man's record may have been before I meet him, his advice always goes sour after he starts passing it on to me.

I've occasionally made quick profits when a price has risen dramatically just after I bought. But the quick profits were only a fringe benefit. The purchase was made because the funds happened to be available then and I saw good long-term potential.

Don't look for inside sources to tell you *when* to buy. Look for an investment that has an unusually high upward potential— based upon general economic factors—and a reasonably small downward risk. Then buy—whether it's too soon or a little too late. Be prepared to wait out the inevitable. You may not make 50% the first year, but you may very well make 300% in four years. And with a large upside potential, many things 'can go against you and you can still make a profit.

Never invest in *anything* that has to pay off within a year, unless you're using excess money you can afford to speculate with. When you take the long view, some of your investments may pay off quickly, but don't depend upon them to do so.

Those who make quick, spectacular profits usually lose them and more on other mistakes. Don't be awed by anyone's record. Invest in those things you understand—*when* you understand them, unless you have *strong* reasons to believe something adverse is going to happen to that market first.

When you invest in this way, the eventual bottom or top of the market is relatively unimportant. You'll have made a healthy profit—almost always far more than those who have had access to inside sources and tips.

RESTRAINT

The third principle is: *Don't gamble with money you can't afford to lose.*

No matter how sure you may be that you're right, never

overlook the possibility that everything may go wrong. There are always unknown factors that may work against you. There are no "sure things."

Too often an investor will become excited about what he thinks is a sure thing. He'll sell his furniture, mortgage his home, sell his wife, and bet all the proceeds on the one big investment that's going to set him up for life. Since he can't lose, he'll probably leverage his investment to the maximum.

Having done that, his objectivity (if he ever had any) disappears. Having bet it all, now he *must* be right. He's vulnerable to anything that might work against the investment. His emotions go to seed, he becomes unwilling to recognize any negative developments, and his insistence that he's right goes up equally with the problems presented.

When he loses (which is inevitable), he'll have to look for a scapegoat—someone who manipulated the market or an immoral government that intervened. But if such things are possible, why didn't he consider them in advance?

The successful investor always begins with certain questions: Where are the funds coming from? Am I prepared to handle a loss if it occurs? How long a period can I afford to wait for the investment to pay off? What will I do if it doesn't turn out as I expect? At what point must I sell out and prevent further losses? What will have to happen for me to decide that I've made a mistake? How can I limit my potential loss?

These questions must be asked *before* you invest. The worst time to make such decisions is after you've bought and the price is dropping.

"Stop loss" orders are often used to limit potential losses, but they're undependable. A "stop loss" is an instruction, given in advance, for the broker to automatically sell the investment if the price drops to a certain point.

Often, however, a stop loss is an opportunity for the man who's supposed to execute it for you. A trader on the floor of the exchange might execute the order when the price is only close to the prescribed point. *He* buys the investment from you at the "stop loss" price. Afterward, it can be said that the price dropped that low, but the sale of your investment may have been the only trade executed at that price.

Also, a "stop loss" can't protect you if the market is dropping too fast for the order to be executed at the price you've been depending upon.

A safer way is to establish a price *range* that you consider dangerous to you. If the price drops near that range, watch it closely. If it starts to enter the range, sell rather than risk a sudden drop. When the price rises away from the range, buy back. You'll suffer a few dollars loss between the selling and rebuying prices, but that will be a small insurance cost to prevent the risk of a sudden drop that would be more than you can afford.

Don't risk precious funds on investments where short-term movements would affect you adversely. You must be prepared for downward fluctuations. If you can't afford those, invest only in media that have small fluctuations; pick the investments that have small downside risks rather than those with large upside potentials.

There's no such thing as absolute safety in this world. Many things have proven to be safe over the last thirty years—but only in retrospect. In advance, there was always a risk involved.

The important thing is to understand what you're looking for. Don't play with funds that are irreplaceable. Always make sure you know the risks involved. Then choose the investments with risks you can tolerate, and avoid those where losses would injure you.

SANITY

Most investments follow a standard pattern. You buy something you believe will soon be discovered by other people in the marketplace. You hope to buy before they do, and then watch them stampede the price upward.

This system has worked sometimes for some people during the

past twenty-five years. But even during "good times," many part-time investors have achieved little success with it.

I believe that the people who've made the most money over the past two decades—and especially over the past five years—have been those who have *not* used that system. They haven't looked for a market stampede; they've looked for investments that have sound economic reasons for appreciation. They've looked for supply and demand factors, and ignored the opinions of other investors.

It's really very foolish to believe that you can outguess several million other people in the marketplace (especially if you're a part-time investor). How can you, with a few hours' study each week, expect to see in advance an opportunity that's going to ignite the motivations of everyone else?

Look for economic situations that will force a price upward even if everyone else believes it will go down. Most investors are wrong most of the time anyway.

Once you find such a situation, take an investment position and wait it out. Others may have paper profits in the short term, and may think you're foolish for not grabbing the "hot" item while it's available. But over a period of four years or so, you may make 300% (or more) on your investment—while others have been looking for a quick profit of 50–75% in a year and not getting it.

If investing is a game to you, it's a different story. Then go ahead and try to outguess others. Enjoy yourself; indulge yourself; use a ouija board or anything else that captures your fancy. Gambling is an honorable recreation; and it's also a good living—for *professional* gamblers.

I like to gamble. I play with money I can afford to lose—both in Las Vegas and in the investment markets. But I'd never be so foolish as to use money that's precious to me, money I've stashed away to see me through the times to come. Even when my gambles produce good profits, I don't get carried away and risk precious funds.

If you can't afford to play with your money, stay away from investment conversations with gamblers, keep clear of the hot tips and the go-go excitement. Stay in a quiet place, keep your head clear, and decide what it is you really want. Whether it's profit or protection, it's very likely you'll want to invest your money in good long-term opportunities and then forget about them.

There are such investments available—even today. They won't require that you outguess other investors; neither will you need to be on twenty-four-hour guard duty, watching over them to be sure that nothing goes wrong.

This investment principle is: *Don't base your hopes on a market stampede.* Instead, bet on your understanding of the General Market, your knowledge of what economic changes are inevitable. And don't worry whether others agree with you.

You won't need up-to-the-minute information. You won't be swayed from your judgment by adverse news. And you won't need to be concerned about rumors and market tips. You can invest, relax, and profit.

DIRECTION

The fifth principle is: *Don't add nonessentials to your expectations.*

Define what it is you expect to happen. Then invest in a way that doesn't rely for success upon anything outside of those expectations.

As an illustration, suppose you had decided in 1971 that the price of silver would go up because of supply and demand pressures. Let's say you made the decision when the price was about $1.60, and you expected silver to be worth $2.50 by 1973.

To bet on your expectations, you called your broker and he recommended the stock of Sunshine Mining Company, a leading U.S. silver producer. You bought the stock at $30 per share.

As it turned out, your expectations were right—the price of silver fluctuated between $2.50 and $3.00 during 1973. *But you didn't profit from the investment.* For Sunshine Mining Company suffered a terrible fire that rendered it inoperative for seven months. When the price of silver was at $2.75, Sunshine Mining stock was at $15—$15 less than when you bought it.

You were right about silver but you still lost money. You lost because you also bet on something else—that nothing would go wrong at Sunshine Mining.

Company profits are dependent upon much more than just the demands for its product. There are other variables: government intervention in the form of taxes and regulations, good or bad management, labor relations (a strike often occurs when it would harm the company most), and the possibilities of natural disasters—fires, floods, earthquakes.

The fire at Sunshine Mining actually helped move the price of silver upward by reducing the supply. But I know of no way the reverse could happen. If something affects the price of silver adversely, it will also affect the producers of silver.

Stocks are *not* inherently bad investments. But the silver example illustrates a case where a stock is a misdirected application of your expectations. Never buy a stock if there's a more direct way to profit from your expectations.

Define, as precisely as you can, what you expect to happen. Then find a way to bet on it that includes as few nonessentials as possible.

COURAGE

The sixth principle is: *Never be afraid to take a loss.*

When you see you've made a mistake, don't wait for the price of your investment to return upward to your break-even point. It may take 26½ years to do so. Once you're *sure* you've made a mistake, the time to sell is *right now*.

The investor who buys at 40, expecting the price to go straight up to 50, and then sees it drop to 30, may wait for it to go back to 40 before selling, but he'll probably wind up selling at 20.

The fallacy is his belief that he can't afford to lose the 10 points between 40 and 30. But that isn't realistic; *he's already lost it*. Now he has only 30—not 40. The important question is: What should he do with the 30? The 40 no longer exists.

Sometimes, it's a matter of ego; no one likes to admit he's made a mistake. So he hopes that if he hangs on, it'll go to 60 and prove him right. But all successful investors make mistakes. They're successful because they *recognize* their mistakes and cut their losses before the mistakes become too expensive.

On the other hand, be sure you *have* made a mistake before you sell in panic. If you bought at 40, believing that it must go to 100 over a long-term period, don't panic if the price goes down to 30. That isn't proof you were wrong. A drop only proves a mistake if you had believed that it *couldn't* drop. In the latter case, you've been proven wrong and it might go down further.

It's important to decide *at the time you buy* just how far down you can tolerate a temporary loss position. Part of it may depend upon the length of time to which you've committed the investment. If it's a one-year investment and you can only tolerate a 25% loss, you should sell when the price drops from 40 to 30.

But if you're investing funds that don't have to be touched for several years, you can allow the price to drop 25% because it will have plenty of time to recoup. In that case, you shouldn't reopen the decision unless something totally unexpected happens that could alter the entire economics of the investment.

It takes as much courage *not* to sell when it's unwarranted as it does to sell when you should. The kind of courage that applies depends upon the expectations and objectives you had when you originally made the investment. And those aren't likely to change easily.

Never be afraid to take a loss once you've determined that you're in the wrong place; you only compound your loss by hanging on to a losing plan.

That principle has always been important. Today, it's more vital than ever, for most people *need* to make important changes in their investments right now. The time has come to get out of traditional investments.

If making a change means acknowledging a loss, don't let

your ego get in the way; don't wait "just a little longer" in hopes of recouping your losses. You'll be more likely to recoup your losses by putting your money in investments that have a better chance to appreciate.

INDIVIDUALITY

The final principle is perhaps the most important: *Don't copy others.*

You are a totally unique individual. No one is in exactly the same situation as you. There are an infinite variety of differences —in emotional nature, income, family situation, knowledge, hopes, and dreams. You couldn't possibly get what *you* want through an investment program that was designed to fit someone else.

Suppose you know someone who always seems to make big profits from his investments. He has access to valuable information, always knows what's going on, and regularly averages 100% or more profit each year. So you ask him to tell you what he's investing in, and you do the same. Now you're on the right track —doing something big and profitable for a change.

But a strange thing happens. He goes on about his business just as before; nothing's changed. *You*, however, are having trouble sleeping nights. You begin to realize that his investments are a little risky for you. You've put yourself in a highly vulnerable position and it's taking a toll on your emotions.

A year later, the investments are cashed in. He *was* right; the investments have paid off. And he uses his profits to buy a beautiful new house. But you use *your* profits to go to the hospital and have your ulcer removed.

You can't satisfy your objectives by emulating someone who's different from you. His needs and requirements are different; he can do things that you can't—and vice-versa.

I know two men who both agree that explosive times are ahead. One of them has put all his savings in a Swiss bank. The other couldn't sleep nights if his money were somewhere across the ocean. He has to have his life savings where he can look at them every so often.

So he's turned his savings into silver coins and buried them all in the backyard. Every once in a while, he and his wife dig up the coins to be sure they're still there.[1]

Which one is doing the right thing?

In my opinion, both of them are. Each has recognized the situation and *recognized himself*. Each has utilized a method that's realistic for him—a way that eliminates intolerable risks and accepts risks that he's willing to live with.

The final outcome of an investment isn't all that matters. You have to consider the period between now and then. Will you rest easy? Will you get along with your spouse? Will you have made long-term investments with funds that might be needed in the short term? There are plenty of other questions you should consider, too. But only you can decide which questions are important—let alone the answers.

I'm often asked, "What are *you* doing with your money right now?" Not only is that my own business, but it's also based upon my own considerations. I often do things I wouldn't recommend to most of my clients.

Every investment should be tailor-made. I often receive phone calls or letters asking for advice. But how can I know what someone should do when I don't know anything about him?

I make recommendations only after a four-hour consultation with an investor. During that time, I hope to understand enough about him to be able to offer advice that he can live with, recommendations that truly fit his objectives.

I hope to put enough information in this book to help you decide for yourself what you must do. I can tell you what I think is most likely to happen in the future; and I can show you a number of alternatives from which to choose. But *you* must do the choosing.

You have to decide which of the problems are the most dangerous and must be hedged against. You have to decide how

---

[1] Name and address *not* available on request.

much you can afford to speculate. You have to decide how much must be put in safe places—and which places are the safest for you.

Look around—listen to suggestions—look for alternatives—even listen to advice. Know what's possible and what's available. But you decide what must be done. To delegate that decision is to place your future in the hands of someone whose interests are different from yours.

After determining the available alternatives, the guiding principle must be to choose from among them those that will allow you to feel *comfortable*. That's what it all boils down to. You must choose in a way that will permit you to relax, to ignore the day-to-day news, to know that you've fulfilled your most important objectives, to be able to enjoy your life in the way that's most important to you, to feel comfortable about what you're doing.

You are a unique individual. Don't believe that anyone else knows what's best for you.

SUMMARY

The seven important investment principles are:
1. Don't act as if you know everything.
2. Don't try to buy at the absolute bottom or sell at the absolute top.
3. Don't gamble with money you can't afford to lose.
4. Don't base your hopes on a market stampede.
5. Don't add nonessentials to your expectations.
6. Don't be afraid to take a loss.
7. Don't copy others.

These rules may seem negative and restrictive, but only by obedience to these rules does an investor create the opportunity to make the profits he seeks.

There are still opportunities for profit and protection today. To take advantage of them, you must first define your own objectives. Then you can choose realistically from the multitude of alternatives available.

You won't succeed by reacting emotionally to hot tips and mass stampedes. But you have every chance of success if you keep your head.

PART IV *Investments of the Past*

19

Fixed Dollar Investments

THIS PART OF THE BOOK will review briefly the traditional investments. In general, they offer very little of either profit or protection, for reasons we've already seen. The trend that existed from 1945 to 1970 has been reversed.

This chapter will review fixed dollar investments; and the next chapter will cover other types of traditional investments. Chapter 21 will offer suggestions for employers and employees concerning the difficult task of making a living during these times.

IMPOTENT DOLLARS

Fixed dollar investments are those in which you have a contract that calls for future payment to you of a specified number of dollars. These can be grouped in three broad categories:

1. *Cash:* checking accounts, savings accounts, cash outside of banks, and Treasury bills.

2. *Intermediate term investments:* bonds (either corporate or governmental) and mortgages or other debts owed to you.

3. *Long-term retirement plans:* Social Security, pension plans, annuities, cash value in a life insurance policy, and any other retirement programs computed in dollars.

It should be obvious that all these investments are highly vulnerable to what lies ahead of us. Dollars will be worth progressively less in terms of purchasing power. From 1960 to 1970, loss of value from inflation was an irritant one accepted in exchange for the safety offered by these forms of liquid savings. But now inflation is no longer an irritant. Your losses will be far more than 3–5% a year; they'll be anywhere from 20% to total destruction.

Traditionally, it was wise to get into a strong cash position prior to a depression. But I see little hope of falling prices and bargains during the next depression. Most likely, inflation will continue right through it.

Fortunately, there are other alternatives available for each of these forms of savings. We'll discuss those in Part V. And since much of what needed to be said about fixed-dollar investments was covered in Chapter 17, I'll offer only a few added comments here.

CHECKING AND SAVINGS ACCOUNTS

With the future so uncertain, it *is* important to have liquid funds that you can use at any time. However, you won't achieve that by having money in checking and savings accounts in U.S. dollars in U.S. banks or savings and loan associations. The dollars will progressively deteriorate.

In addition, I have no faith that the banks are any safer now than they were in the 1930s. I'm not predicting a string of bank failures but, at the same time, the banks are just as vulnerable as they've always been.

Only two things have changed since the 1930s: inflation is greater; and the government has created a program based upon a curious idea called the "sticker principle."

The sticker principle could be described as follows: "We don't want the banks to fail, and bank runs lead to failures. So we'll put a sticker in the window of each bank saying that all accounts are protected by the Federal Deposit Insurance Corporation. If someone gets nervous about the solvency of the bank, he'll see the sticker and be reassured. He won't start a run on the bank. If there are no bank runs, the banks won't fail. The sticker will have been truthful; the accounts *are* protected—by the sticker." [1]

The Federal Deposit Insurance Corporation doesn't have a vast quantity of dollars available to meet bank runs. At the close of 1971, the bank deposits insured by the FDIC totalled $393.3 billion; the deposit insurance fund was $4.7 billion, only 1.2% of the total deposits. [2]

And of the $4.7 billion reserve fund, only $10 million was in cash. Almost all the rest was invested—in (you guessed it) U.S. government bonds. Insurance premiums paid to the FDIC have been used as another method of financing the government's spending programs.

The FDIC has the authority to borrow up to $3 billion from the federal treasury in times of emergency. That increases the potential reserve fund to $7.7 billion, or 2% of the insured deposits. Obviously, any funds provided by the U.S. Treasury will be printing press money.

If a small bank fails somewhere, because of embezzlement or poor management, the FDIC is right there in a hurry, with cash for the depositors—with reporters and photographers standing by to record the historic event. But what would happen if two or three of the nation's largest banks were in trouble? The potential reserve fund wouldn't go very far.

The Federal Savings and Loan Insurance Corporation is in a similar position. At the close of 1972, $194.5 billion in insured deposits were covered by a reserve fund of $3.1 billion, or 1.6%. [3]

The government can't protect against the consequences of its inflation indefinitely. To expect it to do so is to depend upon the undependable for your security.

My policy is to leave no more in my checking account than

---

[1] I once had a similar idea for an insurance company. Thinking it might be profitable, I presented the plan to my attorney and asked him what he thought it would get me. He said, "Twenty years." Unfortunately, the government doesn't operate by the same laws it applies to individuals.

[2] Annual Report of the Federal Deposit Insurance Corporation, 1971.

[3] Federal Home Loan Bank Board *Journal*, April 1973.

I'm willing to lose. I use it to pay bills, but transfer any excess accumulations to a Swiss bank for savings. I have no savings accounts in U.S. banks or savings and loan associations.

Some people have suggested having credit cards (American Express, Diner's Club, etc.) to use as purchasing power if banks should close. I don't agree. If banks are closed, a merchant can be reimbursed by the credit card company only if it has a huge sum of cash outside the banks and a means of getting the money to him. Neither condition is very probable. So you can assume that merchants won't accept credit cards during a bank holiday.

BONDS

The interest received from American bonds is insignificant compared to the current rate of inflation. It should be recognized, too, that if conditions worsen companies can go under and governments can "temporarily" suspend bond redemptions.

It's possible to obtain interest-paying deposits, bonds, and annuities denominated in foreign currencies. They will be discussed in Part V.

MORTGAGES AND OTHER DEBTS

This is a poor time to be holding IOUs from anyone. Paper assets will be meaningless if your debtors are insolvent.

If you hold mortgages, the real estate may not be the security it seems. If you have to repossess, you may be acquiring a white elephant.

RETIREMENT PLANS

For reasons already stated, conventional retirement plans (company pension plans, annuities, cash value life insurance policies) offer very little security today. If you even receive the payoff, the dollars may pay for only a small fraction of the living standard you expected for retirement.

If you're involved in a voluntary program—such as an annuity or life insurance policy—it would be prudent to withdraw the accumulated savings and use them in one of the ways that will be described in Part V.

If the retirement plan is a mandatory company program, use every avenue to try to withdraw from it. Your contributions to the plan can be used more advantageously. If you can't withdraw money from it, try to borrow from it. If you can do that, send the money to a Swiss bank to be used for one of the conservative alternatives that will be covered in Part V. The same advice applies if you're already retired and receiving a pension. Try to get a cash settlement or, if that fails, try to borrow from it.

If your retirement money is completely locked up, there's still another avenue. In Chapter 30, I'll describe a method by which you can preserve the purchasing power in a pension you can't touch.

The government has endorsed certain types of retirement programs for self-employed individuals. You're allowed to contribute a given sum of tax-free dollars each year to the plan. The tax advantage is an incentive to a self-employed person; but the tax avoidance is allowed only if the money is invested in certain ways. None of those ways is very attractive today. Far better to pay the slightly higher taxes and put retirement funds where they'll appreciate more and be safer.

SOCIAL SECURITY

I wouldn't want to be dependent upon Social Security under any circumstances. It's a government program, and governments can change the rules anytime it suits them. If you've been counting on Social Security, act now to find alternative ways of guaranteeing income for later years. Use every avenue you can find to get as much money from Social Security now, and to avoid paying any money into it in the future.

CHANGES NEEDED

If you have funds tied up in any of these fixed-dollar investments, now is the time to get them out. "Normal" rates of inflation will soon be past history. You need something far more durable than the dollar to depend upon.

If necessary, consult an attorney or accountant to find ways of getting your funds freed from any places where they may be locked in now.

The trouble involved will be far, far less than the trouble you'll have if your wealth is destroyed.

20

Other Traditional Investments

LET'S LOOK NOW at the traditional investments that aren't measured in fixed dollar amounts—stocks, mutual funds, real estate, commodities, diamonds, art, and numismatics.

There's no way to know in what sequence the events of the future will unfold. So if safety is the objective, an investment can be attractive only if it can withstand *all* possibilities—the dollar decline, an orthodox depression, an inflationary depression, and runaway inflation.

STOCKS AND MUTUAL FUNDS

While the dollar has been falling in value, the stock market has virtually stood still in dollar prices. Anyone who has invested in a broad range of stocks has probably lost purchasing power over the past three years.

During the next few years, there will be opportunities for some companies to profit as they lose foreign competition—thanks to higher foreign currency prices. Anyone determined to stay in the stock market should investigate such situations to look for possible gainers.

Safety, however, won't be found in the stock market. As indicated in Chapter 17, during the German inflation the stock

market caught up with runaway inflation only in the final stages
—a period suitable only for gamblers. In the 1970s, price freezes,
other regulations, strikes, and readjustments to inflation are making it more difficult for companies to make profits.

And hovering over the stock market at all times is the ever-
present threat of a crash.[1]

In early 1969, I had as a client a "little old lady" who wasn't
from Pasadena, but who lived only about ten miles from there.
She lived frugally off the income from an estate worth at that
time about $200,000. I advised her to liquidate $100,000 worth
of blue-chip stocks and transfer the money to a Swiss bank.

Afraid to make a decision on her own, she asked me to visit
the family attorney with her. When the attorney heard what I
had in mind, he swore at me and said I was irresponsible for
suggesting that she engage in such gross speculation. Didn't I
realize that this poor woman could afford to be in only the safest
possible investments?

For some reason, she disregarded his advice, liquidated the
stocks, and transferred the money to Switzerland—one-half to be
kept in Swiss francs and one-half put in silver. Today, the
$100,000 has grown to around $160,000 plus interest (which continually increases in dollar value).

The stocks she had held previously are now worth about
$85,000 and the dividends have decreased. The money she trans-
ferred is now worth almost twice as much as it would have been
if she'd left it where it was. To continue living at her 1969
standard, she *has* to have the increased income and capital appreciation.

She did what was safe; to have remained in the stock market,
knowing what she did at the time, would have been the gross
speculation.[2]

---

[1] If you had bought at the high in 1929, it would have been 1952 before
your stocks returned upward to their original purchasing prices. In the meantime,
however, inflation had destroyed almost half the value of the dollar. So it was
around 1958 before you would have broken even on your original investment.

[2] It's possible that the attorney could say now that the move was made too
soon—that he would have recommended the same course of action two years
later. But by then the stock market had dropped and her stocks would have sold
for less.

It took courage to do what she did. She didn't understand the situation fully, but she knew there was plenty wrong.

There may be further "booms" in the stock market yet. But they won't change my opinion that it's already time for a part-time investor concerned about safety to get out. And since mutual funds depend upon the stock market, everything said about stocks applies equally to them.

COMMODITIES

Undoubtedly, the next few years will bring acute shortages of several, if not many, commodities. A few fortunate people may make big profits anticipating the shortages.

For most people, however, the task will be too difficult. You will need excellent timing—the ability to anticipate price controls, specific dollar drops, nationalization possibilities, rationing, and numerous other forms of intervention that are hard to imagine now.

Commodities bought overseas will not only circumvent most of the interference, but will also profit from the U.S. intervention. Again, however, it will take full-time professional competence to take full advantage of the situation.

REAL ESTATE

As an investment, real estate is probably one of the poorest prospects for the future. Its greatest drawback is its illiquidity. You can't sell a plot of land, an apartment house, an office building, or a home at a moment's notice. It may be months after you decide to sell that you finally find a buyer—and perhaps a month or two after that before you get your money. Liquidity and flexibility are very important right now and real estate just doesn't qualify. Real estate prices may continue to rise over the next few years, but I doubt that they'll go up fast enough to keep up with other prices.

In addition, income property is particularly vulnerable. Rents are a ready target for price controls; but many of a landlord's costs escape the controls since a building's services are usually performed by independent contractors. So the landlord's income is limited while his costs continue upward.

Home ownership is another matter. If you think of owning your own home as a form of consumption (buying the home with money you otherwise would have spent on other consumption items), there's no reason not to own a home. But if you consider home ownership as an investment, I'd suggest you sell now. Otherwise, you'll have precious funds tied up in it that you may never get back. A crash could destroy your equity overnight. If there's no crash, real estate values may continue to rise—but not as fast as the cost of living.

In addition, if runaway inflation leads to a total collapse, your home might be worthless to you one day. You may have to walk away from it during the violence and chaos following an unresolved runaway inflation.

If you're determined to own a home, spend on it only those funds you can afford to lose. Treat it as a form of consumption. Otherwise, find a comparable house to rent.

ART AND NUMISMATICS

Works of art, in general, have probably kept ahead of the general price rises. But I find it increasingly difficult to consider art objects as secure investments over the next few years. They are vulnerable to both deflation and runaway inflation. In either case, you might have to wait twenty years to get your investment back when measured in real purchasing power.

Even in good times, art isn't equal to its reputation as a good investment. Spectacular price increases of a few selected works are highly publicized; but the millions of paintings and art objects in the hands of most investors show little appreciation. The normal art customer buys retail and sells wholesale—with a very significant spread in between.

Art is wonderful as a form of consumption. As an investment, only the wealthy and perceptive are qualified to play. So buy the kind of art you like to look at, but don't consider it the road to riches.

Numismatics (collecting rare coins) add up the same way as art. Gold coins and silver coins will become more valuable but only because of their gold or silver contents. A numismatic coin sells at prices far beyond its gold content. During hard times, you can expect the coin to fall in value to its usefulness as gold or silver. Far better to buy gold or silver coins now that have little or no numismatic value figured in the price.

DIAMONDS

Diamonds have a romantic reputation. Stories abound of people who have bribed guards with the family jewels or retained their wealth by smuggling diamonds out of the country.

And in certain circumstances, they may be very valuable in the future. Diamonds traded internationally can profit from the continuing decline of the dollar—as you can get back more dollars than you paid, even if the actual market value of the diamond hasn't increased. In other words, they can be used as a hedge against the dollar.

But diamonds can't be expected to hold their value during a worldwide depression or a runaway inflation. If the runaway inflation is limited to the United States, diamonds could be kept in a Swiss bank as wealth to be used much later.

It should be understood, however, that the diamond market is largely a professional one. You can get sealed packets from DeBeers that are traded internationally and don't require an appraisal. But otherwise, you run into the same problems that you do with art—you need professional competence, and you may wind up buying retail and selling wholesale.

The principal value of diamonds today is for the very wealthy who may need to store a great deal of wealth in a small area of space. For that purpose, diamonds are better even than gold coins.

A BYGONE ERA

It requires a lot of mental energy to reorient your thinking away from the investment traditions of the past thirty years. But the time has come when that's necessary. The old ways won't provide the simple opportunities for capital appreciation that they once did.

However difficult it may be to bid goodbye to the bygone era, it must be done. We've already seen how little protection the traditional investments have provided in the past three years. They haven't produced the profits necessary to keep up with skyrocketing prices and shortages.

And although an inflationary depression now seems to be the most likely possibility, a gigantic crash still remains as a constant threat. Once inflation has gone far enough (and it already has), it doesn't require a normal deflation to bring on a crash. Inflation must be constantly expanded to sustain itself, and so a mere slowdown in the rate of expansion can be enough to allow the General Market to reassert itself—causing a crash.

The money managers have been playing with the economy for the past few years—speeding up inflation to keep "business booming" (is it?) and then slightly slowing the rate of increase to cool things down. What if they miss their signals? What if they pull back just a little too much? If that happens, the house of cards could come falling down in a hurry—with the traditional crash and all.

Every day that you continue playing around with the stock market or hanging onto paper-profit real estate, you're faced with the frightening prospect that one day—suddenly, without warning—you could discover it's too late to get out.

You can always live with the knowledge that you got out too soon; but you're not likely to forgive yourself if you get out too late.

"*Grin and Bear It*" by George Lichty, Courtesy of Publishers-Hall Syndicate

"..A depression can't happen and even if it does I assure you it will never be called by that name!"

21
Making a Living

UNLESS YOU'VE ALREADY ACCUMULATED and protected enough wealth to last through the next ten years or so, producing income of real value will be a prime concern in troubled times.

During the next few years, the General Market will be attempting to reallocate resources in more useful ways. Although the government will be fighting back, many industries that seemed to be much in demand during the past few years will face rough going.

You'll have to be very agile—whether you're the owner of a business or an employee.

EMPLOYMENT

If you aren't self-employed, the best thing you can do is to try to be.

If you're employed by a company, you're going to be dependent upon the economic wisdom of the managers of that company. And that's a very vulnerable position.

The future will belong to those who can perceive real consumer demand and are flexible enough to respond to it. Those who simply go along, depending for protection upon the safety of a labor union or a large company, are going to find their security blankets tattered and torn before much longer.

There's never a shortage of consumer demand (despite the

cliché explanations of recessions as "shortages of demand"). Desires are unlimited. There's always a market for someone who has initiative and who respects the changing minds and tastes of consumers.

If that sounds like Horatio Alger stuff, so be it. Those who say that modern times are so complicated that one can't pull oneself up "by the bootstraps" don't understand economics.

They fail to recognize that the marketplace is constantly changing. When markets shift, they feel an individual has a "right" to his comfortable niche and shouldn't be dislodged from it. They overlook the fact that, to protect the producer from changing employment, all consumers must suffer a lower standard of living to subsidize him.

No one has a right to any job or business. Those who respond to consumer demands earn the rewards; those who prefer not to worry about consumers' desires are always in an insecure position.

If you're employed by someone, you're dependent upon him to understand consumer demand, to be willing to respond to it, and to do it efficiently. That's a normal risk an employee takes during normal times. In abnormal times, it's a dangerous situation. You're much better off marketing your services yourself. It doesn't matter what your specialty is—engineer, secretary, salesman, bookkeeper. Whatever it is, it's possible to be an engineering service, a secretarial service, a sales consultant, a bookkeeping service.[1] I know dozens of people in those kinds of occupations who do that now.

There are numerous advantages to this approach. For one, you're in a much better tax position. As a business, you can deduct many of your home expenses as office expenses (since that's where your office is).

Another benefit is that you usually make more money. You contract with companies to produce a specific result for a specific fee. You're no longer bound by industry-wide standard wage rates, labor union contracts, or other standards that limit your hourly income. By working well and quickly, you can earn far more per hour than you did on an hourly basis. At the same time,

[1] Your present employer may be your first customer.

your customer will wind up paying less per function performed than when he pays an hourly-wage employee to do it.

The most important advantage of this system is the flexibility it provides for you. You're no longer dependent upon someone else getting work for you. You can adapt to changing times much more easily. Can you imagine the manager of a company with 5,000 employees, facing shifts in demand, perceiving how to use the skills of all 5,000 in a new market situation?

You'll be mobile; you'll no longer have to work in any given place at any given time. You can move as necessary to meet consumer demand wherever it can be found.

There are millions and millions of employees who don't feel responsible for their own welfare. They rely for protection upon others—their employers, the government, "they."

Those people aren't equipped to face the kind of future promised by the coming years. But *you* can accept and implement the responsibility for your own life.

And when you depend upon yourself, you'll probably find that you feel much less insecure. There's no greater security in the world than the realization that you can cope with anything that comes, that you can take care of yourself, that you're not dependent upon anyone or anything, that you can accept losses when they occur and continue to move forward, that you're no longer vulnerable to the mistakes of others.[2]

If you become self-employed, many of the comments offered to businessmen on the following pages will concern you. If you remain employed, the following section can be used as a guide to determine how prepared your employer is to face the coming years.

YOUR BUSINESS

If you own your own business, the same considerations of flexibility and liquidity will be most important. It is impossible

[2] These matters of self-employment and security are covered at greater length in *How I Found Freedom in an Unfree World*, listed in the Recommended Reading.

to foresee exactly *how* all coming changes will affect you. You must be in a position to move in any direction the future dictates —without being immobilized by mistaken investments and decisions of the past.

To achieve that flexibility, certain procedures are advisable:

1. Keep your cash reserves invulnerable. They'll be much safer in a Swiss bank in Swiss francs. As of 1973, there's no law prohibiting that.[3]

2. Try to convert all long-term assets—real estate, bonds, etc. —to liquid assets. Place these assets in appropriate media selected from Part V of this book.

3. Protect the value of your receivables; otherwise they will depreciate by the time you receive the dollars. A method for doing so will be described in Chapter 30.

4. Try to phase out areas of your business that have been aided by inflation or are dependent ultimately on governmental programs. Investigate new markets that may be more durable.

5. Consider your customers very carefully. Don't make long-term contracts with companies or individuals who may not last through the life of the contract. Be cautious about extending credit. Make sure the debtor will have the means to pay his debt.

6. Try not to rely on only one market for your future. Keep looking for new areas that may be less subject to governmental intervention, less luxury-oriented.

7. Be very, very cautious about new long-term investments. Be willing to pass up "opportunities" in favor of retaining a flexible position.

8. Wherever possible, rent equipment instead of buying it. Make the rental contracts as short as possible. Avoid lease-purchase arrangements; they're merely a disguised form of purchase.

9. Reduce fixed overhead as much as possible. Instead of hiring new employees when needed, try to *contract* for things you need—from secretarial services, temporary help agencies, etc.

[3] If it should become illegal to have a foreign bank account, you can convert your reserves to Swiss franc banknotes, gold coins, or silver coins and store them in a safe deposit box, safe, or vault.

If it seems more expensive, remember that many of those costs are already buried somewhere in your expense statements.

And one last suggestion. If you've been getting attractive offers from people who want to purchase your business from you, take another look at them. This wouldn't be a bad time to sell out, use the proceeds to make safe or profitable investments, and take a break from your business for a few years—while you see just how the future unfolds.

If you convert your paper wealth to real wealth, you may be in a very fortunate position in a few years to pick up where you left off. But your position will be far better then—because you'll be one of the few people around with real, tangible wealth to invest.

DEBTS

It's often said that it's better during inflationary times to borrow as much money as possible, use someone else's capital to make profits, buy commodities at present prices, and repay in cheaper dollars.

I can neither bless nor condemn the idea. It's wholly a matter of personal taste. Some people manage to keep a cool head and an optimistic attitude while juggling a series of debts. Others never rest easy if they have such liabilities.

I personally prefer the flexibility of a debt-free life. The only debts I incur are in margin accounts where the debt is secured and offset directly by the investment. I want to be in a position where I can respond quickly and freely to events as they occur—unhampered by debts incurred for past decisions.

If you now enjoy a relatively debt-free, conservative life, recognize your individuality and don't expect to reorient your emotions to conform to someone else's idea of financial sophistication.

If you're comfortable with debt, and willing to risk the possibility of a crash with falling prices, you might gain advantages by borrowing now and repaying cheaper dollars.

MAKING A LIVING

Whatever your occupation or position, flexibility and liquidity must be the guiding standards of your professional decisions. Only those who are free to move as the times dictate will master the coming years.

If you're immobilized now by your job, by contractual commitments, by debts (corporate or personal), or by long-term investments, begin now to free yourself. If the overall job seems too big to be tackled, remember that every inch of freedom you gain can be used to your advantage.

"Grin and Bear It" by George Lichty, Courtesy of Publishers-Hall Syndicate

"How do I know we're in the grip of a recession? ... because my brother-in-law thinks it's safe to look for a job, that's why!"

PART V *Recommended*

Investments

22

Looking Forward

NOW THAT WE'VE COVERED the principles underlying today's crises, and seen the magnitude of the situation, it's easier
to know what will work and what won't.

The next fifteen chapters will be devoted to the alternatives
available for protection and profit. They revolve around gold,
silver, and foreign currencies. There are a great many methods
by which one can invest in each of these hedges, and the mechanics of each method will be explained in detail.

It's difficult to categorize all the information in separate com-
partments; some things apply to more than one of the investments. To avoid repetition, most items will be stated only once,
but may be referred to again in another chapter.

I suggest that you read the entire section at least once, mark-
ing the methods that might be appropriate for you. You can
return to them later to review them again and decide which alternatives seem best suited to your objectives.

Before committing yourself to any plans, review the principles in Part III. Make sure what you do is truly appropriate for
you. Be certain you understand and accept the risks involved.

Above all, make sure that the final decisions are *yours*, not
mine or those of anyone else. Only then will you have an investment program that will permit you to be comfortable about the
future.

23

Swiss Bank Accounts

BECAUSE A SWISS BANK ACCOUNT can be used for many things, we'll examine it first. Then we can discuss what you can put into it.

Contrary to popular opinion, Swiss bank accounts aren't the exclusive province of millionaires, gangsters, and tax evaders. In my own experience, I've dealt with hundreds of individuals who have Swiss bank accounts. Most of them are typical people in middle-class financial brackets. I even know of one man who opened a Swiss bank account with $50.

Although it may seem very mysterious to you now, such an account is no different from banking by mail with any bank. The mysterious part can be cleared up easily; the rest is normal banking procedure.

BENEFITS

The advantages of using a Swiss bank account are:

1. You'll have funds outside your own country, where they can't be confiscated by a government using totalitarian controls in an attempt to repair the damages of its own mistakes.

2. You'll be dealing with a banking system that is, in some respects, sounder than the U.S. banking system. The Swiss banks usually maintain higher reserves against their deposits. And, unlike in U.S. banks, the withdrawal restrictions stated for each type of account are taken seriously; the banks don't lend funds that may be claimed at any time by a depositor.

3. You can keep your wealth in foreign currencies that increase in value as the dollar declines.

4. Your privacy will be respected. Even the Swiss government has no access to information about your account.

5. You can use the account to make investments anywhere in the world—whether those investments be stocks, foreign currencies, bonds, gold, silver, other metals or commodities, real estate, mutual funds, etc.

6. If you choose, you can utilize the financial opinions of the bank's management in making your investments.

7. If you choose, you can utilize the account to try to avoid taxes you believe to be confiscatory.

The Swiss banking industry enjoys the world's best banking reputation and is an important part of the Swiss economy. It has earned this status mostly because of two characteristics—sound management and respect for privacy.

PRIVACY

If you should read a newspaper report that new agreements provide that the Swiss government will supply information to the U.S. government about Swiss bank accounts, the report is probably erroneous.

Swiss law stipulates that no bank employee may reveal information about an account to anyone outside the bank—not even to the Swiss government. He may not even reveal whether you have an account in the bank. Violations of this law involve fines up to 50,000 Swiss francs and possible jail sentences of up to six months.

There are exceptions. The law provides that bank information must be revealed to the Swiss government if *prima facie* evidence shows that the bank customer may have acquired the money through robbery, extortion, kidnapping, or drug trade. In such cases, the Swiss government will cooperate even with foreign governments.

However, the Swiss government will not cooperate with a foreign government *if the issue involved is not a crime by Swiss law*. And, in Switzerland, it isn't a crime to send money out of the country, to own a foreign bank account, to have a secret bank account, to own gold in any form, or even to evade taxes. Tax evasion is a civil matter; the government will sue an individual in civil court if it believes he hasn't paid enough taxes.

Thus, the Swiss government will not cooperate with any foreign government to obtain bank account information regarding any case involving tax evasion, gold ownership, or foreign exchange evasions. And to obtain the information on any *other* pretext, a *prima facie* case must be shown to a Swiss court.

It's very, very unlikely that the Swiss government will change those conditions. To do so would destroy a banking status acquired over hundreds of years. And banking is one of the most important industries in the Swiss economy.

If you hear something that suggests all this has changed, write to a Swiss bank for verification.

Some Swiss banks won't open numbered accounts or buy gold for an American citizen. Others will do so after informing the customer that the liabilities are solely his.

SOUNDNESS

The Swiss banking system is generally sounder than other banking systems. A Swiss bank usually won't extend itself to take risks on your behalf, although it will help you risk your own money if you so desire.

There is less banking regulation there, which means that banks compete with each other on the basis of safety and service —instead of being submerged into a monopoly system.

I know of no banking system in the world that operates with 100% reserves. There's always a component of inflation. But the Swiss system is by far the best I'm aware of.

TYPES OF ACCOUNTS

Like American banks, Swiss banks offer a variety of accounts. They vary according to the interest paid and the withdrawal restrictions. The higher the interest, the less liquid the account.

Except for withdrawals to make certain types of investments within the bank, the withdrawal restrictions are enforced in Swiss banks.

For savings or liquid funds, there are several basic types of accounts. The interest rates and conditions vary from bank to bank, but the following will provide a general guide (as of August 1973):

1. *Current Account:* This is the European equivalent of a checking account. Most non-resident customers have little use for a checkbook; instead, they issue payment instructions by letter, wire, or telephone. Any amount can be withdrawn from a current account at any time. Usually no interest is paid—although, occasionally, some banks pay ½% or 1% interest on large accounts. Some banks have a minimum required to open an account, but many will open a current account with $25 or more.

2. *Deposit Account:* This is like a savings account. Withdrawals are restricted, and the restrictions vary widely between banks. A typical withdrawal restriction plan would be: up to $3,000 may be withdrawn within any month without notice; three months' notice required for larger amounts. Some banks use a different approach: up to $1,000 per month without notice; up to $2,500 with thirty days' notice; over $2,500 with sixty days' notice.[1]

Interest rates of Swiss franc deposit accounts were around 3% per year during 1973; higher rates were paid if the account was kept in other currencies. Interest is paid annually on December 31—either credited to your balance or mailed to you, as you request. The larger banks do not establish minimum amounts

[1] The withdrawal restrictions are actually stated in terms of Swiss francs; my figures are the 1973 dollar equivalents.

necessary to open deposit accounts; in smaller banks, a minimum of around $1,000 may be required.

3. *Savings Account:* This is similar to a deposit account except that it usually pays 4% interest and you may withdraw more than $1,000 only with six months' notice.

4. *Investment Savings Account:* This is like a savings account except the withdrawal restrictions are even tighter—no more than $350 within any six month period; and six months' notice required for larger amounts. Interest rates average 4½% for balances under $3,500; 5% for balances over $3,500.

5. *Fixed Deposit Account:* This is similar to a deposit account except that you agree to leave the money in the account for a fixed period of time; the period may be three months, six months, one year, etc. Interest rates are generally about the same as for investment savings accounts.

6. *Cash Bonds:* Many banks issue their own bonds. If you purchase them you tie up the funds for a lengthy period of time, but receive high interest. The periods range from three to seven years, and the interest runs from 4¾% to 5¼%.

7. *Custodial Account:* This isn't a normal type of bank account. Its purpose is to keep valuables for you in the bank's vault, in a warehouse elsewhere, or in a safe deposit box in your name. You receive no interest, and instead pay a fee for the safekeeping. The account can be used for keeping cash, gold, silver, art objects, whatever. If it's cash, the bank doesn't lend it to anyone else. If the bank should fail, the property is not considered part of the bank's assets, and so you aren't vulnerable in any way.

GENERAL INFORMATION

There are no minimum requirements for adding to any of the accounts—except for cash bonds which are in fixed amounts.

Most accounts are subject to small handling charges ($1 per three months or six months, for example).

Swiss law makes some provisions regarding the disposition of the bank's assets in case of bankruptcy. Savings accounts and investment savings accounts are privileged up to 10,000 Swiss francs (about $3,500). That means that the bank's assets must be used to pay out up to 10,000 Swiss francs to holders of each of those accounts before funds can be paid elsewhere. Also, no assets held for customers in custodial accounts can be used to settle the bank's affairs; those assets belong to the individual customers.

Interest rates are traditionally low in Switzerland compared to most other countries. The principal reason for this is the small debt owed by the national government. In other nations, the government is continually in the marketplace borrowing money to refinance its debt; it competes with other borrowers to drive interest rates upward.[2]

If your objective is absolute safety against all kinds of possibilities, a custodial account of Swiss francs or gold makes the most sense.

However, most investors will also be concerned about liquidity, convenience, and possibly income. For convenience and liquidity, a current account is best; for income, consider types 2 through 6.

If you want some liquid funds plus interest, you can put part of your savings in a current account and the rest in one of the interest-bearing accounts.

WITHHOLDING TAXES

There is a Swiss withholding tax of 30% on interest or dividends received through a Swiss bank by non-residents.

The tax applies to interest earned on a Swiss bank account and to dividends paid by companies that do business in Switzer-

[2] A client called me during 1973 to say that he didn't think he could afford to keep his Swiss account with such low interest rates. He'd overlooked the fact that his deposit had appreciated by 40% in the preceding two years, thanks to changing currency rates, which was equivalent to a 20% interest rate.

land. It does *not* apply to interest earned on certain types of accounts we haven't discussed yet. On South African gold stocks, the tax is 15%. There is *no* tax on *profits* earned on gold, silver, or other commodities or stocks, or to profits made on changes in currency prices.

The withholding of the tax appears on your bank statement at the same time the interest is credited. The bank forwards the money withheld from all its accounts to the Swiss government in one lump sum without providing the names of any customers. If you have no desire to get the 30% back,[3] the matter ends there, and your privacy is in intact. If you don't want to pay the tax, you can file for a refund. The Swiss and American governments have a double-taxation treaty—which is a means of assuring that a citizen of either country doesn't pay a double tax by being taxed on the same money by both governments.

To recover the money, you file a form R82 with the Swiss government (the form is available from the Swiss bank you deal with). The Swiss government will then remit ⅚ of the tax involved to you or to your bank; this reduces the withholding tax to 5% from 30%. Since the form asks where you filed tax returns for the past two years, it's entirely possible that the information will be available to the U.S. government—and your privacy will be secure no more. So you have to decide which is more important, the refund or the privacy.

It should also be noted, however, that any interest you receive anywhere in the world is subject to tax if you're an American citizen or resident. So you're legally required to report such interest on your tax return. If you do so, there's no reason not to file for the refund from the Swiss government.

The refund is available only to individuals in countries that have double-taxation agreements with the Swiss government. Canada, for example, doesn't have such an agreement and so no refund is possible.

---

[3] Please understand that the tax is 30% of whatever you earn, not 30% of the total funds in the account. Thus, if you earn interest of 3%, for example, the tax will be equivalent to ⁹⁄₁₀ of 1% of the funds in the account (100% × 3% × 30% = .9%).

STATEMENTS

Most banks issue statements twice-yearly for the types of accounts we've covered. The statement may seem a little strange at first, but it's quite simple. It tells you what your balance was at the beginning of the statement period, enters all withdrawals and deposits during the period, adds any interest earned, subtracts any other charges, and shows your new balance.

The balance figure is the number of units of the currency in which your account is kept. You can translate that to dollar value by checking the current price of that currency in the *Wall Street Journal*. For example, if the balance is 100,000 Swiss francs and the current price of the Swiss franc is $.3485, your account is worth $34,850 (100,000 × $.3485 = $34,850).

You may be disoriented slightly by one European practice. In stating figures, commas mean what decimals mean to us; and decimals mean what commas mean to us. Thus, you might see a balance of 68.923,41—which means 68,923.41—or you might see it stated 68'923.41. You might see it the American way—or even something still different. Some banks have arranged statements for American customers to conform to American usage. As long as you realize that the commas and decimals may not be used in the same way you do, you'll be able to figure out the specific method used quickly enough.

Swiss bankers generally operate in three languages: German, French, and English. Some bank statements will be written in all three languages, others in only one of the three. Again, some banks have created English-language statements for American customers.

If your statement arrives in a foreign language, a few key words are all you need to understand. There's a glossary of the important words with their meanings on pages 194–195.

Foreign words are likely to show up only on statements and deposit or withdrawal confirmations. Bank brochures and correspondence to you will be in English unless you request otherwise.

Glossary of Terms Used by Swiss Banks

German	French	English	Meaning
Abschluss-Datum	Date de clôture	Closing date	Last day of period covered
Anlagesparkonto	Compte d'épargne-placement	Investment savings account	See page 190
Datum	Date	Date	Date item entered on statement
Einlage	Dépôt	Deposit	Addition to your account
Einlagekonto	Compte de dépôt	Deposit account	See page 189
Festgeld	Compte de dépôt à terme	Fixed deposit account	See page 190
Filiale	Succursale	Branch office	Location of branch
Haben	Crédit	Credit	An addition to your equity
Habenzins	Intérêt créditeur	Credit interest	Interest in your favor
Hauptsitz	Siège social	Head office	Main office of bank
Kommission	Commission	Commission	Transaction fee
Kontoart	Genre du compte	Type of account	Current, deposit, etc.
Kontoinhaber	Titulaire du compte	Account holder	Name of customer or account number
Kontokorrent	Compte courant	Current account	See page 189
Obligationen	Obligations	Bonds	Bonds
Porto	Port	Postage	Mailing fee

Glossary of Terms Used by Swiss Banks (*Cont.*)

German	French	English	Meaning
Rückzug	Retrait	Withdrawal	Payment to you
Saldo	Solde	Balance	The amount in your account
Soll	Débit	Debit	A deduction from your equity
Sollzins	Intérêt débiteur	Debit interest	Interest paid by you
Sparkonto	Compte d'épargne	Savings account	See page 190
Spesen	Frais	Expenses	Costs incurred on your account
Text	Texte	Text	Type of transaction—deposit, withdrawal, etc.
Währung	Monnaie	Currency	Currency to which all figures on the statement refer
Wert	Valeur	Value date	Date the transaction actually affected your account for interest purposes
Zahlung	Paiement	Payment	Payment

NUMBERED ACCOUNTS

There are many misconceptions regarding the famous "numbered account." All Swiss bank accounts have numbers—just as with bank accounts everywhere.

By Swiss law, a bank employee cannot reveal any banking information to anyone outside the bank. So the privacy of *all* accounts is legally protected. However, there have been occasional instances of bank employees being bribed to reveal important information.

The so-called "numbered account" is handled only by number within the bank; bank employees don't know the name of the customer. The names are kept in the bank manager's safe and only two or three bank officers will have access to that information.

The numbered-account customer transacts all business with the bank by using the number only. Usually, he signs the number in his handwriting to confirm that a withdrawal request has actually come from the true holder of the account.

Because of the extra effort involved, most banks will open a numbered account only if the funds exceed a certain minimum —varying from $10,000 to $50,000. Such accounts are almost always opened in person or through a courier.

Understand that numbered accounts aren't necessary for 99% of a bank's customers. Usually, the funds involved aren't sufficient to warrant bribery of a bank employee.

Some banks won't open numbered accounts for Americans.

NEGATIVE INTEREST

To halt the inflationary tide created by an influx of non-resident accounts coming from weak currency nations, the Swiss government in 1972 imposed a negative interest tax on current accounts and interest-bearing accounts.

The tax applies only to Swiss franc accounts, and it depends upon the number of francs involved.

If you open a new account, the first 50,000 Swiss francs (approximately $17,000 in 1973) earn the normal interest paid on the account. The next 50,000 Swiss francs earn no interest. All francs in excess of 100,000 earn no interest and are subject to a tax of 2% per calendar quarter.

If the account was opened by June 30, 1972, whatever balance you had on that date is exempt from these provisions. So you can add 50,000 Swiss francs to that balance and receive interest on all francs in the account. You can add an additional 50,000 Swiss francs that will earn no interest and won't be taxed. All additions over 100,000 francs will be taxed.

If you keep the account in a currency other than Swiss francs, the Swiss bank will probably keep your balance in an account of its own in a bank in the country of the currency involved. Several other countries have imposed negative interest taxes also; so even if you keep the currency account in a Swiss bank, you may be affected by the tax if the Swiss bank is.

Negative interest tax policies are changing so rapidly that I can provide only a transitory summary here. Swiss franc deposits are definitely restricted, as already explained. But the Dutch guilder restrictions have been removed, Belgian franc restrictions are rarely enforced, and the German mark has had no restrictions. However, the uncertain policies have discouraged Swiss banks from handling some of the currencies. Any Swiss bank can tell you what it offers currently.

I don't know how long the negative interest taxes may continue. I'm surprised they've lasted beyond the time the nations involved quit supporting the dollar. But as long as the taxes continue, there are ways of avoiding them. Here are some of the ways:

1. You can open several accounts, using various family names and family combinations. Each account can be limited to 50,000 Swiss francs (or 100,000 if interest isn't important to you).

2. You can open accounts in several strong currencies.

3. You can open accounts in several different banks.

4. If you have a large sum of money, and interest isn't important to you, you can ask the bank to convert the sum to Swiss francs and keep the money in cash in the bank's vault in your name. The tax applies only to money in accounts.

5. You can keep funds in an Austrian bank where there are no negative interest or withholding taxes.

There are probably other alternatives I'm not aware of. A Swiss bank can advise you of the current availability of any alternatives that would bypass the tax.

Needless to say, there's no tax if you keep the money in U.S. dollars; the interest rates are higher, too. But don't be encouraged to keep the money in dollars; as the dollar drops, the higher price of the Swiss franc will more than compensate for the loss in interest.

Always keep your assets in a strong currency and your liabilities in dollars.

TYPES OF BANKS

Banks in Switzerland are loosely categorized according to type, but many banks fit more than one type. Of the approximately seven types, there are three that can be useful for non-residents:

1. *The Big Banks:* There are three banks referred to by that label: Union Bank of Switzerland, Swiss Bank Corporation, and Swiss Credit Bank. The assets of these banks are far greater than any of the others. They are "retail" banks in every sense of the word—with branches all over Switzerland and banking facilities that resemble American banks.

These banks offer most of the services that any Swiss bank offers, and appeal to customers of all income classes. Most types of accounts can be opened without minimum amounts required.

The banks accept new accounts by mail from anywhere in the world. However, they will ask that your signature be notarized by a branch or office of the bank in the United States, by the Swiss Consulate office, or by a U.S. bank that's a correspondent of the Swiss bank. If you have the signature verified at a U.S. office of the Swiss bank or at the Swiss Consulate, no record is kept of the notarization.

The big three banks all have offices or branches in the United States—in New York and some other cities. These offices can be contacted for information. However, there's no need to open an account through them; it's just as easy, and more private, to handle it by mail directly with the offices in Switzerland.

It should be understood that Swiss bank branches in countries other than Switzerland are subject to all laws of the country where they're located.

The big banks are accessible and friendly. However, it's more difficult to establish a relationship with one individual within the bank, someone you can write to whenever you have questions—and that's usually helpful.

Sometimes, references are made to the "big five" Swiss banks —in which case the reference includes Swiss Volksbank and Bank Leu.

2. *The Private Banks:* This type of bank is a unique institution. It's usually operated by a family, with the ownership passing from generation to generation.

The private banks are *not* corporations and so they don't have limited liability, as corporations do. The owner of a private bank is responsible for all liabilities to the extent of his personal fortune. Because the liability isn't limited, financial statements aren't published.

Private banks aren't retail banks. Their offices are more like the offices of a large company; there are no lobbies filled with tellers as in regular banks. They perform all the same services that the other banks do, but they choose their customers carefully. Generally, they're interested only in large accounts, and especially trust accounts in which they will manage a customer's investments for him.

Private banks rarely accept new accounts from strangers by mail. They may accept an account if it comes with references—

from mutual friends or present clients. They also accept new accounts when opened in person, after an exploratory interview. Minimum accounts are usually 100,000 francs or more (around $35,000).

A private bank can be useful for the individual who has a large account and desires professional management.

3. *Other Banks:* The expression "other banks" isn't meant to cover a miscellaneous assortment of banks; it's a specific banking category. In general, the other banks are similar to private banks, but more open. Many of them are owned by non-Swiss, and many of them cater to non-Swiss customers.

Their requirements for new accounts are usually larger than those of the big banks, as they're not generally retail banks. They can be most useful for non-residents.

Among the other banks are branches of U.S. banks. I mention them because I've seen recommendations made that U.S. citizens deal with these banks—because they may be more Americanized and easier to deal with.

However, I haven't found that to be an advantage. Several non-American banks have taken useful steps to make things easy for American clients. In addition, because of the restrictive Swiss immigration policies, American banks there are staffed almost entirely by Swiss citizens.

American banks in Switzerland operate under Swiss law so privacy is respected. However, the U.S. branches are required to report the names of all debtors to their central offices in the United States; this would include customers with margin accounts, for example.

FINANCIAL STATEMENTS

All banks, except the private banks, issue financial statements. If you're trying to judge size, however, the statements can be misleading. For Swiss procedures differ from American practices. A large part of a bank's business may be in the form of custodial accounts or private investment portfolios that aren't part of a bank's assets or liabilities; consequently, the bank's operations may be considerably larger than the figures on the statement indicate.

The two most useful standards to apply to a Swiss bank financial statement are: (1) How large are the reserves? and (2) What is the comparison between unsecured loans and secured loans (secured by collateral such as gold, silver, other commodities—usually held by the bank against the loan)? Some banks have a high proportion of unsecured loans which might not be recoverable in the event of a financial crash.

After finding banks that measure up by these standards, pick the bank that seems to offer most of what you require.

OPENING AN ACCOUNT

If you go to Europe, you can open an account in person—at which time you can get answers to any questions you may have. Barring that possibility, the easiest way to open an account is by mail.

A list of Swiss banks is given in Chapter 33. Additional names can be obtained by checking a directory of foreign banks—available at many banks and libraries. You can write to any of these banks for information as follows:

> Please send me current information regarding the types of accounts you offer and current interest rates.

You'll receive a brochure, in English, providing that information—or a polite letter informing you that the bank isn't accepting new accounts at the present time. If the latter, try additional banks.

If you don't want to inquire first, or if you've received a welcome that satisfies you, you can open the account by writing a letter, as follows:

> Enclosed is a bank money order for US$0,000. Please open a

Swiss franc [4] deposit [5] account for me in the name(s) of [names desired]. Please send all correspondence to me in English at the above address.

Thank you for your attention to this matter.

Take the funds you'll use to open the account to a U.S. bank and get a bank money order for the amount in U.S. dollars (the Swiss bank will convert the dollars to the currency of your choice). Enclose the money order with the letter and mail it to the bank (airmail postage to Switzerland in 1973 was 21¢ per half-ounce).

You can also transfer the money to Switzerland by wiring it through a U.S. bank that's a correspondent of the Swiss bank. The wire can be sent from any bank, to be routed through the correspondent bank to the Swiss bank. The bank wire only sends the funds and identifies the sender; you then send your instructions by mail or cable.

Upon receipt of your letter and/or funds, the bank will send you several things: (1) a credit slip showing the amount of the deposit in Swiss francs; (2) a lengthy statement detailing the current Swiss banking conditions, which you're requested to sign and return; (3) a signature card on which you indicate the signatures of any individuals empowered to transact business on the account; and (4) an application form which will ask various questions concerning the way you want the account handled. While you're attending to these matters, the money is already securely in the bank in Swiss francs.

You'll be given an account number which should be used in all future correspondence, and in making deposits and with-drawals—to prevent mistakes. All future deposits can be made by sending a bank money order with a note indicating the account to which it is deposited, or by bank wire. The deposit will auto-matically be made in the currency of the account.

The bank may notify you that it's opened a *sundry* account for you. That's a temporary account awaiting the finished paper-work to open the permanent account. The sundry account will

[4] Or other currency.
[5] Or other type of account.

be kept in the currency you've chosen, however, so you're covered while completing the paperwork.

Correspondence will be in English, unless you request otherwise. Letters will usually be signed with an illegible scrawl—as some banks seek to discourage customers from writing to a specific person at the bank.

Any account can be opened in one name, several names, or in the name of a company.

Funds can be withdrawn by so requesting in a letter. You can ask the bank to mail a check to anyone anywhere in the world, in any currency. The check it sends will usually be drawn on a bank close to the recipient. You can also request that the funds be wired, specifying a bank near the recipient to receive the funds.

With many banks, you can also request a withdrawal by wire or telephone. But such withdrawals will be sent only to *you* at the address recorded on your application form—since the withdrawal is being made without your signature.

Amounts of more than $5,000 sent to or from the United States are required by law to be reported to the U.S. government. You may legally be able to avoid this by sending several checks, each a day apart, and each no more than $5,000.

CAN YOU BRING THE MONEY HOME?

There is almost no chance that the Swiss government would ever freeze non-resident bank accounts in Swiss banks, or that the U.S. government would ever prevent reentry of funds into the United States.

If the Swiss government were to prevent funds from leaving Switzerland, it would destroy a banking reputation built carefully over hundreds of years. Anything is possible in this world, but so obviously self-destructive an act is very improbable.

On the other hand, it's very possible that the U.S. government will one day prevent funds from *leaving* the United States; so it's important to get your savings out while you still can. But I've never heard of a government preventing *reentry* of funds. In fact, there are many cases where after it became illegal to have foreign bank accounts, the government promised amnesty to those who brought their funds home.

DIVERSITY

You may want to use more than one bank—as further protection against the improbable. You may also want to use more than one currency. And you may want to have at least one account in a country other than Switzerland. To my knowledge, Austria is the second best place; while banking secrecy isn't a matter of criminal law there, the banks won't reveal account information without a court order. There are other countries that have tried to establish Swiss-type banking systems to attract funds, but all are too new to be considered reliable.

ADDITIONAL ALTERNATIVES

In addition to the types of accounts we've already covered, there are some more alternatives available to you.

1. *Trust Accounts*: Generally, trust accounts mean what discretion accounts mean in the United States—accounts in which the bank is empowered by the customer to make whatever investment decisions the bank believes would be profitable for him.

There are some exceptional cases where this is advisable, but generally I don't recommend it. Swiss bankers are not infallible. They're usually objective but not, in my opinion, well grounded in economic principles. For example, during a visit to Switzerland in August 1973 after the dollar had risen to where a Swiss franc cost only 33¢, I heard several Swiss bankers say that the dollar was still undervalued and would rise considerably further. When I wrote this book, in early September 1973, the results weren't in. But now you know whether or not they were right.

At the operating level, a Swiss bank is staffed with salaried employees. I respect them and would prefer them to American bankers or brokers if I required someone to make decisions for me. But for most people, the object is to put one's funds in long-term positions and leave them there. There's no need for continual transactions. If you tell the banker to sell your Swiss francs, gold, or silver when *he* thinks the time is right, he may sell when he expects a small technical correction—which isn't what you're after.

2. *Swiss Bonds*: It's possible to buy bonds issued by the Swiss government, by cantons (the Swiss equivalent of states), by municipalities, and by corporations. The bonds are denominated in Swiss francs, so they have the opportunity to appreciate for anyone who will one day convert the proceeds back to dollars.

As of July 1, 1972, Swiss law restricts sales of bonds to non-residents. However, if a bank sells a bond for a non-resident, it can purchase an equivalent value in bonds for another non-resident. So if you want to purchase bonds, the bank will put you on a waiting list.

When new bonds are issued, the government allocates a certain percentage that may be sold to non-residents. The amount has recently been in the neighborhood of 40%, but the figure varies with each issue.

The 30% withholding tax applies to interest earned on the bonds, but you can get it back (see page 192).

On bonds running twelve to fifteen years, the interest rates in 1973 were generally as follows. Swiss government 5¼–5½%; municipalities 5½–5¾%; first-class corporations 5¾%; normal corporations 6%. The indication then was that rates would probably rise by ¼% soon.

As the next depression will probably affect Switzerland, I'm not fond of corporate bonds, and only a little more enthusiastic about government bonds.

3. *Swiss Stocks and Mutual Funds*: The restrictions upon non-resident purchases of Swiss bonds apply in the same way to non-resident purchases of Swiss stocks.

It's probably just as well, because I don't consider Swiss stocks to be any safer than American stocks. In addition, you'll probably have to rely upon someone else's opinion to select the stocks, since it will be difficult to get enough information to make a good judgment.

Many Swiss banks have their own mutual funds. Of those that I've seen, I'm not impressed with any.

4. *Eurocurrency Accounts:* Eurocurrency is money outside its nation of origin—such as dollars in Switzerland or Austrian schillings in Germany.

The Swiss bank can arrange to purchase currency for you and deposit it in a bank that's outside of Switzerland and outside the nation issuing the currency. I've received minimum requirement quotations from banks ranging from $1,000 to $100,000; so if you're interested ask a bank what it requires.

A Eurocurrency deposit can be arranged for one, three, six, nine, eleven, or twelve months. Since the U.S. Interest Equalization Tax applies to deposits of twelve months or more, it's best to limit the contract to no more than 360 days. You can instruct the bank to automatically arrange a new one for you upon termination of the old one.

There is no negative interest tax and no Swiss withholding tax on Eurocurrency contracts. Since the Swiss bank only places the contract for you with a non-Swiss bank, the Swiss bank isn't responsible in case the non-Swiss bank fails; the liability is yours.

The interest rates are higher than on savings accounts. Here are some sample interest rate quotations given on August 14, 1973:

Currency	3 Months	6 Months	9 Months	12 Months[6]
Swiss Francs[7]	6½–7%	7¼–7¾%	7¼–7¾%	7¼–7¾%
German Marks	7½–8%	7¾–8%	8¼%	7¾–8¼%
Dutch Guilders	8½–10%	8½–10%	8½%	8¾–9¼%
Belgian Francs	7⅞%	8%	8¼%	8¼%
U.S. Dollars[6]	11½–12%	11¼–11¾%	11%	10½–11%
British Pounds[6]	16½–17½%	15½–16½%	15–16%	14–15%

[6] Not recommended.
[7] There seems to be some question whether Swiss banks will arrange Eurocurrency deposits in Swiss francs. Some banks quote rates; others will not.

5. *Certificates of Deposit:* This is a similar contract except that the bank arranges to deposit the money in the country in which the currency is issued. There is no withholding tax and no negative interest tax. Again, the Swiss bank isn't responsible if the bank where the money is deposited fails. Generally, minimum amounts required are smaller, and interest rates are smaller. Here are some sample interest rate quotations given on August 14, 1973:

Currency	3 Months	6 Months	9 Months
German Marks	5½ %	5¾ %	6%
Dutch Guilders	5½ %	5¾ %	6%
U.S. Dollars[8]	11⅜ %	11⅜ %	10½ %
British Pounds[8]	9%	9½ %	10%

YOUR OWN SWISS BANK ACCOUNT

However large or small your wealth, you can have the protection and opportunities offered by a Swiss bank account. The procedures are relatively simple, and such an account is the important first step in any investment program of the 1970s.

In addition to the services already covered, a Swiss bank can handle for you most of the investments that will be covered in Chapters 24, 25, 26, 29, and 30.

Here are some guidelines to keep in mind when establishing an account:

1. Small accounts are usually accepted by mail without further red tape. Larger accounts, usually $50,000 or more, are sometimes placed in a sundry account while the bank asks for references and checks them.

2. After the account is established, if you'll require fairly frequent transactions in commodities, Eurocurrency contracts, etc., it's better to establish a relationship with one individual with whom you can correspond and ask questions. It's much easier to do this with a smaller or medium-size bank.

[8] Not recommended.

3. Make it as easy as possible for the bank to accept your account. Use the bank's terminology in your opening letters (see the sample on pages 201–202). Try to keep everything within the bank's normal routine, and don't ask for anything unusual until after the account is established. For example, don't try to open the account by sending $300 and requesting a numbered account in gold bullion.

4. *Don't ever do anything you don't understand.* If a particular service or contract is attractive to you, don't commit yourself until you're sure you understand it fully. Otherwise, you may find later that the bank did the *opposite* of what you'd intended.

There are hundreds of millions of people around the world who wish they'd found a haven for their savings outside their own countries *before* it became illegal to do so. Once the door has been shut, you can get funds to Switzerland only by smuggling them (difficult and risky) or by paying a private courier (expensive).

There's no way to predict when exchange controls will be imposed in the United States or any other country. But as the currency situation worsens, the pressure to shut the door on exiting funds will be great. It's always better to send the funds out too soon.[9]

---

[9] Regarding the negative interest tax, see the footnote on page 322.

24

Foreign Currencies

FOR SAVINGS, the most stable form of value is a strong currency. There are drawbacks to any currency, as we'll see, but a currency like the Swiss franc offers a very small downward risk and a very high upside potential.

Very likely, silver and gold will show much greater appreciation than foreign currencies over the next few years. But both of those commodities have already risen far enough that there's room for severe drops during temporary fluctuations.

In the sample investment programs, I'll recommend gold and silver for even the most conservative investors. But if safety is your object, and you can do only one thing, I'd recommend that you put all your savings in a Swiss bank in Swiss francs.

STRONG CURRENCIES

Literally, there's no such thing as a strong currency today. To properly earn that title, a currency should be merely a warehouse receipt, convertible into gold at a permanent rate at any time by anyone who wants gold. Free market changes in the price of gold would have no effect upon such a currency because it would be nothing but a warehouse receipt for gold. Rising gold prices make convertibility difficult *only* because a government has issued more currency than it has gold in storage.

There's no strong currency in the world because all governments inflate their currencies. Those who have said that a little bit of inflation is a good thing must be biting their tongues today. For the monetary crises are hurting even those nations where inflation has been comparatively mild.

There is, however, a vast difference *between* currencies. And when you convert assets from U.S. dollars to a currency that's *much less weak,* you're taking a long step upward in safety.

A good example is the Swiss franc. It started from a very strong position and progressively weakened—partly through efforts to support the dollar and partly because of typical governmental efforts to "stimulate" the economy.

Fortunately, the Swiss government ended its support of the dollar in February 1973. I can only hope it won't resume the support. The Swiss franc was strong enough to withstand a lot of abuse, but it can't withstand such abuse indefinitely. The franc will continue to depreciate against gold, but will undoubtedly appreciate against the dollar.

For simplicity, I'll refer to currencies like the Swiss franc as strong currencies. They are the safest haven today. Even though some of them have already risen 30–42% against the dollar, it's doubtful that temporary fluctuations could cause them to drop by more than 15% from any price at which you buy them. Gold or silver, on the other hand, could easily suffer temporary drops of 25–30%—even though they should go up by 100–300% eventually.

"HOT" AND "COLD" CURRENCIES

The investor interested in long-term safety and appreciation should try to stay clear of the many forecasts of short-term currency price movements. At any given time, there will be currencies due for short-term increases or drops. But to speculate on those short-term movements is a field all its own—and for the part-time investor it's filled with more traps than opportunities.

For one thing, once the impending increase is "common

knowledge," the marketplace will have already caused a higher price that covers most of the anticipated increase. And the individual who rushes in then will have an opportunity for very little profit but will be vulnerable to a large loss if the forecast proves wrong.

During the past few years, most of the currency news has revolved around the excitement of the German mark and the Japanese yen. While the mark has appreciated equally with the attention given it, the yen has been surpassed by two currencies given much less attention—the Swiss franc and the Austrian schilling. And for the long term, the yen is probably greatly overvalued and will eventually drop.

If you're attracted by the excitement of a hot currency, you could buy just before it cools off. And an easy way to take a quick loss is with a cold currency.

Full-time currency speculators are the only people who have any business switching back and forth between currencies to take advantage of short-term movements. Part-time investors will almost always be burned if they try to keep up with them.

So it's important to ignore short-term reports and recommendations. Understand your objectives; if they're long term, find a good, sound currency, put your money there, and wait it out.

In January 1973, a financial newsletter that recommends gold, silver, and strong currencies advised its readers that the Swiss franc was temporarily *over*valued and should be sold *short*. Within a month, the Swiss franc had *risen* by 20%. Since short contracts usually require 10% down payment or less, anyone who took the advice would have been liable for losses equal to 200% of his investment.

If the newsletter reader didn't use margin, but merely converted to dollars for the temporary period, he would have lost a good part of the Swiss franc gain he'd been awaiting.

Any adviser can make a mistake. The harm comes in reacting to short-term possibilities when your real objective is long-term safety and profit.

GOLD, GOLD, GOLD

Perhaps the most important point this book is attempting to make is that gold will reign supreme long after most paper currencies have been turned to ashes. There are two possible ways this supremacy will assert itself:

1. The governments of the world will quit trying to do the impossible. They'll finally realign their currencies in accordance with their *actual* (not "official") gold contents. This will be necessary to restore convertibility of the weaker currencies; otherwise, a weaker nation would lose all its gold quickly after restoring convertibility. The new currency price will have to be based upon the amount of currency in circulation versus the gold backing—as compared with similar evaluations of all other currencies. Or . . .

2. The governments will continue to try to ignore gold, and their currencies will continue to depreciate. In that case, people in the marketplace will gravitate toward those currencies that are the best true substitutes for gold.

Either way, currency prices will change. And the long-term changes will be in the direction of the actual gold contents of the currencies. Strangely, I don't think it impossible that the first alternative might come to pass. A point may be reached where the nations with stronger currencies will force the weaker ones to go along.

Although currencies may make minor changes in either direction in the short term, the long-term future belongs to the currencies that maintain high gold contents. And there are vast differences in that respect among the major world currencies.

EVALUATION OF CURRENCIES

To determine the best currencies for long-term investment, we can establish four standards:

1. If you believe that gold is the only real money, the first measurement must be the *gold backing* of the currency.

2. Is it *convenient* to obtain and hold the currency? Is it readily available in Swiss banks, for example?

3. Is there a *large enough market* for the currency to enable you to convert it back to dollars whenever you choose?

4. How *reliable* is the currency? Is it possible that its present gold content is only a temporary condition? What is the government's history regarding currency manipulation, monetary freedom for its citizens?

The prime consideration is the gold backing. When you find several currencies that appear to be solid in that respect, you can then choose among them to satisfy the other standards.

GOLD BACKING

To determine the gold backing of a currency, we need to know two things: (1) the amount of currency in circulation, and (2) the size of the gold reserve. In turn, the currency in circulation is determined by two components: the demand deposits in banks and the currency circulation outside of banks.

Since demand deposits (checking accounts or current accounts) are subject to withdrawals of currency that are legal tender, the deposits are as much a part of the money supply as the currency outside of the banks. Both of those factors serve as substitutes for gold.

There are other factors that are sometimes included in money substitute totals—time deposits (savings accounts), cash values in life insurance policies, savings and loan deposits, etc. But these figures are difficult to obtain in many countries, and often they're duplications of the demand deposit figures.

However, we don't need a precise figure of the amount of inflation that has taken place (I know of no formula for relating the precise amount of inflation to any future event). What we need is a standard by which we can *compare* various currencies.

The central banks of each nation regularly publish totals of demand deposits, currency outside of banks, and gold reserves. The table on pages 216–217 provides that information for twenty-six major currencies. Most currencies that have received any attention from investors or the press have been included. Central and South American currencies were excluded because none of them offers an investment opportunity. Comparable information for Hong Kong and Rhodesia wasn't available.

The gold reserves do *not* include the foreign currency holdings that governments ordinarily count as part of their monetary reserves—even when those foreign currencies are supposed to be convertible to gold. There's no way those currencies could be exchanged for gold without running the gold price up significantly or causing substantial devaluations before the convertibility could be completed.

Here is an explanation of the table:

Demand Deposits are checking account or current account balances in all commercial banks in each nation. The figures are in millions (for example, there are 250 billion U.S. dollars or 36 trillion Italian lira).

Currency Outside Banks includes all currency printed by the government less the amount reported held by commercial banks. It would include deposits of the currency in banks outside the country. The figures are in millions.

Total Money Substitutes is the total of *Demand Deposits* and *Currency Outside Banks*.

Gold Reserves are calculated by multiplying the number of ounces of the government's gold by its official gold price. (For example, as of December 31, 1972, the U.S. government held 273,684,211 ounces of gold—multiplied by the then official rate of $38.00 equals $10.4 billion.) The gold reserve doesn't include foreign currencies or SDRs—only gold. The figures are in millions.

Gold Backing is the percentage of the nation's money substitutes that are actually backed by gold at the official rate. The figure is obtained by dividing the total money substitutes into the currency value of the gold reserve.

All figures are as of December 31, 1972. Sources for the figures are given on page 386.

From the table, we can draw some conclusions:

1. There's one currency—the Lebanese pound—that has substantial gold backing.

2. There are six other currencies that have substantial backing when compared with the rest of the list.

3. There are two marginal currencies—the German mark and the French franc.

4. The rest of the currencies have relatively insignificant gold backing.

5. Way down the list, in position 24, is the highly-touted Japanese yen with less than 1% gold backing. I suspect that the much-acclaimed Japanese economy, based upon an oriental form of welfare-statism, will not hold up over the coming years—despite the many predictions that it will be the world's leading economy by the end of the century.

It should be noted that all these figures are pretty slippery. To begin with, they come from biased sources—the governments involved. And each may have its own way of tabulating the figures. Some are seasonally adjusted and some aren't, for example.

I ran into this problem in 1969 when preparing the *Devaluation* book. I tried many sources to obtain readable figures for the Swiss franc, but to no avail. Finally, at a U.S. office of a Swiss bank, the manager read the figures to me from a German-language publication of the Swiss National Bank. The figures showed 82% gold backing, compared to 4% backing of the U.S. dollar at that time.

Since then, I've realized that the figures must have been wrong, but I couldn't determine what figures I *had* received. Finally, Franz Pick pointed out to me that the demand deposit figures were for the cantonal banks—no other banks, including the big banks, were included.

I apologize for publishing that erroneous information—but not for recommending the Swiss franc as a result. It's still a recommended currency and has risen 42% against the U.S. dollar since publication of the book.

Gold Backing for 26 Major Currencies

(as of December 31, 1972—all amounts in millions)

Rank	Currency	Demand Deposits	Currency Outside Banks	Total Money Substitutes	Gold Reserve	Gold Backing
1.	Lebanese Pound	1,215	1,034	2,249	1,078.02	47.93%
2.	Dutch Guilder	11,890	11,410	23,300	6,681.01	28.67%
3.	Swiss Franc	31,500	17,930	49,430	11,879.79	24.03%
4.	Portuguese Escudo	85,570	36,120	121,690	27,823.05	22.86%
5.	South African Rand	2,170	627	2,797	533.16	19.06%
6.	Austrian Schilling	53,350	45,470	98,820	18,454.03	18.67%
7.	Belgian Franc	203,200	216,800	420,000	73,410.10	17.48%
8.	German (West) Mark	85,600	45,700	131,300	13,973.10	10.64%
9.	French Franc	174,550	84,130	258,680	19,573.14	7.57%
10.	Turkish Lira	9,630	16,940	26,570	1,904.04	7.17%
11.	Greek Drachma	25,490	50,560	76,050	3,984.09	5.24%
12.	Swedish Krona	6,490	14,360	20,850	1,044.43	5.01%
13.	Italian Lira	36,052,000	8,471,000	44,523,000	1,820,136.31	4.09%

Gold Backing for 26 Major Currencies (*Cont.*)

Rank	Currency	Demand Deposits	Currency Outside Banks	Total Money Substitutes	Gold Reserve	Gold Backing
14.	Canadian Dollar	16,890	4,550	21,440	830.46	3.87%
15.	Mexican Peso	37,900	26,880	64,780	2,350.06	3.63%
16.	United States Dollar	250,180	56,600	306,780	10,400.00	3.39%
17.	Spanish Peseta	723,800	327,800	1,051,600	34,881.06	3.32%
18.	Israel Pound	3,550	2,040	5,590	182.28	3.26%
19.	Australian Dollar	5,227	1,665	6,892	220.40	3.20%
20.	English Pound	9,342	4,079	13,421	307.03	2.29%
21.	Yugoslavian Dinar	31,400	23,400	54,800	952.02	1.73%
22.	Danish Krone	25,910	5,350	31,260	480.94	1.54%
23.	Norwegian Krone	10,500	8,750	19,250	247.21	1.28%
24.	Japanese Yen	26,820,000	7,706,000	34,526,000	246,714.50	.71%
25.	New Zealand Dollar	956	238	1,194	.88	.07%
26.	Irish Pound	301,800	191,300	493,100	6.52	.0013%

I caution you, also, to watch out for misleading figures that are occasionally published. Often, they're based on incomplete factors. For example, I occasionally see references to the Swiss franc having 120% gold backing. Such percentages usually don't allow for demand deposits—which are just as much claims against the gold reserve as the currency outside banks.

FUTURE EXCHANGE PRICES

Sooner or later, gold will be the measuring standard for all currencies. To maintain its value, a currency will have to be convertible into gold. And if a government has inflated its currency to where convertibility isn't possible, there are only two ways it can remedy the situation.

One way is to deflate the currency—by withdrawing it from circulation as it passes through the government. Because a deflation will trigger a depression, it's not too likely that the U.S. government will choose this alternative. If it does, the dollar will rise in price. If you're holding a foreign currency at that time, you won't lose wealth by the dollar rise, however. You'll exchange back to dollars at a higher dollar rate, but the dollars will each be worth more because of the deflation.

The other way to permit convertibility is for the government to devalue its currency. It does this by lowering the gold content of each currency unit, thus making each ounce of gold back more currency units. When that happens, there's a change in its currency exchange price. In that case, you can reconvert to dollars and receive more dollars than you converted originally.

The same result is achieved by allowing the currency to float downward until it levels off. Then the government devalues by an amount comparable to the drop in its currency's price. In that case, the exchange price, and the profits therefrom, have occurred *before* the devaluation.

If the government does nothing to restore convertibility, the currency will continue to sink in international exchange. So any strong foreign currency you hold will reconvert to more of your own currency eventually. And those who have turned to gold-backed currencies for safety will have the greatest purchasing power.

The "official" gold content of a currency is meaningless, due to inflation. But the *actual* gold content can be determined by dividing the number of money substitutes in circulation into the number of ounces in the gold reserve. That will show the actual number of currency units circulating for each ounce of gold.

For example, as of December 31, 1972, the "official" U.S. gold position was 38 paper dollars circulating for each ounce of gold in reserve. The actual position was 1,121 dollars in circulation for each ounce of gold. That makes each dollar worth $\frac{1}{1,121}$ ounce of gold.

At the same time, there were 595 Swiss francs in circulation for each ounce of gold in reserve. Each Swiss franc had a gold content of $\frac{1}{595}$ ounce of gold.

Currency prices must gravitate toward levels consistent with those actual gold contents. It doesn't matter if 100% gold backing is considered necessary or 25% backing is considered respectable; *any* standard of gold backing will cause the actual gold contents to determine the currency exchange prices.

With 595 Swiss francs and 1,121 dollars each representing one ounce of gold, a respect for gold will make each Swiss franc the equivalent of 1.88 dollars. That means a Swiss franc price of $1.88. In the summer of 1973, the price was $.33, a long way from its potential.

There are many factors that can prevent the Swiss franc from reaching $1.88 eventually—or cause it to go much further.

For one thing, the component factors are constantly changing. As nations inflate or deflate their currencies, and increase or decrease their gold reserves, the *currency units per ounce* figure changes. In addition, the governments involved may take misguided measures to prevent their currencies from appreciating —in an attempt to aid exports—but those impediments will, by necessity, be temporary. And, too, the marketplace may not demand prices that reflect gold contents precisely.

But the trend will inevitably be in the direction of a currency price based upon actual relative gold content. So $1.88 is a *potential* price for the Swiss franc—the objective toward which the General Market will be gravitating. And as long as the Swiss government doesn't try to outdo the U.S. government in currency perversion, that potential is a realistic one.

The table on page 221 applies the same standard to the twenty-six currencies. In each case the *actual currency units per ounce* figure is divided into the same figure for the U.S. dollar.[1] The result is the *actual dollar value* of that currency, which represents a potential dollar price for the currency. We can then compare that potential with the currency's dollar price in June 1973, to see how far the currency price will have to move, up or down, to achieve its potential.

That figure appears as a percentage in the column *Change Necessary Against $*. The Swiss franc, for example, will have to rise 473% to reach its potential. Until that potential is reached, there will be recurring problems between the governments trying to enforce a lesser exchange rate upon the marketplace.

It can be misleading to read all the figures in dollar terms only, even if that's the currency you now hold. For instance, the Mexican peso shows a potential increase of 7%. That could lead you to believe that the peso won't depreciate. But the last column indicates that the peso can depreciate 55% against all the other currencies on the list. The peso won't provide the purchasing power you need to meet future shortages and much higher retail prices in dollars and pesos.

So the last column measures the currency's potential change against the potentials of all twenty-five other currencies.

It should be noted that a U.S. runaway inflation would increase the potentials a million times or more for any nation that isn't also afflicted with runaway inflation. But the foreign currency potentials *relative to each other* should remain somewhat the same.

The table reveals seven currencies with outstanding potential.

---

[1] The true figure for the dollar is 1,120.93. Figures on all tables have been rounded for convenience, but unrounded figures have been used to make the calculations.

Potential Currency Changes

Rank	Currency	Actual Units/Oz.	Actual $ Value	Price 6/18/73	Change Necessary Against $	Change Necessary Against All
1.	Lebanese Pound	244	4.5906	.4015	+1,043%	+380%
2.	Dutch Guilder	430	2.6068	.3685	+ 607%	+197%
3.	Portuguese Escudo	4,529	.2475	.0430	+ 476%	+142%
4.	Swiss Franc	595	1.8846	.3290	+ 473%	+140%
5.	So. African Rand	156	7.1822	1.4950	+ 380%	+102%
6.	Austrian Schilling	4,741	.2364	.0530	+ 346%	+ 87%
7.	Belgian Franc	9,744	.1150	.0268	+ 329%	+ 80%
8.	German Mark	1,151	.9741	.3910	+ 149%	+ 5%
9.	Turkish Lira	7,424	.1510	.0725	+ 108%	− 13%
10.	French Franc	2,569	.4363	.2375	+ 84%	− 23%
11.	Greek Drachma	21,761	.0515	.0336	+ 53%	− 36%
12.	Swedish Krona	3,651	.3070	.2384	+ 29%	− 46%
13.	Italian Lira	540,535	.0021	.0016	+ 27%	− 47%
14.	Canadian Dollar	977	1.1475	1.0005	+ 15%	− 52%
15.	Mexican Peso	13,094	.0856	.0801	+ 7%	− 55%
16.	U.S. Dollar	1,121	1.0000	1.0000	—	− 58%
17.	Israeli Pound	4,894	.2290	.2381	− 4%	− 60%
18.	Spanish Peseta	73,865	.0152	.0180	− 16%	− 65%
19.	Australian Dollar	932	1.2027	1.4250	− 16%	− 65%
20.	English Pound	638	1.7583	2.5830	− 32%	− 71%
21.	Yugoslavian Dinar	37,186	.0301	.0643	− 53%	− 80%
22.	Danish Krone	17,241	.0650	.1729	− 62%	− 84%
23.	Norwegian Krone	19,664	.0570	.1836	− 69%	− 87%
24.	Japanese Yen	1,637,938	.0007	.0038	− 82%	− 92%
25.	New Zealand Dollar	45,364	.0247	1.3350	− 98%	− 99%
26.	Irish Pound	1,102,225	.0010	2.5850	− 99.96%	− 99.98%

The potential must be large enough to withstand reversals in an uncertain world. A potential increase of 300% or more against the dollar gives you plenty of breathing room; if a lot goes against you, the net result within the next few years should be a minimum increase of 100%.

The German mark stands eighth on the list, quite far behind the rest. But I'll include it with the top seven—for reasons I'll explain shortly.

One factor that should be considered is the freedom the currency has to move to its ultimate potential. That freedom may be inhibited by a government bent on influencing its balance of payments. A partial indication can be seen from its movement during the past three years. The table on page 223 shows the changing currency prices from 1970 to 1973.

Again, the figures are presented in dollar terms. And because that can be misleading, they're converted in the final column to show each currency's change against all the other currencies on the list.

The prices listed are for a three-year period. However, I've used June 18, 1973, because it precedes a period in which the strong currencies rose substantially against the dollar, and then dropped again to levels similar to June 18. Where the prices will be when you read this, I can't say; but you can check the current prices in the foreign exchange section of the *Wall Street Journal*.

It should also be noted that the German mark price in dollars increased by approximately 10% from June 1969 to June 1970. So over a four-year period, it has increased by over 50% against the dollar—and is the leader in currency appreciation.

It's interesting to compare the tables on pages 221 and 223. They reveal currencies that have been popular during the past three years, but whose long-term potential is decidedly downward. For example, the Japanese yen has gone up 36%, but has a downward potential of 82%. And the Norwegian krone, the Danish krone, the Australian dollar, the Spanish peseta, and the New Zealand dollar have all done well during the past three years; but all have depressing prospects for the future.

Additional standards for evaluation were listed on pages 212–213. Each of the eight strongest currencies will be discussed in terms of the four standards. We'll begin with the two currencies that I don't recommend.

SOUTH AFRICAN RAND

The gold backing of the rand is impressive, but it's misleading. South Africa is the leading gold producing area of the world. By governmental edict, all gold mining companies must market

Currency Price Changes, 1970–1973

Rank	Currency	Price 6/30/70	Price 6/18/73	Change vs. $	Change vs. All
1.	Swiss Franc	.2317	.3290	+41.98%	+20.82%
2.	German Mark	.2755	.3910	+41.94%	+20.79%
3.	Austrian Schilling	.0388	.0530	+36.60%	+16.25%
4.	Japanese Yen	.0028	.0038	+35.84%	+15.60%
5.	Dutch Guilder	.2759	.3685	+33.55%	+13.65%
6.	Belgian Franc	.0201	.0268	+33.04%	+13.22%
7.	Norwegian Krone	.1400	.1836	+31.14%	+11.60%
8.	French Franc	.1813	.2375	+31.02%	+11.50%
9.	Lebanese Pound	.3072	.4015	+30.70%	+11.22%
10.	Danish Krone	.1335	.1729	+29.56%	+10.25%
11.	Australian Dollar	1.1180	1.4250	+27.46%	+ 8.47%
12.	Spanish Peseta	.0144	.0180	+25.00%	+ 6.37%
13.	Swedish Krona	.1930	.2384	+23.52%	+ 5.11%
14.	Portuguese Escudo	.0352	.0430	+22.16%	+ 3.96%
15.	New Zealand Dollar	1.1220	1.3350	+18.98%	+ 1.25%
16.	Irish Pound	2.3700	2.5850	+ 9.07%	− 7.18%
17.	English Pound	2.3954	2.5830	+ 7.83%	− 8.24%
18.	So. African Rand	1.3985	1.4950	+ 6.90%	− 9.03%
19.	Canadian Dollar	.9669	1.0005	+ 3.48%	−11.94%
20.	Italian Lira	.0016	.0016	+ 2.39%	−12.87%
21.	Greek Drachma	.0329	.0336	+ 2.16%	−13.06%
22.	U.S. Dollar	1.0000	1.0000	—	−14.90%
23.	Mexican Peso	.0801	.0801	—	−14.90%
24.	Turkish Lira	.0775	.0725	− 6.45%	−20.39%
25.	Yugoslavian Dinar	.0760	.0643	−15.39%	−28.00%
26.	Israeli Pound	.2875	.2381	−17.18%	−29.52%

Figures may not agree because of rounding.

their outputs through the South African government. Because the gold reserve figures include gold that may soon be sold, there's no way to know how much respect the government has for its gold reserves.

In addition, the government has done a lot of tinkering with the currency. It was officially pegged to the British pound until August 1971, and when the U.S. went off the gold convertibility standard, South Africa decided to peg the rand to the U.S. dollar, instead—if you can make some sense out of that.

South African residents are severely limited in their financial dealings. They can't own the country's major commodity, gold. In many ways, they're more restricted than U.S. citizens.

Given the overall mismanagement of the currency, it can only be assumed that its high gold reserves are merely an inventory of gold awaiting sale in the marketplace.

The currency is not easily available through Swiss banks or anywhere outside of South Africa. Even if it were, the rand isn't a very safe bet.

PORTUGUESE ESCUDO

Citizens of Portugal have a little more monetary freedom than those in South Africa, but the overall situation is much the same. The government is attempting the erection of a gigantic welfare state. According to *Pick's Currency Yearbook*, the price inflation is running 20% per year.

The currency isn't widely traded.

If the escudo were the only strong currency available, a closer look would be warranted. But there are much better possibilities.

RECOMMENDED CURRENCIES

There are good reasons for considering each of the remaining six currencies. The Swiss franc and the Dutch guilder are both strong currencies with good potentials. The Austrian schilling and the Belgian franc are also strong but a little harder to deal with. The German mark has some advantages; and the Lebanese pound can be considered for speculative purposes. Here are the salient characteristics of each of those currencies.

SWISS FRANC

The Swiss franc is the elite currency of the world, and for good reason. While the Swiss government is still a government, with all that the word implies, it has done much to encourage good monetary conditions; or rather, I should say that it has done little to impede progress.

Zurich has become the gold center of the world, replacing the London market over the past few years. The lack of restrictions upon private ownership of gold or foreign exchange dealings provides a wide market among Swiss residents to deal in currencies and gold. This base is augmented many times over by millions of Swiss bank customers from all over the world.

Unfortunately, the Swiss government has recently undertaken numerous social programs that cost a lot of money, and which have caused the national budget to run in the red. Combined with its support of the dollar for several years, this has made the Swiss franc less attractive than it was a few years back.

In addition, the Swiss government has imposed the bank balance restrictions on non-residents that were covered in the last chapter. But there are ways of getting around the restrictions, as we've seen.

Overall, the Swiss franc is still the most attractive currency for protection and conservative profit purposes. If it continues downhill, it will probably take several years for its status to change. Switzerland is now in approximately the same position the United States was twenty years or so ago.

The Swiss franc is not involved in any fixed exchange rate systems.

DUTCH GUILDER

Monetary freedom also exists in the Netherlands, although the government has been more of a welfare state than the Swiss government. The guilder has been free to move upwards during the past three years, increasing in value by one-third over the dollar.

In September 1973, the guilder was upvalued an additional 5%, and its price exceeded $.39. It still has a long way to go upward, however; and now there are no negative interest taxes on guilder accounts.

The guilder operates in two separate fixed exchange systems —the European Common Market and a separate arrangement among the Benelux nations (Belgium, Holland, and Luxembourg). Each supports the others' currencies, but the currencies float freely against those of outside nations.

BELGIAN FRANC

The Belgian franc has moved upward freely since the Belgians stopped supporting the dollar. The franc has an excellent upside potential and is freely available throughout Europe. The only limitation is the government's imposition of a negative interest tax on non-resident balances of over 500,000 francs (approximately $13,500), and that is rarely enforced. A Belgian franc account can be used for some of the excess that might be taxed in a Swiss franc account. Swiss banks handle the Belgian franc.

There are no limitations on the monetary freedom of Belgian residents. The franc is part of the Common Market and Benelux fixed exchange systems, as is the guilder.

AUSTRIAN SCHILLING

Austrians face more monetary restrictions than do the Swiss, Dutch, or Belgians. Foreign bank accounts are illegal for Austrian residents; and there are limitations upon the importing and exporting of gold. However, some Austrian banks have proven to be useful depositories for non-residents.

As of 1973, there were no negative interest taxes on non-resident bank balances, and so the schilling can be used to handle excess funds in a Swiss bank.

The currency is part of the Common Market fixed exchange rate system, but floats against all other currencies.

GERMAN MARK

The mark has already moved quite a ways toward its ultimate potential. However, I would expect it to continue in that direction for at least the next year or two.

Eventually, however, problems of inflation and a socialized economy are bound to catch up with the situation. The highly praised "German miracle" of postwar recovery has been caused more by extravagant aid from the United States than by free enterprise. To a European, "free enterprise" often means the right to choose your own doctor under socialized medicine.

Because of the foundation upon which the German economy rests, I expect it to be one of the noisiest fallers when the next crash comes. How that will affect the currency will depend mostly on the reactions of those in power at the time. However, the biggest threat will be the impetus to inflate when the going gets rough—so the currency isn't likely to be affected for a few years yet. And when the time comes, you'll probably have some warning.

In the meantime, the mark offers some advantages. One is the likelihood of a continuing price rise for the next year or two. Another is the fact that no exchange restrictions have been placed upon it yet. You can have an unlimited German mark account in a Swiss bank, and several banks continue to pay normal interest rates on those accounts. Generally, the interest rate is ½% or 1% higher than for Swiss francs.

The mark is part of the Common Market fixed exchange rate system. The currency can be traded easily in Switzerland or elsewhere in the world.

For large bank balances, the mark can be used for excess funds while awaiting the removal of the negative interest tax on Swiss francs. For those who don't need several accounts, I suggest using the Swiss franc instead. You may have a few twinges of anxiety if the mark rises faster than the franc over the next year, but in the long term you'll be able to rest more easily with your money in Swiss francs.

LEBANESE POUND

The Lebanese pound must be approached as a pure speculation—but possibly a very profitable speculation. As we've seen, its gold content far surpasses that of any other major currency. The respect for gold is very strong in the Middle East, but the other currencies there are either difficult to trade or too unstable.

The biggest problem for the Lebanese pound has been the perpetual warfare between Israel and the Arab countries. In addition, concern over its export-import balances has kept the government from allowing the currency to float upward to a price more compatible with its gold content. The pound has risen 30% since 1970, but should have risen more considering its gold content.

If the day comes within the next few years when the currencies of the world are realigned in accordance with their true gold values—either by agreement or by marketplace action—the Lebanese pound will probably have an extraordinary increase in price. With an upward potential of over 1,000%, there's plenty of room left to offset problems.

After World War II, the government instituted a bank secrecy act, a very mild version of the Swiss system. Complete monetary freedom was allowed for both residents and non-residents. Since then, the country has been considered the financial center of the Middle East—weathering both a banking crisis and guerrilla fighting in the streets of Beirut.

The Lebanese pound can't be traded easily in Switzerland. To take advantage of its potential, you must open an account in Lebanon—risking further political warfare crises.

The Lebanese pound shouldn't be considered for funds seeking safety; the risks are much too great. But if you'd like to take a flyer with speculative funds, it's an attractive possibility.

RECOMMENDATIONS

It should be noted, first of all, that we live in a world of welfare states. In none of the countries just covered does the average citizen enjoy much more economic freedom than an American citizen does. All the governments involved inflate their currencies, tax fairly heavily, intervene in their economies, and restrict their citizens in other ways.

That noted, however, there *are* differences. In Switzerland, for example, the citizens would feel they were living in a totalitarian dictatorship if they couldn't own gold or have foreign bank accounts. And until a couple of years ago, national budget deficits were unheard of; inflation was caused mostly by banks lending demand deposits.

Switzerland has never joined the International Monetary Fund, nor even the United Nations, and has avoided any treaties that could lead to war. These policies have been part of a deeply-rooted tradition, not just the politics of the party in power at any given time.

That's changing now, slowly but surely. Fortunately, the changes should take long enough that Switzerland is still an attractive haven for funds that need to weather the next few perilous years.

The other countries recommended fall between Switzerland and the United States in terms of safety and reliability. They are liable to be more affected by the coming depression; Switzerland will suffer, too, but not to the same extent as those countries that have been rebuilt with American economic aid and direction since the war.

The recommended currencies are:

1. *Swiss franc:* The basic protection for savings. Its potential price increase is 473%, and so it should appreciate materially over the next few years. But its principal attraction is the opportunity to place your funds where there's little downside risk, no risk of confiscation, and an assurance that upward price movements will more than cover the explosive price increases in the offing for Americans.

2. *Dutch guilder:* The guilder provides a good second currency for excess funds, and for diversification. Its upside potential—607%—is even greater than the Swiss franc, with few offsetting disadvantages. One of those disadvantages is the shorter period of history behind it to provide a precedent for future reliability. The other is that it isn't traded as widely as the Swiss franc. Swiss banks can handle your needs, however, so I recommend the guilder enthusiastically.

3. *Belgian franc:* While not as attractive in either its potential (329%) or safety, the Belgian franc provides a third currency for diversification.

4. *Austrian schilling:* Less attractive yet than the three preceding currencies, the schilling is still quite far ahead of the pack. With better alternatives available, however, it's only to be kept in mind—to be used if special circumstances should require it. It has a long-term potential increase of 346%.

5. *German mark:* With a much smaller potential than the others (149%), the mark can still serve usefully for the next couple of years. Its usefulness right now is the freedom to hold unlimited balances in marks in a Swiss bank.

6. *Lebanese pound:* Useful only for speculation. But for that it's an attractive medium (potential increase: 1,043%).

BANK INSTRUCTIONS

Swiss bank policies with regard to the above currencies vary right now. So you may need to write to several banks if you want accounts in currencies other than the Swiss franc.

The procedure for buying a foreign currency is very simple. Using the sample letter given in the previous chapter, just tell the bank you want to open a German mark current account, or German mark deposit account, or whatever. All funds deposited in that account will be converted automatically to German marks. The same applies for any of the other currencies recommended, except the Lebanese pound—which will have to be handled in Lebanon.

BANKNOTES

It's possible to buy foreign currencies in the United States, to be held at home or in a safe deposit box. Foreign exchange companies, and some banks, maintain inventories of foreign currencies (in cash form, they're referred to as *banknotes*). The inventories are usually small, but large quantities can be ordered for delivery a few days later.

You may be able to think of some reasons why holding foreign cash might be valuable, but I've never come up with any. Only if you may have to travel quickly to the country whose currency you hold does it make any sense.

Foreign currency prices are usually slightly higher when purchasing banknotes in the United States. The banknotes can be stored in a safe deposit box or a safe. However, you may not have any purpose in holding them.

So even if you have only $100 you'd like to see appreciate, it's more profitable to deposit it at a Swiss bank.

SAFETY

The time has arrived when personal financial safety is the overriding issue. One might have squandered a few funds in a misguided attempt to support his government a few years ago, and suffered very little for his folly. Today, the stakes are too high, the funds are too precious, and the ready assurance that you can earn the money back later no longer exists. What you earn during the next two to five years may be the last of your big income days for a while.

There's nothing unpatriotic about using the best banking system or a currency necessary for your financial survival. Would you give up Brazilian coffee, French wines, or Canadian oil in order to be patriotic?

The government should compete for your patronage as anyone else does. If it has debased its currency, its "last refuge" will be to appeal to your patriotism. But patriotism in that case means paying for the government's mistakes.

The U.S. government has already paved the way toward foreign exchange controls by requiring you to report overseas transmissions of more than $5,000, and by requiring you to list foreign bank accounts on your income tax return. The door shutting off overseas transmissions could close at any time. Once that's happened, the price of getting your money out will go up many times over—for smuggling will be the only avenue.

In the meantime, the best time to act is when you know what to do. If the dollar is rising as you read this, don't wait for the currency market to turn around. The best time to make the exchange is while the dollar is quietly rising. For when it turns around, a panic can send the dollar nosediving at any time.

I met a man a couple of years ago who had lived most of his life in Cuba. He had been a millionaire. He'd believed it would be unpatriotic to keep his money anywhere but in Cuba. When Castro seized power, he thought of it as only a change in administration. How could anyone be more totalitarian than Batista?

When he began to realize that it might be valuable to have some of his wealth outside the country, it was already too late. Then they *took* his wealth.

He and his family finally managed to sneak out of the country to the United States—penniless—and he had to begin all over again here.

Today, he's not nearly as rich as he once was. But of the little wealth he's accumulated, a good percentage is in a Swiss bank.

The same story could be told by millions of people from dozens of different countries. Everyone of them had good reason to believe that his country was different. But each of them paid the price for trusting his government.

There's no way that acting too soon can hurt you. But by waiting until it's too late, the results could be disastrous.[2]

[2] After this book was in print, the Swiss negative interest tax was repealed—eliminating the need for the German mark in a diversified program. For more details, see the footnote on page 322.

In addition, the "energy crisis" has depressed the prices of most European currencies temporarily. For long-term investments, they are now better than ever—since bargain prices have been created (which may or may not still exist when you read this).

"Grin and Bear It" by George Lichty, Courtesy of Publishers-Hall Syndicate

"Investment-wise, this fellow has Rembrandt, Goya and Van Gogh licked . . . he uses nothing but 24 carat gold paint."

25
Gold

GOLD AND SILVER are the only real monies with universal acceptance in the world today. And gold is much more honored as money than silver, as it has been through the ages.

When paper money systems begin to crack at the seams, the run to gold could be explosive. There's really no way to determine the upside potential of gold, but a conservative estimate would be $300–$500 per ounce within five years—and possibly even within a year. It wouldn't shock me if it reached $1,000 per ounce within five years—even without runaway inflation.

As recently as a year ago, I placed the upside potential at $140; but I can see how shortsighted that was. By the time it reached $125 I had raised my sights, so I didn't advise anyone to sell.

RECENT HISTORY

The price of gold can increase as the demand for industrial uses of gold increases. But the principal reason for price increases is the depreciation of currency. As a result, the price of gold increases by different amounts in different currencies, as currencies also change in price relative to each other. For example, while the price of an ounce of gold was rising in dollars from $40 to $120 (up 200%) the price in Swiss francs rose from SwF175 to SwF341 (up only 95%). This was because the dollar was dropping against the Swiss franc as well as against gold.

Currencies have depreciated for decades, but the price of gold hasn't gone up accordingly, just as the currency prices haven't reached their natural levels. This is because price controls on both gold and currencies have retarded their growth. Now that they're free to move, it will take very little to set off large upward movements. We've already seen some of those movements in both gold and currencies. And there's a lot more to come.

Price controls for gold were formally established in 1961 with the formation of the Gold Pool. The pool was made up of a number of Western governments; its purpose was to hold the free market price of gold down to $35 per ounce (and its equivalent in other currencies).

The Gold Pool was to buy gold when the price slipped under $35 per ounce (which rarely happened) and to sell gold when the price threatened to go above $35 (which happened frequently). And since the U.S. government contributed approximately half the resources involved, this undoubtedly had a lot to do with the reduction in U.S. gold reserves.

The first major monetary crisis of the present series, the flight from British pounds in November 1964, created the first big attack on the gold supply. Thereafter, the U.S. was forced more and more to go it alone in its fanatical desire to keep the gold price from rising. Finally, in March 1968, the Gold Pool gave up. The demand for gold had reached such proportions that further attempts to defend the $35 price would exhaust the gold reserves of all the participating nations.

Here we see an excellent example of the way individuals act to protect themselves—despite governmental actions and assurances. The price of gold hadn't budged more than a dollar from the $35 price since 1953—fifteen years before. On the surface, it appeared that the price would *never* go up, and the governments were guaranteeing it. But still the demand for gold was overwhelming. Governments can't defeat the General Market.

When the Gold Pool closed down, the new arrangement was called a "two-tier gold system." Governments would thereafter trade with each other at the "official" gold prices ($35 and its equivalent in other currencies), but not enter the free market to buy or sell.

Following the collapse of the Gold Pool, the price moved quickly to the $40 level—which was apparently sufficient to absorb the current pent-up demand. It fluctuated between $35 and $43 until early 1972. Then it made a major move to the $60–$70 range where it remained for a year. In the spring of 1973, the European governments quit supporting the dollar and their currencies moved upward dramatically. Apparently, this revelation of the dollar's weakness was the cause of another major move in gold prices—which reached the $90 level very quickly. In May and June 1973, it moved again to a high of $127, then slipped backward to the $90 to $110 range, where it was when this book was written.

It's apparent that it will take little in the way of events or other revelations of dollar weakness to touch off more major moves upward in gold. Where it will finally level off is almost impossible to predict.

There's no way now that governments can hold the price down by selling gold. The price is already so high that the governments have too little gold to make a substantial effect upon the free market. Only if they devalue their currencies substantially can they sell enough gold to affect the market while retaining enough gold to provide currency backing.

Rumors abounded during the summer of 1973 suggesting that gold sales have been made, or will be made, by the U.S. government and/or other governments. I wouldn't be surprised if the governments tried it, especially the U.S. government. The purpose, I imagine, would be to hold the gold price down long enough to permit the U.S. government to devalue the dollar to an extent that would make the "official" gold price at or above the free market price.

Any sales by governments would depress the price in the short term—either lowering it or at least preventing it from rising, temporarily. But such sales would aggravate the eventual price rise, because the currencies involved would be *less* backed by gold as a result—and the need for individuals to own gold instead of currencies would be greater.

The price drop of July–August 1973, whatever its cause, illustrates the current downside risk in gold. When the price was $35, it was as close to a sure thing as you'll ever find (I thought so *then*, too)—no downside risk and great upside potential.

When the price reached $65, I started warning clients to be more observant of the downside risk. In retrospect, this seems to have been unnecessary—but the downside risk existed, nonetheless. And there's an even greater risk now.

But the risk should be defined. If you're investing money that you won't have to touch for the next few years, gold is an outstanding opportunity. It has an almost unlimited upside potential. The price may fluctuate downward in the short term, but it will be in a highly profitable position long before you need to sell. So the advice is to buy now and wait it out.

On the other hand, if you're investing funds that you may have to use within a year, the risk is far greater. It's entirely possible that you could buy at $100–$125 and have to sell at a price of $90 or even less. The short term is too uncertain and should be used only for speculative purposes. For safekeeping of short-term funds, the Swiss franc is a much better bet; its maximum short-term downside potential is most likely around 15%.

WAYS TO INVEST

Unrefined gold is difficult to store and difficult to resell. There are more convenient ways to invest in gold.

Commemorative gold coins and gold jewelry are too expensive. You usually pay over 100% more than the gold content of the item. There are less expensive ways to own gold.

Mutual funds specializing in gold investments aren't attractive either. There's too much at stake to risk your future on the economic understanding and investment objectives of a mutual fund manager. Once you've established a basic program that gives you

comfortable protection, excess funds can be used for such purposes as a gold mutual fund.

The three principal media for gold investments are:

1. Gold bullion—refined gold bars.

2. Gold coins—minted by governments, used now exclusively
for trading in gold, and selling at prices reasonably close to their
gold contents.

3. Gold stocks—shares of stock in gold mining companies.

We'll look at each of these methods separately. (Brokerage
and storage fees for these investments will be covered in Chapter
29.)

GOLD BULLION

Since 1933, it has been illegal for U.S. citizens to own gold
bullion within the United States. Since 1961, it's been illegal for
U.S. citizens to own it anywhere in the world. The United States
is one of the few major Western nations in which that's the case.

There's no way to confirm it, but most likely there are many
Americans who do own gold through Swiss or Canadian bank
accounts. If you're an American citizen, whether you decide to
own gold will depend mostly upon the risks you're willing to
take.

Gold bullion is the safest way to invest in gold. It includes no
nonessentials; you're buying gold and no other variables.

For non-Americans, it is the recommended way to invest in
gold for protection. For Americans, it's up to each individual to
decide what he wants to do. There are other ways to invest in
gold, which will be covered next.

The easiest way to own gold bullion is to have a Swiss bank
purchase it for you in the London or Zurich markets and store it
for you. The Zurich market is apparently larger than the London
market now, but, since the transactions are handled by phone
between the banks, there's no way to measure the volume. The
banker will decide which market offers the best alternative for
you at the time of purchase.

Some Swiss banks won't buy gold bullion for Americans; others leave it up to you to decide how you'll respond to laws in your own country. It isn't illegal in Switzerland for anyone to own gold. You can request that the Swiss bank not send you any correspondence regarding your purchase.

If you purchase through a Swiss bank, the transaction may be measured in grams, rather than ounces. Here are the necessary translations:

1 gram = .03215 ounces (multiply the number of grams by .03215 to determine the number of ounces).

1 kilogram = 32.15 ounces (multiply the number of kilograms by 32.15 to determine the number of ounces).

Bullion is usually sold in bars of 400 ounces each ($40,000 at $100 per ounce) which is approximately 12½ kilograms. And many banks require a minimum purchase of 400 ounces.

However, there are smaller bars you can buy which the bank will store for you. These come in sizes of 10, 25, 50, 100, 200, 250, 500, and 1,000 grams each. It's doubtful that any bank will purchase and store a bar of less than 500 grams (approximately 16 ounces) if ordered by mail. But you can buy the smaller bars (or wafers) over the counter in a Swiss or Canadian bank. In the smaller sizes, the price is usually about 2% above the bullion price for that day. You can then store the bars in a safe deposit box or take them home with you.

The London gold-bullion prices are published daily in the *Wall Street Journal* and in many daily newspapers. The Zurich prices will always be within a few cents of the London prices. However, you may notice a discrepancy between the price of a purchase or sale made for you and the published price for that day. This is because there are only one or two prices published for each day, while, as with any other market, the price frequently fluctuates within the day. So your transaction may not have been executed at the published price.

The spread between wholesale and retail prices is usually 25¢–30¢.

GOLD COINS

It *is* legal for American citizens to own gold coins dated before 1934—if they're held for numismatic purposes. To date, the U.S. Treasury hasn't required that you prove your numismatic intentions, so long as the coins are dated before 1934. It's an ideal, legal way for Americans to own gold.[1]

There are numerous gold coins, issued by various governments, available for purchase today. The main considerations in choosing among them are:

1. What are you actually paying for the gold in the coin? Coins invariably sell for more than the value of their metallic content. This is because the minting of the coin makes the gold more recognizable, its weight known, and therefore more marketable. The cost of the coin above its gold content is called its *premium;* and you want to pay as small a premium as possible.

2. How *marketable* is the coin? Is its value easily recognizable to others? Is there a large market for the coin so that you can sell it whenever you want to?

The table on page 241 shows a number of coins that circulate in markets in Europe and the United States. It lists the major sellers, together with the premiums they commanded during July–August 1973. Those marked with an asterisk (*) are legal to own in the United States for numismatic purposes.

The premiums quoted are averages of Swiss bank prices during July and August 1973. Prices of the legal coins are generally a little higher in the United States.

The premium can be understood most easily in this way: If a coin had no premium, it would sell at the current price of the gold in it. Thus, the South African KrugerRand, which has virtually one ounce of gold, would sell for $100 per coin if the gold bullion price were currently $100 per ounce. With a 10% premium, it sells for around $110 when the gold price is $100 per ounce.

---

[1] If you're concerned about the fine points of the laws regarding any investments in this book, an attorney can obtain the appropriate statutes for you and discuss their interpretations.

Gold Coins—Weights & Premiums

Nation—Coin	Fine Gold Weight (Ounces)	Premium
Austria—100 Crowns	.98016	7%
Austria—4 Ducats	.18666	78%
Belgium—20 Francs	.44268	11%
*Dutch East Indies—1 Ducat	.11028	52%
France—20 Francs ("Napoleon")	.18666	38%
*Germany—20 Marks	.23045	80%
*Great Britain—Sovereign	.23540	50%
Great Britain—Sovereign "Elizabeth"	.23540	26%
Italy—20 Lire	.18666	110%
*Mexico—50 Pesos	1.20563	21%
*Netherlands—10 Guilders (also called "10 Florins")	.19444	50%
*Russia—5 Rubles	.12445	57%
*Russia—10 Rubles	.24891	72%
South Africa—2 Rands	.23540	31%
South Africa—1 Rand	.11770	31%
South Africa—KrugerRand	.99997	10%
*Switzerland—20 Francs	.18666	75%
*Switzerland—10 Francs	.09333	575%
*U.S.A.—$20 Liberty ("Double Eagle")	.96746	70%
*U.S.A.—$10 Liberty ("Eagle")	.48373	72%
*U.S.A.—$5 Liberty ("Half-Eagle")	.24187	115%

To determine the approximate price of a coin, multiply its gold weight times the current gold bullion price and add the amount of the premium. For example, at a gold bullion price of $115, the Mexican 50-peso coin would sell for 1.20563 × $115.00 + 21% (or × 1.21) = $167.76 per coin. This gives you an approximate idea of the current selling price, but only approximate, as the premiums fluctuate daily.

The wide premium differences between coins are attributable to their numismatic values. As stated in Chapter 20, I don't look for the numismatic market to hold up; so I suggest you look for coins with the smallest premiums.

Unfortunately, the smallest premiums are on the coins that are still being minted, as there's no shortage of supply. All coins dated 1933 or earlier command strong premiums since they're no longer being minted.

Of those coins *not* legal for U.S. citizens, I recommend the South African KrugerRand. It has a premium of only 10%, sometimes less, and is widely traded throughout Europe.

There are three major coins that are traded in large volume in the United States: the British Sovereign,[2] the American Double Eagle, and the Mexican 50 Peso. Of these, the Mexican 50 Peso has a much smaller premium, and so is currently the best way to invest in gold coins as gold. It's illegal to import Mexican peso gold coins into the United States, but legal to own them. So if you buy them and take them out of the country, it's illegal to bring them back.

High premiums are dangerous because they can fall at any time. So it's best to stick with the coins that can be purchased at the smallest premiums.

Most Swiss banks can obtain gold coins and store them for you. You can also buy gold coins from many U.S. coin dealers. Several large coin dealers have emerged, specializing in the trading of gold coins and silver coins—rather than specializing in the trading of single rare coins. The largest of these, the Pacific Coast Coin Exchange, had a volume of over $30 million per month during 1973. So the coin market is large, liquid, and accessible.

In the United States, gold coins are often quoted in *lots*—specific quantities of the coins. Here are the vital statistics for the major coins sold in the United States.

	British Sovereign	American Double Eagle	Mexican 50 Peso
Actual gold weight per coin	.2354 oz.	.96746 oz.	1.20563 oz.
Number of coins per lot	100	20	20
Gold weight per lot	23.54 oz.	19.3492 oz.	24.1126 oz.

[2] The British Sovereign "Elizabeth" is a different coin and has a much lower premium. That's because it's still being minted, and is thus illegal for Americans.

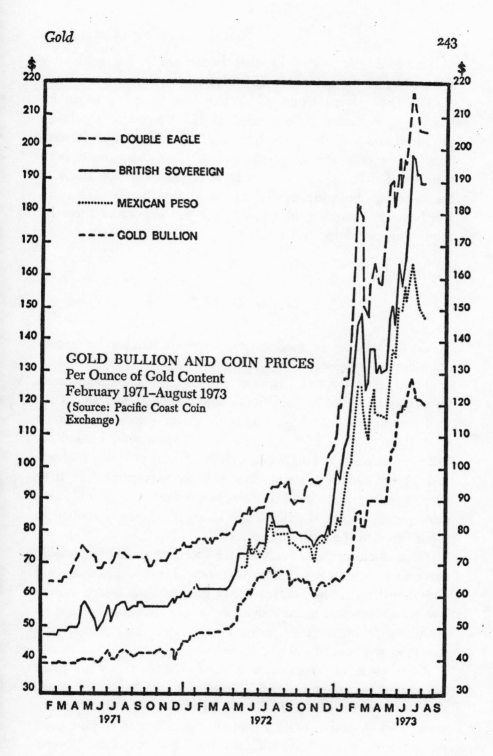

GOLD BULLION AND COIN PRICES
Per Ounce of Gold Content
February 1971–August 1973
(Source: Pacific Coast Coin
Exchange)

--- — DOUBLE EAGLE

——— BRITISH SOVEREIGN

········· MEXICAN PESO

- - - - GOLD BULLION

(All gold weights stated in this chapter are for fine gold, after elimination of the accompanying alloy.)

The U.S. government's gold restrictions have led to an interesting consequence. Counterfeit British sovereigns are being produced and sold. But they have the full gold content in each coin. Then why are they counterfeit? The dates have been counterfeited to appear to have been produced in the 1920s so the coins can be sold "legally" in the United States. The coins still have the proper gold content, but you can avoid them by requesting *circulated* coins only.

GOLD STOCKS

Gold stocks can be used as speculative investments or as conservative investments.

For a conservative investment program, the stocks can be an important source of income. Some South African gold stocks are well known for their high dividends. After prices came down from their extreme highs of July 1973 (when gold bullion hit $127 per ounce), a number of South African gold stocks were still paying 6–10% annual dividends as percentages of their current selling prices. And that was in a period of high gold stock prices, even before the dividends had been given a chance to catch up with the high gold prices.

Gold stocks are also available for speculation. They generally move more intensely in either direction than the price of gold does. Some operating South African gold companies are mining low-quality ore that could show spectacular increases in earnings (resulting in higher stock prices) only after the price of gold stabilizes well over $100 per ounce.

Gold stocks are speculative in another way—a way not often recognized by investors. As I pointed out in Chapter 18, when you buy a gold stock you're betting on more factors than just the price of gold. You're betting that the specific gold mining company won't be adversely affected by labor problems, governmental policies, poor management, natural disasters, etc. Overall, these interferences are more critical in North America; so I recommend only South African gold stocks.

However, the South African government is very much in the picture, too. All gold mining companies are required to turn their production over to the central bank, the South African Reserve Bank. It then sells the gold to the free market or to foreign central banks.

The government pays the mining company the "official" price (the equivalent of $42.22 in rands) upon receipt of the gold. If the Reserve Bank sells the gold to other central banks or to the International Monetary Fund, the mining company receives no additional money. If the gold is sold eventually in the free market, the company receives a bonus payment—which is computed by a complicated formula distributing the added price to the companies that sold gold to the Reserve Bank during the month involved.

So the government acts as a broker for the mining companies. But the companies have no authority to decide when and how the gold will be sold. In addition, the South African government has complicated agreements with the International Monetary Fund regarding allocations of its gold to governments and to the free market.

This governmental program makes the companies extremely vulnerable; in the long term, the companies might be prevented from earning the full value of higher gold prices. So I recommend that gold stocks be liquidated sooner than most of the other recommended investments (this will be covered in Chapter 34).

On the other hand, if the South African government were to sever its ties with the International Monetary Fund, all South African gold could be sold in the free market at much higher prices. That would act as a slight brake on the bullion price, but increase the earnings of the mining companies.

The present program also affects the prices of the gold stocks in other significant ways. For one thing, during the first eight months of 1973, the free market price of gold doubled to $120. But during that period, the South African government sold most of its gold to other central banks at $42.22. It's reasonable to assume that at a stabilized price over $100, a great deal of gold will be sold to the free market at those high prices; but the gold mining companies won't profit from the high gold prices until then.

Gold stock prices generally go up as the price of gold goes up. But the full significance of a higher gold price may not be added to the gold stock price until a few months later, after the company has declared higher earnings for the calendar quarter.

Thus, gold stocks are sometimes opportunities to take advantage of a gold boom after it's already begun. If you run into that situation when you're ready to make an investment in gold, you might wait a week or so to see if the gold stocks come down from their brief highs and settle at a little lower price for a while before higher earnings have been declared.

The opportunities for appreciation in gold stocks are very good. The London *Financial Times* index of South African gold mining shares increased from 45 at the beginning of 1970 to 170 in August 1973 (including a brief high of 203 during the gold boom of July 1973). During the worst period of the last depression, from 1931 to 1935, the index moved upward from 80 to 245—thanks largely to devaluations.

South African gold stocks are traded on the London Stock Exchange and can be purchased there by a Swiss bank. The bank can choose the stocks according to your objectives, or you can pick them yourself. You can send dollars for the purchase or ask the bank to transfer funds from an account you already have there (no matter what currency is in that account).

The purchase will be made in British pounds and pence (there are 100 pence in a pound). You can determine the dollar values of such purchases by checking the foreign exchange prices in the *Wall Street Journal* or a daily newspaper. (Many South African stock prices are listed daily in the *Journal* and in some daily.newspapers.)

Dividends from South African gold stocks are subject to the Swiss withholding tax. Dividends will be credited to your account unless you request that they be sent to you.

If you have a fairly large portfolio of income-producing gold stocks, you can ask the bank to simply send you a fixed amount of dollars every month or every three months. As the bank receives the dividends, they will be credited against the amount sent to you; the difference is a credit to your account or a small loan against it.

You can actually receive more than the amount of the dividends, drawing on your capital in the process. As the loan amount builds to a workable figure, the bank can sell sufficient stocks to liquidate the loan and start over. Thus, you can set up something of an annuity for yourself, drawing on both the income and capital over a period of time.

South African gold stocks are also traded over-the-counter in the United States. In order to facilitate transfer of the stocks and to price them in dollars, the shares are kept in New York or abroad and most trading is done with ADRs (American Depository Receipts), which are receipts for the shares. If it's important to you, you can obtain and hold the actual shares, but you have to go to a good deal of bother and expense to get them.

The U.S. government imposes an interest equalization tax of 11% on the shares. When you buy an ADR the tax has already been paid by a previous owner. During periods of high demand for the stocks, new shares may have to be imported from London —in which case the tax is added at that time. You can usually recoup the added price when you sell.

If you decide to buy gold stocks, make sure you define what you want: dividends, conservative growth stocks, or highly speculative stocks that may show bigger increases at higher gold prices.

WHICH WAY?

You'll have to decide for yourself which form of gold investment is most appropriate for you—bullion, coins, or stocks.

Gold bullion has no nonessential risk. It *is* gold bullion, so your investment will rise or fall with the fate of gold. However, it isn't legal for American citizens to own it.

Gold coins are the nearest thing to gold bullion. But the wide movements in the coin premium over the gold price create an additional variable. If you buy when the premium is 50%, for example, the premium might drop while the gold price is going up—leaving the coin price about where it began. If you can buy a coin legal in the United States when its premium is 25% or less, you'll probably avoid any problems caused by premium drops.

Gold stocks include the most variables; if the company you invest in has troubles, they'll be your troubles. However, the movements in gold stock prices are exaggerations of the gold bullion price movements, and so there are opportunities for greater profits. In addition, gold stocks can be a source of income for your investment program.[3]

The time to invest in gold is, generally, whenever you've decided that you want to invest in gold. Price movements may be pretty unpredictable for a while, so you might get left behind if you try to wait for a temporary low point at which to buy. If you're buying for the long term, don't worry about fluctuations downward after you buy. Just buy, relax, and forget about it for a while.

In the same way, don't buy in panic. If you haven't yet decided what your investment program should be, don't rush to buy gold in the middle of a monetary crisis. Decide to buy gold as part of an overall investment plan. Once you've made the decision, buy then.

If you decide to buy gold coins but find that the premium is abnormally high at present, there's a way you can get around that. Purchase conservative gold stocks instead; then watch the coin premiums until they've returned to a satisfactory range. At that point, sell the stocks and convert the proceeds to gold coins.

In that way, you'll be temporarily covered in case there's a sudden increase in the gold price, but you won't have had to pay high coin premiums. You'll have to pay gold stock commissions,

[3] Margin accounts and forward contracts in gold bullion, coins, and stocks will be covered in Chapter 29.

and you may also suffer some slight losses in the transactions. So the procedure is designed only for periods of unusually high coin premiums.

GOLD IS MONEY

The potential price increase for gold is somewhere between 200% and 500%. Once again, we see an investment that could suffer several reversals and still pay off handsomely. In fact, there's really no limit to the upside potential for gold, because the potential continually rises as governments make more mistakes.

The more governments disavow gold, the more important it becomes for an individual to hold it. Currencies are only substitutes for gold, and when they cease to perform that function, you have to go straight to the source—to gold.

Nothing will prevent the inevitable increase in the price of gold when measured in currencies. But there will undoubtedly be many attempts by governments to stop it. Such attempts will only be interruptions, however, and they'll only make the eventual gold price that much higher.

Those interruptions can cause short-term fluctuations. So don't get carried away betting more short-term funds than you can afford to lose through downside fluctuations.

For the long term, however, gold will reign. It has always been, and always will be (at least in our lifetimes), the best long-term store of value. Any new money system that could truly work would take at least a century to replace gold.

Gold is money.

And that's what you need.[4]

---

[4] In January 1974, the U.S. Treasury amended its regulations to permit ownership of coins minted up to 1959. This has, in effect, "legalized" the Austrian 100 Crown coin (see page 241). The new regulations have caused its premium to rise to 15–20% and other premiums to drop somewhat. A large U.S. coin dealer can give you further information.

26
Silver

THE HISTORY OF SILVER over the past century is a definitive example of governmental intervention in the marketplace. As a result, the government has caused a shortage that will provoke an explosive price situation some time during the next few years.

Now that the government is regulating the prices of all things, there are bound to be numerous opportunities for short-term speculation. However, it will take intense concentration, twenty-four-hour attention, excellent timing, and a little luck to take advantage of these opportunities. For they can come and go before you realize what's happening.

Silver, however, is a different story. The intervention has been so huge, the time period so long, that it has created a monumental imbalance in the supply and demand economics. It's only a matter of time until the imbalance is felt in earnest. For an investor endowed with a little patience and conviction, the payoff may be even greater than with gold or foreign currencies.

HISTORY

The history of silver in the United States is long and involved; I won't attempt to cover it in detail here. There are sources of the full story listed in the Recommended Reading on page 375. I'll hit only the highlights in order to demonstrate the magnitude of the shortage coming.[1]

[1] I'm especially grateful to Jerome F. Smith for bringing much of this information to my attention originally, and I highly recommend his book, *Silver Profits in the Seventies* (listed in the Recommended Reading).

Government intervention in the silver market began in earnest in 1878 when the government began purchasing $4 million in silver each month for the minting of silver coins. The purchase was a statutory requirement, regardless of the current need for coins. The program was changed in 1890 to $4.5 million with no minting required.

Needless to say, these artificial purchases held the price up and stimulated the production of silver. And the U.S. Treasury began to acquire a hoard of unneeded silver.

In 1893, the program was terminated and the price of silver fell. But in 1906, it was resumed and the price of silver started climbing again—from a low of $.47 per ounce in 1902 to a high of $1.37 in 1919.

In 1923, the government dropped out of the silver market for a period of ten years. But it was back again in 1933 and remained there almost continually for the following thirty-seven years.

The new program began with a law allowing foreign nations to repay their debts to the U.S. with silver which the government credited at $.50 per ounce (double the market price at that time). Naturally, the treasury received a lot of silver.

In 1934, the government increased the subsidy to silver miners by buying silver at $.64—well above the market price. This, of course, induced speculators to buy—knowing the government would be pushing the price upward with its unnecessary purchases.

The windfall profits for many speculators were so high that the government was resentful and imposed a special excess profits tax of 50% on all silver gains. Then the president nationalized silver, ordering all domestic holders (other than industrial users) to turn in their silver at $.50 an ounce—$.14 less than the "official" price.

The New York Commodity Exchange was forced to end trading in silver, because a market without speculators is too thin and erratic to be useful.

There was very little industrial use of silver during this period —mainly silverware and jewelry. The acquisitions of silver by the government were used for coinage and to create a large hoard for which there was no apparent use in sight.

In 1935, the price again dropped when the U.S. Treasury suspended silver purchases for one year.

During World War II, silver became an industrial metal—used for machine tool, electrical, and other functions related to the production of war goods. This increased the demand for silver, so the government put a ceiling on silver prices—$.45 early in 1942 and then $.71 later in the year.

In 1946, the Treasury resumed purchases at $.905, but shortly afterward dropped the program and the price began to fall again. Thereafter, the government made periodic purchases, but the picture was rapidly changing. The government was no longer needed to hold the price of silver up.

NEW DEMAND

By 1950, many important silver uses had been discovered in industry, and silver consumption was growing at a rapid rate. By 1957, the market had been completely reversed. For the first time, industrial silver consumption was greater than new silver production, and new uses for silver were being discovered constantly. A silver shortage would have been forecast—except for one thing. By 1950, the government had amassed a hoard of two *billion* ounces of silver, larger than the entire world's production in a six-year period. It was assumed that this silver could make up any deficit between consumption and production for scores of years.

The economics of the situation would have discouraged industries from undertaking products involving silver if they'd thought supply-demand considerations would run the price up substantially. They might not have entered into long-term production plans for new products that required silver (a precious, irreplaceable metal). But the government hoard seemed to assure a never-ending supply of silver at prices around $1 per ounce.

And so during 1961, the U.S. Treasury again entered the silver market. But after eighty-eight years of *supporting* the price of silver, it was now determined to *repress* it.

A large part of the hoard was required to back the Silver Certificate money substitutes then in circulation and for coinage needs. So the government was reluctant to sell too much. It dropped out of the market in late 1961, selling only small amounts occasionally until 1963. During that time, the price rose from $.91 to $1.28.

In 1963, the government took two contradictory measures. It began a "permanent" program to keep the price of silver—world-wide—at $1.293 by selling all that the market could buy at that price. And then, almost as if it were determined to make its job harder, it repealed all restrictions on silver ownership and trading. So the silver markets opened again.

One can only assume that the government really believed it had enough silver to supply the world forever.

The choice of $1.293 as the price to be maintained wasn't whimsical. That's the price at which the silver content of a silver dollar is worth exactly $1. If the price went higher, silver dollars would be hoarded or melted for their silver value. At $1.38, the same condition exists for the smaller silver coins. Four quarters have exactly $1 in silver content if the price of silver is $1.38.

From 1961 to 1967, the prices of everything rose substantially; everything, that is, but silver. And silver became an intrinsic part of many industries; it was used in photography, electronics, brazing, welding, etc. During that period, the U.S. government dumped 80% of its hoard—1.6 billion ounces—on the market to hold the price down. Part of this was in double-time production of silver coins during 1964 and 1965 to flood the country with coins—hoping to stop people from hoarding them in anticipation of a higher price.

Finally, on May 18, 1967, the government sales were cut. Selling was limited to U.S. industrial users with permits; others had to buy their silver elsewhere. The price started rising. On July 14, 1967, the government withdrew further. It limited sales to industrial users to two million ounces per week—to be allocated by sealed bids.

The following year, on June 24, 1968, the government quit redeeming Silver Certificates with silver. Previously, they could be converted to silver at a rate equivalent to a silver price of $1.29. At that time, the free market silver price hit a high of $2.56.

The government then revealed that during the time it had been telling U.S. citizens not to hoard silver coins, it had been quietly collecting several hundred million ounces of coins on its own. And it was going to melt those coins and continue its sale of silver.

This caused the silver price to recede from its high, beginning a long decline. The government finally ended its sales in November 1970. But it's apparent, in retrospect, that a great deal of the silver dumped by the government had gone into standing inventories of industrial users and speculators. As the price continued to decline, many speculators became discouraged and sold silver, providing a steady supply to the market—silver that was originally in the government's hoard.

The decline finally ended at $1.28 in October 1971.

Meanwhile, the imbalance between the production and consumption of silver had worsened. By 1964, the annual industrial use of silver had become 50% larger than the new mine production. An eventual shortage of silver was apparent, but it had appeared that the government really could continue to supply the market for another ten or twenty years.

In 1967, for example, the U.S. government supplied the world market with 195 million ounces. Since world production was only 214 million, the U.S. contribution nearly doubled the available supply.

But now that the U.S. Treasury is *out* of the market, more and more supplies have to be bid away from speculative holdings at higher and higher prices.

Since October 1971, the price has moved upward fairly steadily, reaching $3 in June 1973, before dropping along with declines in gold and foreign currencies during July and August.

CONSUMPTION OF SILVER

The silver shortage is now visible for all to see. Industrial users are looking for substitutes, but they will be easier sought than found. The users are locked into the production of products for which no simple substitutes are available. Since silver is a precious metal, it can be replaced—in many cases—only by another precious metal, such as gold or platinum. And, of course, the prices of those commodities are much higher than the price of silver.

Substitutes may eventually be found, but they'll have to be found one at a time. Each industrial use relies on one of silver's many valuable properties; a replacement for one use won't automatically provide a replacement for another use.

Even where silver is eventually replaceable, the transition may take many years. For example, a silverless photographic film would require a new kind of camera; it would be years before a large part of the presently owned cameras would be replaced by the owners.

Normally, if the cost of a product's vital component goes up dramatically, the product can be priced out of the market. Fortunately, this isn't the case with silver. The companies that use it are dependent upon it; but, at present prices, the cost of silver represents only 1–5% of the cost of producing most products—varying, of course, with each product.

That means a doubling of the price of silver will raise the cost of producing a given product by only 5% at the most. The exceptions to this are silverware and jewelry; there the silver represents as much as 25% of the production cost. The two industries account for 18% of the industrial consumption of silver.

In all the other silver-using industries, higher prices for silver won't affect the demand for silver appreciably.

SILVER PRODUCTION

The production of silver is similarly unaffected by rising prices. This is because of the unique way in which silver is produced.

Most of the pure silver deposits close to the world's surface have already been discovered and mined. Over 75% of the silver produced today is a by-product of the mining of copper, lead, or zinc.

For example, some copper ore also contains silver. A copper miner will extract that silver and sell it for the current market price. His production decisions, however, are based upon current *copper* prices. An increase in the silver price won't inspire him to mine more copper.

Since this is the way over 75% of the world's silver is produced, increases in the price of silver do little to stimulate new silver production.

For the few large companies that are devoted almost solely to the mining of pure silver deposits, higher silver prices will be a boon. But these companies can't be expected to increase production drastically; most of them already operate at full capacity.

There are marginal mines that could be worked again at a price of $5 or $6 an ounce, but they would add far too little production to overcome the world's supply and demand deficit.

Even a substantially higher silver price won't suffice to increase production to the present rate of worldwide consumption.

SUPPLY AND DEMAND

The silver available from new production and from the recycling of old silver has been a little under 300 million ounces per year. Meanwhile, industrial consumption alone has been 350–380 million ounces annually. In addition, governments continue to use silver for commemorative coins, consuming in a

World Silver Supplies and Consumption, 1959–1972 *

	1959	1960	1961	1962	1963	1964	1965	1966	1967	1968	1969	1970	1971	1972
Supplies														
Production[2]	188	208	203	206	215	211	218	221	214	231	245	253	249	243
Salvage[3]	15	21	29	7	11	36	7	59	53	27	12	22	41	56
U.S. Govt. Sales	34	21	63	1	25	151	80	142	195	180	89	67	0	0
Other Sources[4]	21	33	25	85	66	(30)	93	9	(48)	(35)	42	48	95	121
Total Supplies	258	283	320	299	317	368	398	431	414	403	388	390	385	420
Consumption														
Industrial Use[5]	213	225	239	248	261	304	337	355	353	351	367	357	360	382
Coinage Use[6]	45	58	81	51	56	64	61	76	61	52	21	33	25	38
Total Consumption	258	283	320	299	317	368	398	431	414	403	388	390	385	420

[2] Does not include production in communist countries. Sales from communist countries to the non-communist world are included under "other sources."

[3] When salvage by an industrial user is reused within the company, neither the salvage nor the second consumption is recorded on this table.

[4] Includes sales by foreign governments, smuggled silver from the Far East, melted coins, sales from communist countries, inventory reductions, but is now mostly sales from speculative holdings. When *purchases* for speculative holdings outweigh other sales, the figure appears as a minus.

[5] Includes private mints.

[6] Includes all non-communist governments except the United States. U.S. coinage is taken from existing U.S. government stocks.

* Sources: Handy & Harman annual review of the silver market; Samuel Montagu & Co.; *Silver Profits in the Seventies* by Jerome F. Smith.

range of 20–40 million ounces each year. So the supply is 300 million ounces; consumption is around 400 million ounces.

When the silver shortage is felt fully, the situation will be disastrous for many companies. The problem could have been averted to an extent if the government hadn't intervened in the silver market. Some users might have made other long-term plans for products, since the coming silver shortage would have been more apparent. For example, Kodak might not have produced so many millions of cameras that require silver-glazed film.

The government's game-playing misled many industries to believe that low-cost silver would be available indefinitely. Now when prices skyrocket, the government will most likely blame the problem on "greedy speculators" who supposedly run prices upward.

The shortage has been inherent in the situation all along. First, it was offset by the government's massive sales from the hoard it had acquired through subsidies to the mining industry. When the government gave up trying to make up the supply-demand deficit, its place was taken by those who resold silver originally purchased from the government.

In late 1973, it appears that the existing stocks of silver are being depleted rapidly. For example, the inventory in the Commodity Exchange warehouse in New York has dropped over the past year from 125 million ounces to 50 million.

There will always be a certain amount of silver in hoards, awaiting the appropriate time to sell. But even those holdings have apparently dropped considerably since 1971. As the price moves upward, it will take even higher prices to pry the silver loose from private hoards.

THE BIDDING BEGINS

For example, 1974 might find that the demand for silver remains at about 400 million ounces. But there might be only 75 million ounces of hoarded silver available to add to the

300 million produced. That means a *real* shortage of 25 million ounces—with no "benevolent" government to make up the difference.

The industrial users will go into the market, as always, ready to bid for the silver they need. But there won't be quite enough to go around, and the price will be bid upward. But none of the companies involved would be priced out of business by a small increase—so there are no nearby limits to the bidding.

The companies will bid against each other until 25 million ounces of usage is bid out of the market. The bidding will stop only when some marginal companies have to stop manufacturing because of a prohibitive silver price. In this way, the consumption of silver will be forcibly reduced to 375 million ounces.

The following year the situation will be further aggravated. Availability may be reduced by another 25 or 50 million ounces. And more companies will have to drop out—but it will take quite a price to drive them out.

And so the situation will continue for two to five years until the consumption of silver is reduced by a total of 100 million ounces—to equal the production and salvage of silver.

PRICE PROSPECTS

What will be the price that eventually eliminates 100 million ounces of silver consumption? I don't know, but it's going to be a much higher price than we see today. Will Eastman Kodak quit producing film because the price of silver has reached $5 or $6 an ounce? Will IBM stop producing computers if the price reaches $10? It's hardly likely.

There are, as always, unknown factors that may alter the situation unexpectedly. But here again we have an investment in which the upside potential is so great that you can tolerate several reversals and still make a healthy profit.

My guess is that silver will be at least $10 per ounce within the next two to five years—assuming a continuation of the present economy.

If there's a major depression during that time, the price could go higher. Industrial consumption would be cut, but production would probably be reduced even more; silver production relies upon copper, zinc, and lead mining which are traditional losers in a depression. If the depression begins with a crash, it might take silver down partways with it, but the economics would force the price even higher in the long term.

Unfortunately, there are no precedents to guide us. In the last depression, silver wasn't yet an industrial commodity; in addition, prices were mainly determined by the government.

If there's a runaway inflation, silver is one good way to hold a store of value through the worst times. In the aftermath, silver would be in greater demand because of its monetary value.

In one respect, silver has the best prospects of the three major investments. Compared with gold and foreign currencies, silver had realized the least of its potential by late 1973. There's still a great deal of room for it to go upward.

However, silver isn't for the faint-hearted. There are those who've been waiting patiently (or impatiently) for the past seven years while the government has used up its bag of tricks to delay the price increase. There have been false starts and disappointments, and there may be a few more yet.

But for the long-term investor, silver can be an important way to bring about substantial capital growth.

WAYS TO INVEST

There are numerous ways to invest in silver, but only two that I'd recommend.

Silver stocks are out—for reasons mentioned in Chapter 18. You carry too many nonessential risks with your investment when you rely upon a company to profit from a silver price increase. Unlike the situation with gold, you *can* own silver bullion legally. And silver stocks aren't noted for their dividends.

Some companies sell specially minted coins or small silver

bars of three ounces or so of weight. I don't recommend these as ways to invest in silver. You pay for too much more than the value of the silver in the coin or bar. The added premium can be as much as 60% or more. There are better ways.

The two recommended silver investments are:

1. Silver bullion—bars of refined silver.

2. U.S. silver coins—dimes or quarters, dated 1964 or before, which are 90% silver.

Each of these has advantages and disadvantages, compared to the other.

SILVER BULLION

Silver futures and silver purchased on margin will be discussed in Chapter 29. Here we're concerned with the outright purchase of silver bars to be held for the long term.

You can usually purchase silver bullion in any quantity; you receive whatever number of ounces is covered by the amount of money you invest. There are three principal ways you can buy it:

1. You can buy it in the United States and store it yourself.

2. You can buy it in the United States and have the seller store it for you.

3. You can buy it through a Swiss bank and have the bank store it for you.

There are probably only a few investors for whom the first method would be useful. If you plan to go to a hideaway somewhere to wait out the next few years, you may want to take some silver and bury it in the backyard. Even then, silver coins would be more appropriate.

Other than that possibility, the storage would be a problem for you. And bullion is usually bought to be resold later; so it's easier to leave the bullion where it can be easily sold.

Whether you store the silver in the United States or in a

Swiss bank will depend upon how probable you consider another nationalization of silver to be. If that risk bothers you, you'll want to keep the silver overseas.

There's little likelihood that the U.S. government will nationalize silver for the same reasons it did in 1934. The government no longer considers silver to be money, having replaced it with a more accessible commodity—paper. So private ownership and trading of silver is no longer a threat to the government's monetary system.

At the same time, there's now a greater vulnerability in owning *anything*. The government has already shown that it doesn't consider your business to be your business. As price controls create shortages, the government may very well decide that ownership of many commodities will require special permits. There's no way of foretelling that.

Silver trading has already been thrown off the track twice since 1971 by price freezes. The situation will probably get worse.

"Whether" and "when" are uncertain. If the prospect bothers you at all, keep the bullion overseas so that you can sleep nights.

SWISS BANK PURCHASES

If you purchase through a Swiss bank, the procedure is rather simple. Just tell the bank the number of dollars you want to spend, and the bank will purchase the appropriate number of ounces at the current market prices.

You can, if you choose, put price limits on your instructions—telling the bank not to buy above a certain price, for example. However, if the market has passed that price you may wait in vain for your order to be filled.

Bank charges for the service usually amount to a 1% commission when you buy and again when you sell, plus $4.20 per year per 1,000 ounces for storage and insurance. The bullion is stored in the bank's name in a warehouse in London or Zurich.

There's a 3.6% sales tax on silver in Switzerland, but it only applies if you take delivery there. Otherwise, the silver is stored in a warehouse in a free transit zone near the airport.

The money for the purchase can be sent with the instructions, using the money order or wiring procedures given in Chapter 23. Or you can instruct the bank to withdraw the money from an account you already have there.

Most banks will send you a quarterly statement showing your holdings in ounces, billing you annually for the storage charges. The figures on the statement won't change, of course, unless you've bought or sold silver since your last statement.

Some Swiss banks won't buy silver outright for you. They prefer that you enter into a silver claims or forward contract. These are complicated methods for what is essentially a very simple transaction.[7]

If you want a cash purchase and storage, tell them so. And if the bank doesn't offer that, there are other banks that do.

There are two basic silver prices in the market—the London price and the New York price. They're never very far apart, or else it would be profitable for someone to buy in the lower-priced market and sell simultaneously in the higher market. Sometimes, however, the price changes in New York after the London market has closed for the day.

Either of these prices can be found in the *Wall Street Journal* or in many daily newspapers. The London price is listed on the commodity page in the *Journal* in a short news article headed "Silver and Gold Prices." In that article, you'll find a US$ figure for the "spot" price which is the current cash price.

Near it, on the same page, you'll see a large section of figures headed "Futures Prices." In that section, you'll find "New York—Silver." The closing price for the first month listed is the nearest thing to a New York spot price.

The price at which you have bought or sold may not be the same price shown in the newspaper for that day. The published price is only the closing price; there will have been fluctuations prior to the close of the day's market.

[7] I'll explain them in Chapter 29.

U.S. BULLION PURCHASES

You can also buy silver bullion in the United States through the futures market or from some of the coin dealers. If you want to store the bullion yourself, that will be easier than ordering it overseas.

If you buy in the futures market, you must buy in 5,000-ounce contracts in Chicago, or 10,000-ounce contracts in New York. The procedure for taking delivery is a little involved, but any commodity broker can explain it to you. You'll find one in any commodity brokerage house or in the commodity department of any large stock brokerage company. The commission is $45.50 for a New York contract, $35 for a Chicago contract. In addition, you pay transportation costs.

If you buy from a coin dealer, arrangements can be made for shipping the silver to you. Commissions vary from dealer to dealer, but are usually around 2%.

SILVER COINS

The silver coin market is only a little more complicated.

U.S. silver dimes, quarters, half-dollars, and dollars, minted in 1964 or earlier, are 90% silver. They can be melted and refined into silver bullion for a cost of only about 6¢ per ounce. Thus, the value of these coins rises and falls as the price of silver goes up and down.

Because they're coins, they have the added value of being recognizable as silver of a specific weight. Just as with gold coins, silver coins sell at a premium above the price dictated by their silver content.

The premiums for silver dollars have been quite high over the past ten years. Generally, they sell at 100% or more above their silver contents; this is partly because of their scarcity and the resulting numismatic value. If you buy silver dollars, you have to hope that the premium doesn't drop before you sell.

Since there's a great deal of room for the premium to drop, I don't recommend silver dollars as a way of investing in silver.

On a lesser scale, a similar problem exists for half-dollars. They've been a little scarcer than the smaller coins; so they've generally commanded a premium about 2% above the dimes and quarters.

The dimes and quarters are the best buys because they have very little premium. They're sold in bags (regular canvas bank bags) containing a quantity of coins equal to $1,000 in face value of the coins (10,000 dimes or 4,000 quarters). A bag is about the size of a bowling ball and weighs around 55 pounds.

If the coins in the bag were to be melted and refined, they would produce a net total of about 720 ounces of refined silver; this is the silver content of the coins. Whether or not the coins are ever melted, this silver content gives them their special value.

If the price of silver bullion is $2.50 per ounce on a given day, you multiply $2.50 by 720 to determine the silver content of a bag of coins; $2.50 × 720 = $1,800. That's the silver value of the bag. As already mentioned, the coins will command a premium because the silver is more versatile in coin form. If the premium on that day is 4%, the price of the bag will be $1,872 ($1,800 × .04 = $72 + $1,800 = $1,872).

An advantage of silver coins is the floor beneath the price. Theoretically, silver bullion could drop to a price of zero or anywhere above that. A bag of coins, however, could never be less than $1,000. If the price of silver dropped further, you could always use the coins as spending money with a face value of $1,000 per bag.[8]

This provides a theoretical floor under the coins at $1,000 per bag. The *actual* floor, however, is somewhere above that. The theoretical floor at $1,000 provides an incentive for many people to buy, and few people to sell, anywhere near $1,000.

----

[8] The possibility is remote that the U.S. government would prohibit the use of silver coins as legal tender. The coins are so similar in appearance to post-1964 copper–nickel coins that the entire coinage system would have to be replaced to facilitate the ban on silver coins. There's also a law on the books requiring the government to purchase silver bullion if the price drops to $1.25, but that law could be easily repealed or disregarded.

On October 27, 1971, the price of silver bullion dropped to $1.298. At that price, the silver content of a bag of coins was worth $934.56; however, the actual price of a bag was $1,129— 21% higher. This was because there was little risk in holding coins when the price could only drop $129 lower.

This floor makes it possible to provide an absolute limit to your losses. However, the further the price gets away from the floor, the less useful the floor is. If the price were $3,000 per bag, for example, the limit on your losses would be around 65%. At $2,000 per bag, the limit is about 44%.

The silver coin premium has been highest when the price has been near the floor. This can be seen more easily on the chart on page 267. Since silver bullion last passed $2 on the way upward, the premium has ranged from 2% to 6%; so the exact premium figure hasn't been a factor in choosing the time to buy.

SILVER COIN PURCHASES

Silver coins can be purchased in the U.S. or through some Swiss banks. In the U.S., many coin dealers have silver coins to sell or can obtain them for you. Several large companies have emerged in the last five years that specialize in U.S. silver coins.

To let them know what you want, specify "junk" silver. That means the pre-1965 dimes or quarters with no numismatic value.

You can take delivery of the coins or have them stored for you for a nominal annual storage cost. The coins can be shipped easily if you live a distance from the dealer.

If you're concerned about possible nationalization of silver, you should be sure to take delivery and find a place to store the coins yourself. A bank safe deposit box would be safe; a safe deposit box in a non-banking institution would be even better.

Commissions on coin purchases are usually 2%.

You can also buy coins in 10-bag lots through the New York futures market. The commission is only $3.50 per bag but you have to go to a good deal of trouble to take delivery. A commodity broker can explain the procedure.

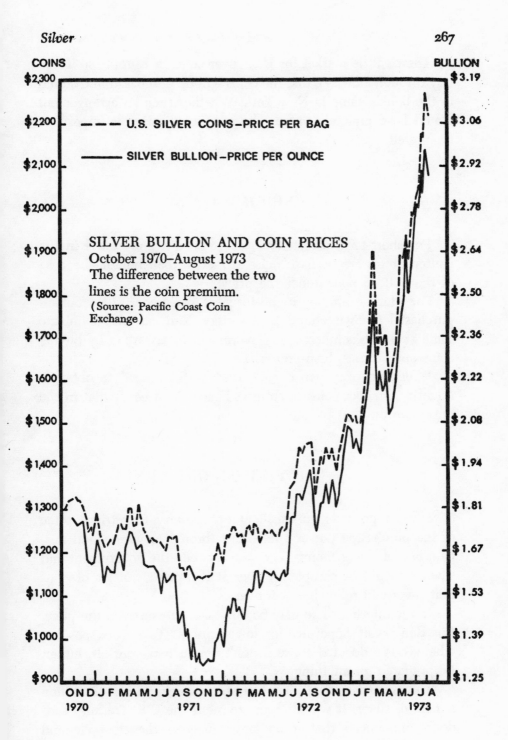

COINS

BULLION

$2,300 — $3.19

$2,200 ---- U.S. SILVER COINS-PRICE PER BAG $3.06

—— SILVER BULLION-PRICE PER OUNCE

$2,100 $2.92

$2,000 $2.78

SILVER BULLION AND COIN PRICES
$1,900 October 1970–August 1973 $2.64
The difference between the two
lines is the coin premium.
$1,800 (Source: Pacific Coast Coin $2.50
Exchange)

$1,700 $2.36

$1,600 $2.22

$1,500 $2.08

$1,400 $1.94

$1,300 $1.81

$1,200 $1.67

$1,100 $1.53

$1,000 $1.39

$900 $1.25

O N D J F M A M J J A S O N D J F M A M J J A S O N D J F M A M J J A
1970   1971   1972   1973

There's little market for U.S. silver coins in Europe; so if you buy through a Swiss bank, the coins will be purchased and stored in the bank's name in New York. Whether such an arrangement would be completely immune to a nationalization is impossible to foretell.

WHICH WAY?

For short-term investments, coins bought and stored in the United States are perhaps more attractive than bullion—because of the built-in floor under the price.

For a long-term, buy-it-and-forget-it investment, silver bullion purchased in Switzerland is less risky. You can also eliminate some of the risks inherent in government intervention by buying coins and storing them yourself.

Whichever way you decide, there's still a need to obtain a quantity of silver coins to store at home. We'll cover that in the next chapter.

SILVER WILL OUT

Silver represents an excellent opportunity to retrieve some of the purchasing power you've lost through governmental mishandling of the economy. The war between the government and silver may not be completely over at this point, but it's obvious that silver will rule when it *is* over.

In the interim, there may be downside pressures on the price. But don't wait hopefully for lower prices. Take your position when you've decided to, and don't overextend yourself, either. Be prepared for anything.

The government still has a strategic stockpile of 143 million ounces of silver. It wouldn't amaze me if the U.S. Treasury suddenly announced that it no longer needed the stockpile and would sell it in the marketplace. It would be an irrational act (the government needs *more* silver, not less), but the government's one redeeming quality has never been rationality.

This is probably the only *real* possibility that could depress the silver price for several months. Other statements you might hear are usually no more than abortive plans or unknowledgeable rumors. Substitutes for silver are periodically announced but die quiet deaths a year or two later, unheralded by the press.

Rumors of sales of silver from India overlook the fact that there's almost always been silver coming out of India, and it has only a slight effect upon the silver price.

The large volume of coins in existence provides no threat to the silver price because there's no profit to be made in melting the coins. The price of coins would have to drop below the price of bullion—something that hasn't happened since it's been legal to melt coins.

Silver offers a way to hedge against a depreciating dollar, to be on the right side of a shortage for a change, to be relatively invulnerable to the next depression, and to preserve a long-term store of value through a runaway inflation.

I don't share the view of many silver advocates that the historic 16 to 1 ratio of gold prices to silver prices will return. That ratio was dreamed up by the U.S. government in an attempt to back two inflated currencies side by side. It's no more a true market phenomenon than that of the price of gold being $42.22. During the last previous free market in silver, just before the legislation of June 18, 1934, gold was selling at $35, silver at $.45—a ratio of 78 to 1. Since then many changes have occurred—including the development of silver as an industrial commodity.

Instead, I believe that silver has a life and a value of its own. It *is* the second most useful money commodity in the world—whether or not governments believe it to be so. And it's a critical industrial commodity that has been thrown out of supply-demand balance by a whimsical government. Its price will go up because it has to.

Whether it will be $\frac{1}{16}$ the price of gold, or more, or less, is unimportant. Both commodities will someday soon be priced at several times their present prices.

27
Coins and Cash

IF A RUNAWAY INFLATION isn't stopped in time, it will lead to the total destruction of the currency. If that happens, individuals will be reduced to a state of cautious barter (since chaos will be the rule). There will probably follow a period in which coins of intrinsic value would be the principal medium of exchange.

Anyone holding silver coins or gold coins during such a time would be in a fortunate position. For he'd be one of the few people owning easily tradeable wealth. Prices of things you might buy with silver coins would be very, very low. You can't buy a can of vegetables for a dime today, but in the aftermath of a runaway inflation you might be able to buy two cans for a silver dime.

Even if runaway inflation is halted before the currency is destroyed, the coins might provide an orderly purchasing medium *during* the runaway inflation. They could enable you to make valuable purchases from people who wouldn't risk accepting rapidly depreciating currency.

I believe that runaway inflation is now a 75% probability; and I believe it's at least 50% possible that it won't be halted in time to preserve the present currency.[1]

Since the potential for runaway inflation is so great, I con-

[1] When I wrote this, there were recurring rumors, unconfirmed, that the U.S. government was selling gold in the free market, a contributing cause of the sliding gold price during July and August 1973. If that was the case, it would make a runaway inflation more probable. The destruction of the currency can be averted only if the government holds back some gold.

sider it prudent to hold a supply of silver coins, and possibly gold coins, against such an emergency. If the emergency never occurs, the value of the coins should go up anyway. The only drawback in such an investment is the bother involved in finding a safe place to keep them.

It's possible that the government could outlaw the use of silver coins during a runaway inflation. That happened during the famous runaway inflation of the French Revolution. But the edict went unheeded—despite the death penalty attached to it.

Legal-tender laws during currency debasement are always an invitation for a black market. And it would be impossible for the government to prevent the use of coins for small transactions.

A COIN SUPPLY

The most useful coins for such a stockpile would be U.S. silver dimes and quarters minted in 1964 or earlier. It's important to have a good supply of small units because there isn't going to be anyone around making change.

The procedure for buying silver coins was outlined in the previous chapter. If you go to a coin dealer, ask for "junk silver" —silver coins without any numismatic value. The coins come in bags containing $1,000 face value (selling for around $2,000 in the fall of 1973). If your resources are too small to afford a full bag, some dealers will sell a quarter-bag ($250 face value).

The amount of silver coins you should obtain will be determined by how great you consider the need to be and by the size of your overall investment program. There's no way to calculate precisely what a bag of coins would be worth after a runaway inflation; but it would be safe to assume that a silver dime (because of its scarcity and usefulness) would be worth at least what one paper dollar is worth now.

If you decide to make a large investment of this kind, you can beat the storage problem by switching to gold coins for everything over two bags of silver coins. Fifty British sovereigns are approximately equal in value to one bag of silver coins but require only $\frac{1}{80}$ of the space.

STORAGE

Storing the coins can be a problem, of course. In addition to a hiding place at home, the first thought is a bank safe deposit box. During the bank holidays of the last depression, the banks were actually open for business—accepting deposits, providing very limited withdrawals, transacting other business, and allowing customers to use their safe deposit boxes.[2] Whether such availability would exist the next time banks are closed is impossible to foretell.

So it would be better to find a safe deposit company in a non-banking institution. Most major cities have at least one safe deposit company, usually in the financial district; such companies are created to store stock certificates for brokerage houses. Look in the Yellow Pages under "Safe Deposit Boxes." If you don't find anything, look around the financial district in your city.[3]

If you have to use bank safe deposit boxes, you might divide the coins between boxes in two or more banks—to avoid being dependent upon one bank's availability.

If you keep the coins at home, you'll have to use some imagination to discover a place you think is safe. If there's enough money involved, you might consider having a safe installed. Even there, use some imagination and choose a place for it that might not be discovered by a casual burglar.

It's probably best to keep the bulk of your coins in a safe deposit box, but you should have some coins at home—perhaps a quarter-bag or more. That way they'll be accessible to you seven days a week; no one can foretell all the possible ways a crisis might occur.

---

[2] A day-by-day account of the period is given in 28 Days by C. C. Colt and N. S. Keith, listed in the Recommended Reading.

[3] A few such companies are listed in Chapter 33.

CASH

Since bank holidays are an ever-present possibility, it's a good idea to have some cash at home and/or in a non-banking safe deposit box.

If all banks should close, cash would be at a premium. You might even be able to use cash at that time to repay debts and make special purchases at a discount. If you have no special desire to take advantage of the situation, a one month supply of cash is probably sufficient to store.

Again, if you keep most of it in a safe deposit box, also keep at least some of it at home where it will be available at all times.

Available cash can be an assurance today. Beyond the possibility of bank closings, there are the threats of civil disturbances and totalitarian governmental policies. Available cash provides mobility, and mobility means safety, the knowledge you'll be able to deal with anything that comes up.[4]

Since you'll be holding U.S. dollars for these needs, the cash will depreciate over a period of time. So don't hold any more than you think will cover all possible needs. And if all prices start moving daily, spend the cash for something useful and let the silver coins suffice from there on.

INSURANCE

These two investments—coins and cash—can be considered insurance policies. If they're never used for this purpose, the dollars will have lost some of their purchasing power; but the coins will most likely go up in value anyway. If silver reaches $10 per ounce, the silver dime you buy today for $.20 will appreciate to $.75 or more.

More than anything else, the availability of coins and cash will allow you to face the future with much less anxiety.

---

[4] As mentioned in Chapter 19, I don't consider credit cards useful for this purpose.

28
A Retreat

IF THE CURRENCY IS DESTROYED through runaway inflation, you may not want to stay where you are now. A modern
community without a currency could be a dangerous place to be.
Without means of paying wages, with no welfare checks, without
the normal necessities of life coming into the city, the possibilities are pretty grim.

I certainly hope this never happens. Much of what I've come
to enjoy in life would be unavailable to me. However, if it should
happen, I'm sure that I'd feel that life is still worth living—and
worth living in safety.

In addition to the runaway inflation possibilities, mob violence
has already become a reality in the past few years. And I suspect
that, as it becomes more difficult for most people to maintain
their accustomed standards of living, such violence will increase.

So you may consider it important to have a plan in mind for
withdrawing from a vulnerable area if any type of civil crisis
should occur. Such a plan is generally called a *retreat*.

A retreat can be a specific place that's been previously prepared as a place to live for a while. Or it may be only a well-
stocked camper that represents mobility to you. Or it might be
a boat that can take you to wherever you think safety is.

Once you start thinking about the subject, you may come up
with an endless number of questions and requirements. There's
no way I can answer all those questions for you; it's the kind of
program each person must think out for himself and prepare for
himself. But there are a few general guidelines that can get you
started. If the retreat is to be a safe place to go where you can

remain for several months, or even years, here are some suggestions:

1. It should be in an area only a few hours from where you live.

2. It should be relatively inaccessible to others. Obviously, if *you* can get there, others can too. But you can pick a place, away from highways and normal streets, where no one is likely to come who isn't looking for you.

3. You should try to find an area in which any other nearby residents are relatively self-sufficient. It would be nice to live near people who would have little reason to turn to looting.

4. You shouldn't pick an area that requires that you live in a way you're not sure you could manage. For example, don't select a spot where the temperature is 30° below during the winter—unless you know you can handle such conditions.

5. Within the area you choose, try to find a place that's relatively unnoticeable, even to those living in the area.

6. The residence there should be stocked, *in advance,* with sufficient food to see you through at least a year (in the case of currency destruction).[1] In addition, the area should provide the means to survive beyond a year—the ability to hunt, fish, and/or grow food.

7. In addition to food, the residence should be stocked with anything essential to your survival: medicines, vitamins, winter clothing, provisions for heating (without normal gas and electricity service), cooking facilities, etc.

8. You should store, in advance, at least part of your coin hoard—for that's where you'll probably need it most.

9. If you can, stock the retreat with items you can trade to others for things you need. Pick trading items that are likely to be in demand by others: extra canned foods, cigarettes, liquor, medicines, gasoline, tools. Choose items that aren't likely to be readily available in that area, that are relatively easy for you to obtain now, and that will be easy to store.

10. And, lastly, you must consider how you'll defend yourself

[1] There are companies that offer freeze-dried and dehydrated foods in large quantities at low cost for long-term storage. A few are listed in Chapter 33.

if it should become necessary. To me, the best defense is to create a situation that avoids all confrontations. But no matter how carefully you plan, you may be faced with the need to defend what's yours.

These are the basic requirements. Beyond that, there's much that can be done to make the retreat more liveable. Prepare it in such a way that you can enjoy it for vacations; that way you won't need a disaster to amortize the cost.

IMPROVEMENTS

Once you undertake the project, you'll continually think of new needs for it and problems to be solved. Get a notebook and write down needs as you think of them—games, books, hobbies, etc. Then occasionally spend a day buying all the things on your list, and visit the retreat to continue stocking it.

The biggest breakthrough you can make is the creation of a source of energy—since you won't be able to depend upon normal power sources. If you have a generator that can produce electricity, you automatically increase your standard of living by 200% or more.

There are numerous ways this can be done. The simplest is through a typical gasoline generator attached to the normal electrical system of the structure. However, it can be difficult to store enough gasoline to last you very long, as gasoline requires a lot of storage space. Diesel fuel is slightly less expensive and is non-explosive.

There are other possibilities, such as having a windmill attached to a battery that can store the energy until you need it. Or a steam generator (off an old boat) if you live in an area abundant with trees. Or if there's a stream on the property and you can create a waterfall a couple of feet in height, you can use the windmill system with a waterwheel.

It's easier if you find a plot of land with a structure of some kind on it already. But if there's no structure, you can erect a prefabricated cabin without any special knowledge.

Once you have a structure stocked with food and other vital necessities, you can relax—assured that your minimum requirements have been satisfied. Then you can add to the retreat as you think of things and as money becomes available to spend on it.

It's not my purpose to answer all possible retreat questions in this chapter. Such a task would require an entire book. But I do want to demonstrate that establishing a safe place is neither impossible nor overly expensive. There are answers to all the questions; and you'll think of them once you devote yourself to the task.

If it seems too ambitious a job to find and stock a hideaway, consider getting a camper or a microbus. Pack a trunk that will have the essential supplies you would need for a quick getaway. Then you can leave at a moment's notice and you'll at least have mobility.

If that's still too much to tackle, at least have a prearranged plan for getting away if it ever becomes necessary—and an area in mind to which you'll go.

Some people I've talked with have made plans to move to foreign countries. I've never found that plan attractive, because I like the North American cities and I'd regret leaving them. If I have to leave them someday to go to a retreat, I'd like to be able to wait until I'm sure it's necessary. A planned move abroad requires that you leave well in advance of any need to. If you were to wait too long, transportation might not be available or you might have to leave too much precious property behind. A retreat within a few hundred miles of your home offers far more flexibility.

PEACE OF MIND

The retreat is the one recommended investment that won't show a monetary profit in the coming years—unless the crises end and you sell it at a profit. It's a form of insurance that's necessary because of the turbulent times.

Like the other recommended investments, it offers peace of mind. If you never need the retreat, you'll still be able to relax more in the meantime if you have it. You won't have that anxious feeling of vulnerability, the fear that tomorrow's news will report a new crisis for which you're unprepared.

And that can be worth a lot.

29
Speculations

EVERY INVESTMENT IS A SPECULATION—although it isn't usually admitted to be so. We live in an uncertain world, and there's no way to arrange any investment so that it can be considered in advance to be a sure thing.

With that said, I consider the investments covered in Chapters 23 to 27 to be the safest available today. While they offer excellent growth possibilities, they also offer the safest havens to the conservative investor who wants to preserve his wealth.

If, in hopes of making a greater profit, you want to be more aggressive and are willing to take a greater risk, there are ways to speculate on these forecasts. This chapter is devoted to the speculative alternatives that are available. They involve the use of margin accounts or futures contracts in order to bet more heavily on gold, silver, or foreign currencies.

MARGIN ACCOUNTS

A margin account is a method by which you increase your stake in a given investment without investing more money. This is done by using credit to increase the size of the purchase.

For example, suppose you've decided to invest in silver bullion. You can do this on either a cash or a margin basis. We've already covered the cash basis in Chapter 26. For a margin example, we'll assume you're going to purchase on margin through a Swiss bank.

Suppose the price is $3 per ounce at the time you buy, and you've decided to invest $6,000. If you buy on a cash basis, the $6,000 will buy 2,000 ounces for you at $3 per ounce. (For simplicity, we'll ignore the commissions and storage charges.)

If you buy on 50% margin, it means that you have to put up only half the money involved instead of all of it. The bank will lend you a sum equal to the amount you invest. It will add $6,000 to your $6,000 and purchase $12,000 worth of silver—or 4,000 ounces at $3 per ounce.

You've doubled your position in the silver market without doubling the amount of money you invest. This means that future movements in the silver price will affect you twice as much—whether the movements are upward or downward. Your profit or loss will be twice what it would have been without the use of margin.

This is also called *leverage,* which refers to the amount by which your position is increased. In the example given, you would have used "two to one leverage" because your purchase was two times the amount of your investment. If you had put up 33% margin, the leverage would have been three to one—a tripling of your purchasing ability.

The word *margin* refers to the amount of your equity as a percentage of the total value of the purchase.

The bank will hold the commodity purchased as security. In the example, $12,000 worth of silver is held as security for a $6,000 loan.

As the price goes up or down, the loan amount remains fixed; it's your equity that changes. If the price of silver were to rise to $4 per ounce, the 4,000 ounces of silver would be worth $16,000. After allowance for the $6,000 loan, your equity would be $10,000—a $4,000 profit. Your margin would have increased, too; it would now be 62½%—your $10,000 equity as a percentage of the $16,000 value of the silver.

If the price goes down to $2 per ounce, the 4,000 ounces would be worth only $8,000. After allowance for the $6,000 loan, your equity would be reduced to $2,000—or a margin of only 25%.

MARGIN CALLS

At that point, the bank will get a little nervous about the security for the loan. For if the price were to drop another $.50, the total value of the silver would be only $6,000—the amount of the loan. And you'd have *no* equity.

So before that happens, the bank will ask you to put up more margin—meaning it will ask you to add to your investment. You may be asked to put up another $2,000 which would be used to reduce your loan. The loan would then be $4,000—which is half the value of the silver at $2 per ounce—and your margin would be 50% again.

This is a *margin call*—a call by the bank to increase your margin so that the loan amount will remain well below the value of the commodity. If you don't respond to the margin call, the bank will have to sell the commodity before the price drops further.

There's no set rule as to when margin calls will be made. Policies vary, and it partially depends upon the type of market involved and the original margin percentage. If the minimum margin requirement is 50%, you can expect a margin call when the margin drops to around 33%. If the original requirement was 33%, you can expect a margin call at around 25%. If the original requirement was 25%, the call will come at around 20%.

If you put up more than the margin requirement originally, the same guidelines apply. Thus, if the margin requirement is 33%, but you put up 50%, you won't receive a margin call until the margin is reduced to around 25%.

If your margin account is in a Swiss bank, you can instruct the bank at the time of purchase to draw money from another account you hold there if it should be necessary to meet margin calls. If you do that, it will be the bank's responsibility to see that margin calls are met. You'll receive a notice whenever they've transferred funds from one account to another.

INTEREST

Since you're borrowing money from the bank, you pay interest on the loan. The loan isn't like an installment contract or mortgage where you have a fixed interest rate and make regular repayments. The loan remains in force until the commodity is sold—at which time the loan is repaid from the proceeds.

Because the loan isn't for a specific period of time, the interest rate isn't fixed; it may go up or down several times before you liquidate the loan. During volatile times in the money markets, the interest rate may change every month. But usually it remains constant for six months or so at a time.

The bank might require that you pay the interest every calendar quarter, at which time it will bill you. Or it may allow you to have the interest added to the loan balance each quarter. In that case, the loan increases and you pay progressively more interest. Also, if the price of the commodity isn't rising, the higher loan balance will lessen your margin percentage and precipitate a margin call sooner.

The interest expense adds to the cost of the investment, of course. If your expectations for the investment prove to be right, the added expense will be immaterial compared to your greater profits. But if the investment doesn't pay off, the interest expense will further compound your losses.

DOLLAR LOANS

If you buy through a Swiss bank, you may be offered a choice of having the loan in U.S. dollars or in Swiss francs. The interest rate on the francs will be less than that for dollars.

Always choose U.S. dollars for the loan.

Your assets should always be in strong currencies; your liabilities should be in weak currencies. As the value of the Swiss franc goes up, so does the amount of the loan you must someday repay—when measured in dollars.

In the silver bullion example I've used, the loan was $6,000. If you'd taken the loan in Swiss francs in 1972, the amount would have been 24,000 francs, because the exchange rate at the time was approximately four to one. A year later, the exchange rate was only three to one, so the 24,000 francs were worth $8,000. Your loan, measured in dollars, would have increased by $2,000 —33%—because the price of the Swiss franc increased by that much. If there had been no change in the currency price, you would have saved $360 in interest costs because the Swiss franc interest rate was lower. Obviously, the odds are in your favor by keeping the loan in dollars.

RESPONSE TO MARGIN CALLS

A standard rule of investing is that you should "never meet a margin call." The principle is that the requirement for a margin call proves your investment to have been a mistake, so you should sell the commodity and take your loss.

I agree with the rule *only* if the premise of the investment was that the price wouldn't drop far enough to require a margin call. But investments are often made that allow for short-term drops before an eventual upward price rise; you don't have to approach an investment with the belief that you've bought at the absolute bottom.

In that case, you should decide when you invest how far down you're willing to let the price drop before you'll give up; and you should decide how much additional margin you'll invest before selling out. If you make those decisions and stick to them it isn't a weakness to meet a margin call. In fact, it can be a strength—you're keeping your eyes on the original long-term objective.

SPECIFIC MARGIN INVESTMENTS

The information covered on the past several pages is the basic theory of margin buying—no matter what the commodity involved or where it's purchased.

You use margin buying if you're able to tolerate a greater loss, should it happen, and are anxious to make a larger-than-normal profit.

Here now are the details regarding the use of margin for each type of investment.

SILVER BULLION

You can buy silver bullion on margin—either in the United States or in Switzerland.

There aren't many Swiss banks that will handle a margin account of the kind described here. Most of them would prefer that you take a silver claims account or a forward contract. Both of those are contracts for a specific period of time. The interest rate is established in advance and applies to the full term of the contract—no matter when you sell. The contracts are difficult to follow, making it easier for you to go wrong. In addition, in either of these types of contracts, the silver isn't considered yours until the contract expires and you take delivery of the silver. So if the bank should fail, you may not have any recourse. In a margin account, the silver is considered yours.

For those Swiss banks that will sell silver on a margin basis, the minimum margin requirements vary between 25% and 50%. Interest rates for U.S. dollar loans were 12–13% in August 1973. However, that was a time of unusually high interest rates everywhere. In recent years, the rate has normally been 8–10%.

Commissions vary; some banks act as dealers and include the commission in the quoted price. Others add 1% to the purchase and to the sale. Storage costs are generally $4–$7 per year per 1,000 ounces.

Minimum purchases also vary. I've received quotations ranging from $1,000 to $10,000 as a minimum investment.

At least one of the large coin dealers in the United States will sell silver bullion on a margin basis; there are probably others who will also. If you buy on margin, the dealer holds the silver until the loan is paid off.

Interest rates on dollar loans are usually lower in the United States. In August 1973, the rate was 10%—compared with 13% in Switzerland. Margin requirements are 25%, with a minimum purchase of 1,000 ounces (at $3 per ounce, the minimum investment would be $750). Storage costs are around $10 per year per 1,000 ounces. Commissions are generally 2% on the purchase and again on the sale.

SILVER COINS

As we saw in Chapter 26, there's a floor beneath the price of silver coins at $1,000 per bag—the value of the coins as spending money. This can be especially helpful in margin buying.

You can borrow $1,000 per bag, pay the interest quarterly, and be assured that you'll never receive a margin call. Since the price can't drop below the amount of your loan, the bank will never have reason to be nervous about your margin position.

There's no U.S. silver coin market in Europe, so very few Swiss banks handle silver coins. The few who do will buy them in New York and store them there. If margin is available, the maximum loan is usually $900 per bag. At a price of $2,000 per bag, your investment would be $1,100—or a margin of 55%, less than two to one leverage. Interest rates and other conditions are the same as with silver bullion.

In the United States, there's a very large silver coin market, and there are many dealers who sell coins on margin. As with bullion, the coins are held by the dealer until the loan is paid off. Interest rates are slightly less than with silver bullion—in August 1973, they averaged 9½%. Storage costs are generally $10 per bag per year. Commissions are 2% each for purchase and sale.

Margin requirements are very liberal. They are usually stated in terms of the loan available per bag, and that generally increases as the price of coins goes upward. It usually works out to about a 20% margin requirement. Needless to say, you can put up more margin than that—which will make margin calls less likely.

Minimum margin purchase is usually three bags.

GOLD BULLION

It's possible to purchase gold bullion on margin through a Swiss bank—although most banks prefer to use forward contracts.

Minimum margin purchase is usually 800 ounces ($80,000 at $100 per ounce), and the margin required may be anywhere between 20% and 50%. Interest rates on U.S. dollar loans in August 1973, were 12–13%, but many banks wouldn't grant dollar loans for gold accounts.

Some banks act as gold dealers, in which case the commission is included in the quoted price. Others charge ⅜% on the purchase and ⅜% on the sale. There are several different ways the storage costs might be computed; usually it runs about 0.15% of the value of the gold per year.

Gold bullion can't be bought in the United States. But there are Canadian banks that sell gold. I'm not aware of any, though, that will sell on a margin basis. If there are, it's doubtful that a U.S. citizen could arrange a margin contract. Gold can be purchased over the counter on a cash basis in Canada.

GOLD COINS

The gold coin market is very large in Switzerland, but there are few banks that will sell coins on a margin basis. If you're interested, you might find one by inquiring of several banks.

Where margin accounts are available, the margin requirement varies between 30% and 50%. Other terms are similar to those for gold bullion.

There's a large market in gold coins in the United States, and several dealers sell gold coins on a margin basis. Minimum purchase is usually three lots of the coin involved (300 British sovereigns or 60 Mexican 50-peso pieces). Commissions are 2% each for the purchase and sale. Interest rates in 1973 were 10½%. Storage costs are nominal. The minimum margin usually figures out to around 20%.

GOLD STOCKS

Gold stocks can be purchased on margin through many Swiss banks. The usual margin requirement is 50%. Interest rates in August 1973, were 12–13%. The normal commission is 1% each for buying and selling. There's a nominal charge for safekeeping of the securities. Minimum purchase requirements vary from $2,000 upward. The most important requirement is that the stocks be bought in 100-share lots.

If the gold stocks produce dividends, the amounts are credited to your account, reducing your loan balance. Interest charges are debited quarterly.

It isn't illegal for a U.S. citizen to purchase stocks through a Swiss bank. But it *is* illegal to neglect to report the dividends as income, to use less margin than current U.S. regulations call for, or to fail to pay the interest equalization tax.

Gold stocks can be purchased on margin through a U.S. stock broker. The current legal requirement is 70% margin, and interest rates were around 10% in August 1973.

CURRENCIES ON MARGIN

I know of no place where you can purchase foreign currencies on margin. However, a currency futures contract through a Swiss bank is very much like a margin account. That will be explained on page 293.

FUTURES CONTRACTS

A futures contract is similar to a margin account, but there are some substantial differences.

In a margin account, the commodity is actually purchased and stored by the dealer or bank; and someone lends you money. In a futures contract, the commodity may not even exist until the contract expires; and no one lends you money.

The futures market can be explained most easily by example. Suppose you're an industrial user of silver, and you know that you'll need 10,000 ounces of silver a year from now. You'd probably like to know today what the silver will cost you next year.

Of course, no one knows what the price of silver will be a year hence, but you can still fix the cost to you. For there's probably a silver mining company that's concerned about the price it will receive next year.

So you and the silver producer make a contract for 10,000 ounces of silver to be delivered to you one year from today—at a price agreed upon now. The price will probably be about 8% higher than today's price—because you won't have to pay for the silver for a year, thereby saving the interest cost on the money you'd probably borrow if you had to buy now.

This is a futures contract. You make a deal for a purchase one year away. Instead of paying the full cost of the contract, you and the producer each post a small bond to guarantee that you'll consummate the contract when it expires.

It would be difficult if you had to look for someone to contract with everytime the need arose. So a futures market exists in which all people with such needs gather to make contracts.

With only silver producers and silver users in the market, it would be too small to be workable. You might want to make a purchase but find that there was no one interested in taking the other side of the contract that day. So speculators operate in the market. Anyone who thinks a price is too high or too low can buy or sell accordingly to take advantage of the price. If he's right, he'll profit; if he's wrong he'll lose.

A speculator can either buy or sell—depending upon his view of the future price. He doesn't need to have the commodity to sell, and he doesn't need to take delivery of the commodity if he buys. Instead, he eventually liquidates his position by doing the opposite of his original contract; before the contract expiration date, he sells every contract he's bought to someone who also wants to liquidate his position.

There will usually be contracts traded for several different expiration months. For example, in January there might be contracts trading for February, March, May, July, September, December, and the following March and June. You can buy or sell a contract of any of the months traded. If you don't intend to consummate the contract, you cancel it out before the expiration date by selling those you've bought or by buying back those you've sold. By the expiration date, only those who intend to deliver or take delivery are left in the market.

MECHANICS OF THE MARKET

If you *buy* a contract, it's called going *long*. It means you expect the price to go up, and you hope to sell the contract later at the higher price.

If you begin by *selling* a contract, it's called going *short*. This is because you're selling something you don't actually have. You do this because you expect to buy an offsetting contract when the price is lower.

Whether you buy first or sell first, you'll eventually have an equal number of purchases and sales. The difference between the buying and selling prices is your profit or loss.

Contracts for the different months will almost always move up and down together in price. All the prices reflect the same thing—the collective market's expectations for the price of the commodity. The price difference between the nearest month's contract and that of one year away will be approximately equal to the current general interest rate plus the cost of storing the commodity for one year. This difference between the various month's prices is called the *interest differential* or *carrying charges*.

Actually, the current price is the price the market expects one year from now less one year's holding costs. If collective market opinion expected the price to double within the year, the current price would be bid upward until it was 8–10% less than double its former price. Speculation always brings the future into the present.

If you buy a futures contract, you're required to put up a deposit. The requirement is usually in the range of 7–15% of the value of the contract—depending upon the commodity involved. Thus, a futures contract for 10,000 ounces of silver at a price of $2.70 would have a total value of $27,000; and you could expect the deposit required to be about $2,700.

This isn't margin buying in the literal sense, because no one is lending you money. Nevertheless, the word *margin* is used to refer to the deposit. The margin requirement in the above example would be $2,700—the amount you must invest at the outset. Margin requirements are stated as amounts of dollars—not percentages. The dollar figures change only when the price of the commodity has become significantly higher or lower.

Just as in margin buying, if the price goes against you, you'll get a margin call. If you've bought long, and the price drops 5%, you'll have lost half of your original margin already (5% of $27,000 = $1,350 which is half of $2,700). You'll be asked to add as much money as your contract has lost—to restore your dollar equity to its original amount.

If you sell short, the same procedure works in reverse. If the price goes *up*, you'll be losing money and you may get a margin call.

A general rule in futures markets is that when you lose 25% of your equity, you receive a call to pay enough money to restore the margin to the original dollar amount.

Margin calls are payable on demand. If you don't respond, the broker must sell out the account. If he allowed the price movement to go too far, you could wind up with a minus equity, and he'd be liable for the difference if you didn't pay up.

When you finally liquidate the contract by doing the opposite of your original purchase or sale, the price at which you bought is compared with the price at which you sold. The difference is your profit or loss. The margin you've invested is returned to you plus the profit or minus the loss.

Each futures market imposes *limits* upon daily price movements. For example, the New York silver contracts can't move more than 10¢ up or down from the previous day's closing price. Thus, if the London price were to go up 15¢ in one day, the New York price could only rise 10¢. But since no one would sell at a price lower than the London price, trading comes to a halt. The objective of the limit rule is to prevent wide swings in price that might be reversed soon afterward. It prevents margin calls that might become unnecessary a day or two later.

The markets with less volume are especially vulnerable to limits. Often, there are days with no trading because there might not be enough participants with opposing views to keep the price stable. So the price is quickly bid up or down the limit. This can jeopardize the ability to trade in and out of the market quickly.

In the same way, as a general rule you should try to trade in the contract months that have the largest volume of contracts outstanding. That way you'll be best able to get out when you want; the large volume of active participants assures a market for your transaction when you're ready to get out.

There's no interest charged on a futures contract because there's no loan. Instead there's the interest differential—the difference in price between the various contract months. The longer the period of time involved, the higher the price.[1]

When you buy through a margin account, you buy at the current price and pay interest on the money borrowed. When

[1] In seasonal commodities the collective judgment of the market often anticipates a lower price in the future. In those instances, the future price will be lower than the current price.

you buy a futures contract, you pay no interest but you buy at a price that equals the current price plus the interest rate.

Contracts are purchased through a commodity broker. There are a number of large commodity brokerage companies in the United States, and most large American stock brokerage firms have commodity departments. Commissions on futures contracts are nominal; the single commission covers both the purchase and the sale.

Margin requirements are invariably less in futures markets than in margin accounts. This means greater leverage, but it also means that small short-term price movements are far more critical. If you use only 5% or 10% margin, you're not really betting on the long-term future of the commodity; you're betting on the movements of the next few days. For a very small drop in price could prompt a margin call.

Consequently, the futures markets in Switzerland or elsewhere in Europe are of little use. You'd have to put up much more than the normal margin, since you can't respond as quickly to developments. If you're in the futures market, you have to be prepared to change your plans within a trading session; obviously, you can't do that if the account is in Switzerland.

The only exception is currency futures, for reasons that will be explained shortly. Otherwise, only the futures markets in the United States and Canada will be covered in this chapter.

Futures markets exist in metals, farm commodities, livestock, and currencies. We're concerned here with those involving silver bullion, silver coins, gold bullion, and currencies.

SILVER BULLION

Silver is traded at the New York Commodities Exchange. Contracts are 10,000 ounces each. Margin requirements range between 7% and 10% of the value of the contract. The interest differential is usually 6–8%, but was as high as 9% in the summer of 1973. The commission is $45.50 per contract.

Silver is also traded at the Chicago Board of Trade on the same basis except that contracts are 5,000 ounces and the commission is $30.

SILVER COINS

Silver coins are traded at the New York Mercantile Exchange. Each contract is 10 bags (approximately 7,200 ounces of silver); prices are quoted per bag. More information on the makeup of silver coin bags is given on page 264.

Margin requirements are generally between 4% and 10%. The interest differential was about 1% higher than for silver bullion during 1973. The commission is $35 per contract.

GOLD BULLION

Gold is traded at the Winnipeg Commodity Exchange in Canada. It's illegal for an American citizen to trade in gold bullion, even on a futures basis. In fact, the West Coast Commodity Exchange in Los Angeles created a gold *coin* futures market in 1971, but it was shut down by government edict within a few weeks.

Contracts in gold bullion are 400 ounces each. Margin requirements are very low—5% to 10%. The interest differential hit 14% in August 1973. Normally, it's around 10%. The market is relatively new and the volume is quite low; usually there's only one month trading with much volume.

CURRENCY FUTURES

Currency futures are traded in exactly the same way that commodity futures are.

Currency futures are traded at the International Monetary Market of the Chicago Mercantile Exchange. The procedure is the same as for commodity futures. Three of the recommended foreign currencies are traded.

Swiss francs: Contracts are 250,000 francs ($83,333 at $.33 per franc); the margin requirement ranges from 2% to 4%. There's usually active trading in two of the contract months at any given time.

Dutch guilders: Contracts are 125,000 guilders ($46,250 at $.37 per guilder); the margin requirement is between 3% and 6%. The market in guilders is new, so the volume is slim but constantly growing.

German marks: Contracts are 250,000 marks ($100,000 at $.40 per mark); the margin requirement runs between 1½% and 3½%. There is usually active trading in two of the contract months at any given time.

Commissions on all contracts are $45. The interest differential runs between 3% and 5%, lower than in commodity futures. And the margin requirements are lower, too, because currencies move less aggressively than commodities. The possibilities of a margin call are just as great as they are in commodities, however.

You can also buy currency futures through many American banks. However, I don't recommend it. Your costs are usually much higher—reflected in a higher interest differential—and there are no compensating advantages.

The interest differential is higher at a Swiss bank, too, but there are good reasons for paying the higher rate. If you're investing for the long term, it's safer to do it through a Swiss bank than in the U.S. futures market. There's no chance for governmental intervention to injure your investment. And if it's a big change in the currency price that you're looking for, the higher interest differential will be less meaningful if you're right. The differential in August 1973 was 5–6% at a time when it was 3–4% in the United States.

A disadvantage is that minimum contracts are often 1,000,000 units of the currency at most banks. If you purchase a contract for 1,000,000 Swiss francs, for example, that's equivalent to

$330,000. And the margin requirement is generally 10%—which would be $33,000 in that case. The 10% margin requirement makes a margin call less likely—but by no means impossible.

If you already have an account at the bank where you buy the contract, you can have the funds transferred from that account. The funds will be converted from the foreign currency of the existing account to U.S. dollars to be used as margin. You want to have no more money in dollars than is necessary at any time, so you can instruct the bank as follows:

> Transfer funds from my Swiss franc current account in the amount necessary to meet the minimum margin requirements. As necessary in the future to meet margin calls, transfer additional funds; but please keep no more funds in dollars than the amount required to meet the minimum margin requirements of this contract.

If you don't have funds in another account at the same bank, you should deposit *at least* 15% as margin, and 25% would be even safer. You would still make a considerable profit if there's a major change in the currency price.

The bank treats the contract much like a margin account. It actually buys the currency involved and holds it. The interest differential is fixed, however, and remains so throughout the life of the contract.

Usually, the maximum length of a contract is one year. When the contract is close to expiration, you can negotiate a new one with the bank. In this way, you can hold a leveraged position in a foreign currency for several years.

You can write to several banks, requesting information about currency contracts—minimum margin requirements, minimum contract sizes, currencies available, maximum length of contract, etc. You can also ask for the price of a one-year contract on a given day. Then you can compare the price with the published spot price of that day to determine the interest differential.

When you've decided what bank you want to deal with, it's best to call the bank to get a firm quote on the day you want to buy, and then give your approval on the telephone. You can do that only if the money is already at the bank, however. Call between 5:00 A.M. and 8:00 A.M. Eastern Standard Time—as those are the hours when prices are available and can still be executed that day. The man you talk to will have a calculator on his desk and can tell you the interest differential in the quoted price. He'll probably give the quote in Swiss franc prices, but he'll convert it to dollar figures if you ask him to.

Because the interest differential is a large part of a currency contract, try not to buy when the interest rate is abnormally high. The banker can advise you if that's the case and can tell you what he thinks the prospects are for the immediate future.

There's no way to obtain daily prices for your contract once you've bought it—as you can with other investments. So check the spot currency prices in the *Wall Street Journal* or the daily newspaper. They will be *under* the current value of your contract because there's no interest differential—but that factor will be reduced as the contract year progresses.

Most Swiss banks offer contracts in Swiss francs, and some banks offer contracts in other major European currencies. You'll have to deal with a Lebanese bank to get a contract for Lebanese pounds. The principles of the contract are the same, however.

Currency futures contracts can be an excellent speculation. There are pitfalls, however. The margin requirements are low, and if you buy just before a price drop you can lose your equity quickly. Since short-term movements aren't easily predicted, approach the contract as a long-term investment; put up plenty of margin and wait for a major price change to make a large profit.

As I said earlier, when the dollar rises, the move is orderly; when the dollar drops, it's often a panic. So you can't wait for the price of a foreign currency to start moving upward before you buy. In the U.S. currency market, the price may be up the limit for several days in a row—in which case there's no chance to buy.

You can only buy when the price is steady for a while or when the foreign currency is dropping. Since there's no way to know how far the currency will drop, the second alternative can be a dangerous time to buy. So the most opportune moments are when the foreign currency is relatively steady for several days after having dropped.

If you find such a time, take your position and wait it out. The price may drop further yet, so you have to be prepared. But only approach the investment on the basis of a time period of a year or more. Chances are there'll be a major move upward during that time.

One last piece of advice: *never go long on the dollar*. Even if you think the dollar has dropped too far temporarily, don't bet on it. There have already been dollar drops followed soon by more dollar drops; it's an easy way to lose a small fortune.

KNOW YOUR OWN LIMITS

Futures markets are exciting places. It's easy to become intoxicated by the excitement of the game and get carried away. Define your own limits and stick to them. Don't use more leverage than is appropriate for you. Don't go by the minimum margin requirements unless you intend to do short-term trading; you still get a lot of leverage if you deposit two or three times the minimum requirement. And that way you won't be wiped out by short-term fluctuations.

If you're looking for a long-term upward price movement, you're probably much better off using a margin account in a Swiss bank. The U.S. futures market isn't the place to take a long-term position. The few operators who make the most money there think entirely in terms of small, short-term price movements in either direction. They may have no opinions regarding the long-term prospects for the commodity involved.

Most people who jump into the futures market, using the minimum margin, don't realize the game they've entered. They are now playing poker with professionals—by the professionals' rules—and the odds are stacked against them.

The part-time investor who wants to speculate can do much better with a margin account.

Another factor to be considered is the vulnerability of the U.S. futures markets to government intervention. They could be closed without warning at any time by a new government venture into economic wonderland. You're vulnerable to this, even if you take a long-term position and put up plenty of margin.

Far better to do it through a Swiss bank where you don't have to worry about those things.

There's a place in the futures market for those inclined to speculate. But you should be absolutely sure you know what you're getting into. You must know that your investment is appropriate to the time and attention you're going to give to it and to the risks you're willing to take.

SHORTING THE STOCK MARKET

Selling short in the stock market would appear to be a good way of taking advantage of a crisis. I would agree, but only if I knew for certain that the next depression will be ushered in with a crash, and if I knew when that crash would be.

But I don't know these things. And since there are much more likely prospects, I prefer to invest elsewhere.

OTHER INVESTMENTS

Continued investments in real estate, mutual funds, and the stock market have to be labeled very speculative today. As the crises continue, any of those investments could collapse at any time. They've become speculations.

I don't recommend any of them. I mention them here only because you *are* speculating if you're involved with any of them. You're playing with time—hoping to make a little more on them and then get out before it's too late.

Stocks from the Dow Jones Industrial Averages aren't "blue

chip" investments today. A blue chip investment would be gold bullion or Swiss francs held in a Swiss bank.

Especially vulnerable is real estate, because you can't liquidate it in a hurry. It may continue to go up substantially over the next few years—but then, so might a penny uranium stock. If several years from now you look back and see that real estate *did* go up, it won't change the status of *risk* that must be placed upon it today.

I have, at times, recommended to some clients that they retain a fairly large position in the traditional investments. But that was only when the client had so much money that he could afford to play both sides of the future. His prime concern was to conserve enough wealth to live comfortably for the rest of his life. And if he had twice that amount now, he could afford to bet half in each direction—rather than risking everything one way or the other. As you can imagine, I've had very few clients who could afford that luxury. For the rest, the risk in staying with the traditional investments was too great.

SPECULATIONS

The speculations covered in this chapter are opportunities that can be approached with money you can afford to lose. But you should never consider using funds that are precious to you.

Even if you use only gambling funds, there's always the danger that you may get carried away. If the price goes against you, you may be unwilling to accept your loss. If that happens, you'll be tempted to draw upon precious funds to meet margin calls —hoping the price will turn around tomorrow morning.

There's always a place for the brave, the iron-willed, the adventurous. They are the people from whose ranks will come the next batch of millionaires. They'll bet heavily because they aren't afraid to lose everything. And if they win, they'll win heavily.

If you fit that category, if you'd be willing to risk everything you have now because the desire for a large fortune is greater than the fear of losing what you have, there are opportunities today.

If you hope for substantial growth, but aren't willing to bet everything you have, there are still ways to take reasonable chances and increase your position. For such a person, conservative margin accounts are the answer.

30

Annuities, Life Insurance, and Pension Protection

IF YOU NEED AN ANNUITY or life insurance, it's possible to have either of them without being vulnerable to a shrinking dollar. The policies can be written in Swiss francs, so that the proceeds will be paid in a more stable currency—thereby assuring that you'll receive the purchasing power that you expect.

If you're contributing to a retirement plan from which you can't withdraw, it's possible to protect the purchasing power of the proceeds by using Swiss franc currency contracts.

These alternatives will be covered in this chapter.

ANNUITIES AND LIFE INSURANCE

There are at least two large Swiss life insurance companies that have services available to foreign customers.[1]

The companies will correspond with you in English, and the procedures are virtually the same as if you were to buy an annuity or a life insurance policy from an American company. The principal difference is that you pay all premiums in Swiss francs and the proceeds are payable in Swiss francs.

An annuity is an arrangement by which you pay a stated amount—either in regular payments or in one lump sum—and

---

[1] Names and addresses are given in Chapter 33.

you receive a guaranteed income from a designated age for as long as you live.

Annuities have become rather unpopular in the United States because the dollar depreciates between the time you put the money in and the time you take it out. With a Swiss franc annuity, you're assured that the depreciation won't be nearly so drastic.

However, while the Swiss franc is far more stable than the dollar, it can be expected to depreciate, too. So a Swiss franc annuity is recommended only for someone who may begin using it soon—age fifty-five or over. You can give a sum of money to the annuity company and be guaranteed a lifetime income in Swiss francs. And the annuity can be combined with life insurance coverage for a beneficiary.

In the same way, life insurance has become less popular for Americans because the eventual payoff to the beneficiary will be made in depreciated dollars. A Swiss franc life insurance policy helps to offset the depreciation. And because the Swiss franc also depreciates, you can get a policy in which the premiums and the coverage increase each year by 4%.

For people under fifty-five, seeking life insurance protection for a beneficiary, I suggest using straight term insurance—a policy in which no cash values accumulate. Use the other investments recommended in this book to accumulate capital. Term insurance in Switzerland is called *death risk insurance*.

For insurance policies, a medical examination is required for policies of 75,000 Swiss francs (approximately $25,000 in 1973) or more, and for all policies if the insured is over forty-five years old. If a medical examination is required, you can be examined by a doctor recommended by the nearest Swiss consulate.

There are no maximum limits to policies. The minimum is a policy with a premium of 50 Swiss francs ($16.67) per year—or about 5,000 Swiss francs ($1,667) coverage.

The premiums can be paid quarterly, semi-annually, or annually. You can arrange with the Swiss bank where you have an account to pay the premiums for you automatically. That would be especially valuable if, in the future, the U.S. government should prevent you from sending funds out of the country. For the same reason, a foreign customer is required to give a Swiss address in addition to his own address. You can use your Swiss bank's address for that purpose.

When the benefits are to be paid, you can instruct the life insurance company to convert the proceeds to any currency you choose before mailing them to you. Thus, you can receive annuity payments in dollars—but the funds aren't converted to dollars until payable.

There are four basic plans available. Here are the highlights of those plans:

1. *Endowment or Annuity Plan:* The face value of the policy is payable when the policy matures (in a lump sum or in lifetime payments) or is paid to the beneficiary if the insured dies before the policy expires.

2. *Endowment Plan with Upvaluation:* This is the same as the first plan except that the premium and the face value of the policy each increase by 4% every year after the second year. This provides added protection against any Swiss franc depreciation.

3. *Endowment Plan on Two Lives:* This plan is similar to the regular endowment plan except that two people can be insured. The face value of the policy is paid whenever the first person dies or when the policy matures. It's also available with the upvaluation provision.

4. *Term Death Risk, Fixed Amount:* This is straight term insurance, payable upon death, with no cash values accumulated for the insured if he survives. This plan is also available with constantly decreasing coverage at a lower cost.

In addition to these plans, the company can tailor-make almost any kind of policy to suit your requirements.

If you deal with a mutual company, there is a profit-sharing provision, just as there is with mutual life insurance companies in the United States. The profits can be used to reduce premiums or to increase the coverage.

When you write for information and rates, include the following information:

1. Sex.
2. Date of birth.
3. The amount of coverage you have in mind.
4. The type of plan you want.
5. The length of the plan. If it's term insurance, the number of years; if it's an endowment, the age at which you want to start receiving payments.
6. Any other information that might help the company to advise you of the appropriate plan.

I don't recommend that you base all your plans for future income and capital on a Swiss annuity. It's best not to be overly dependent upon any life insurance company. The other recommended investments will be safer, more flexible, and can serve the same purposes. But an annuity might be an appropriate part of the investment program for someone of advanced age.

And a life insurance policy to benefit your spouse, family, or a business arrangement will make more sense if it's payable in a currency that won't depreciate as fast as the dollar.

INCOME PROTECTION

If you're expecting a large sum of money to be paid to you in the future in U.S. dollars, you can protect the value of it through currency futures. This can be useful if you're involved in a retirement plan you can't get out of, if you have a large debt payable to you in the future, or if your business has a large volume of long-term receivables.

The futures market was explained on pages 288–292; currency futures were explained on pages 293–297. A currency contract can protect sums payable to you in case the dollar drops further before you receive your money.

Begin by determining the number of dollars involved. Translate that figure into Swiss francs by finding the current exchange rate in the *Wall Street Journal* or the daily newspaper. Purchase a Swiss franc futures contract for approximately that number of Swiss francs.

If the money owed to you will be paid within fifteen months, you may want to purchase the contract in the United States where the cost is less. If a longer period of time is involved, do it through a Swiss bank.

If you can, deposit at least 15% as margin so you'll be free of margin calls. It should be a one-time expense, returned to you later. If the price of the Swiss franc goes up, periodically withdraw all equity above the original amount; transfer those withdrawals to a Swiss bank to be held in a foreign currency.

If a pension is involved, try to calculate the total number of dollars you expect to receive eventually. Buy a contract for an equivalent number of Swiss francs at current exchange rates. Since it will be a long-term matter, buy the longest contract you can obtain through a Swiss bank, and replace it with a new one when it expires. The same procedure can be used if you're *already* receiving a pension and expect to live for a long time yet.

For some people, the deposit involved may make the plan prohibitive. Don't do it if you can only scrape up the minimum margin required. It would be much more practical to have a smaller contract, but with a safer amount of margin. Make sure you understand the plan thoroughly before you proceed.

If the amount of money involved is enough to warrant using this system, it can be an effective way to make sure that the money you're paid in the future will be worth approximately what you're counting on.

The Swiss franc will probably depreciate, too. But money payable in Swiss francs should be worth far more than money payable in dollars.

31
Creating an
Investment Program

NO ONE CAN MAKE YOUR DECISIONS FOR YOU, because no one can know enough about you to determine what you need the most. Only you can take into consideration your objectives, your fears, your emotions, your interests. You have to create an investment program that will make you *feel good* about the situation. And no one but you could possibly consider all the facets of you that should contribute to the final decisions.

In Chapter 32, I'll present some sample investment programs —to help you visualize the various ways the recommended investments can be combined to satisfy different objectives with various amounts of available funds. Those programs are offered only as *examples,* however.

In this chapter, I'll present the investments in a way that will show their potential uses. And I'll offer some guidelines you can use to create a program for yourself.

Let's begin by reviewing the recommended investments:

1. Gold—in the form of bullion, coins, or the stocks of South African mining companies.

2. Silver—in the form of bullion or coins.

3. Foreign currencies—mainly the Swiss franc, the Dutch guilder, the Belgian franc, the German mark, and, for speculative purposes, the Lebanese pound. These can be handled through bank accounts, Eurocurrency contracts, bonds, and certificates of deposit.

4. Coins—for spendable assets during a runaway inflation —principally silver, supplemented by gold.

5. Cash—a small reserve of U.S. currency for mobility and as a hedge against bank holidays.

6. A retreat—as a hedge in case of currency destruction, civil disorder, or totalitarian governmental policies.

7. Swiss annuities and life insurance policies—to guarantee income or to assure funds to someone else in the event of your death.

8. Speculations—margin accounts or futures contracts in the first three items on this list.

OBJECTIVES

Creating an investment program means answering two questions: Which of these investments are appropriate for you? How much of your assets should go into each?

You can answer those questions only if you first define your objectives as clearly as possible. Here are some further questions that might help you better understand what you want:

1. Which possible future events frighten you most (bank closings, purchasing power depreciation, government interference, loss of income during a depression, shortages, etc.)?

2. How precious are the funds you have? Do you believe you can survive easily if you should invest and lose what you have? Or is preservation of your present assets vitally important?

3. Do you require income from your investments?

4. How much of your funds can you invest and forget about for several years? How much might you have to withdraw and use for other purposes within the next year?

5. What kind of risks can you handle emotionally? Remember past experiences; don't undertake projects that require emotional capabilities you've never tested.

6. What is your family situation? Does your spouse share your concern for the future? Which investments should be

eliminated because they might cause marital discord? Which investments can you undertake without family problems?

7. How closely are you willing to watch the investments? Can you pay close attention and make changes as required? Or would you rather create a program you can then forget about?

Each of these questions must be considered. If you ignore any of them, you'll make decisions that you may not be able to live with in the future.

ADVANTAGES

To continue, we can group the investments by their advantages. In each case, it's assumed that you'll someday cash in the investment for U.S. currency. So the returns are in terms of the U.S. dollars you'd receive.

1. *Minimum short-term (less than one year) downside risk:* Swiss francs, Dutch guilders, Belgian francs, German marks.

For funds that you may have to withdraw within a year, you'll want to pick investments that have the least possibility of short-term loss. All the recommended investments will fluctuate, but the foreign currencies have the least possibility of loss in the short term. The maximum loss you might suffer by selling soon after you buy is probably about 15%. And that would happen only if you needed money in a hurry. After you've had the currencies for a year or more, there's little likelihood that you'd sell them at a loss.

2. *Minimum chance of intermediate-term (twelve to thirty months) loss:* The currencies listed in advantage #1, plus gold, gold coins, and conservative South African gold stocks.

3. *Minimum chance of long-term (thirty months or more) loss:* All recommended investments (except cash), but mostly the currencies already mentioned.

4. *Liquidity:* Swiss francs, Dutch guilders, or Belgian francs in a current account in a Swiss bank.

Liquidity means the ability to withdraw your money at any time you need it without suffering a loss thereby. The minimum short-term loss was covered in advantage #1; the current account provides immediate withdrawals without restrictions.

5. *Income:* Swiss bank deposit accounts, Eurocurrency contracts and certificates of deposit in Swiss francs, Dutch guilders, Belgian francs, or German marks (subject to interest-paying limitations you'll be advised of by the Swiss banks); conservative South African gold stocks; Swiss franc annuities or bonds.

6. *Protection of future U.S. dollar income:* Swiss franc futures contracts through a Swiss bank or in the U.S. market.

7. *Good long-term capital growth:* Gold bullion, gold coins, conservative or growth South African gold stocks, silver bullion, silver coins, Swiss francs, Dutch guilders, Belgian francs, Lebanese pounds.

8. *Maximum long-term growth:* Margin accounts in gold bullion, gold coins, gold stocks, silver bullion, silver coins; long-term futures contracts in Swiss francs, Dutch guilders, or Lebanese pounds; speculative gold stocks.

9. *Short-term maximum profit potentials:* Futures contracts in gold bullion, silver bullion, silver coins, Swiss francs, Dutch guilders, German marks, or Lebanese pounds.

10. *Protection against governmental interference:* Any of the preceding investments handled through a Swiss bank; gold coins or silver coins stored by yourself in a safe place; small amounts of U.S. currency stored by yourself; a retreat.

11. *Accessible purchasing power in emergencies:* U.S. currency stored in a safe place; silver coins and/or gold coins (in case of runaway inflation).

Holdings in a Swiss bank wouldn't be useful during bank closings because there'd be no way to get the money to you. If it were sent by mail or wire, someone would have to cash the check or money order—an unlikely possibility. In the case of runaway inflation, you would want to leave any holdings as they were until after the crisis was over; they'd be a long-term store of wealth that would be valuable after the crisis.

12. *Safety in case of turmoil:* A retreat; silver coins and gold coins—to assure purchasing power to reach the retreat and to enhance your living standards once there.

13. *Absolute safety against the inconceivable:* Silver coins and gold coins buried in the safest place you can find.

You'll notice that a U.S. bank deposit isn't listed among any of the advantages. I wouldn't keep any savings in an American bank. Keep a checking account to facilitate the payment of bills, but limit deposits to what you expect to use within the month. Don't accumulate money in a U.S. bank account that you can't afford to lose.

DISADVANTAGES

We should also group the categories by their risks, so that you can avoid doing anything you want to guard against.

1. *Maximum potential short-term (one year or less) loss:* gold bullion, gold coins, gold stocks, silver bullion, silver coins; margin accounts or futures contracts in any investment.

2. *Loss of purchasing power:* U.S. currency, the retreat.

3. *Vulnerability to governmental interference:* Storage of gold coins, silver bullion, silver coins with a U.S. dealer; ADRs for gold stocks; futures contracts bought in the U.S.; Eurocurrency contracts and certificates of deposit in other than Swiss francs.

4. *Vulnerability to theft:* Anything you store yourself—coins, bullion, cash, anything at the retreat.

5. *Vulnerability to bank failures:* Anything held in a U.S. bank account; possibly anything held in a bank safe deposit box; Eurocurrency contracts and certificates of deposit arranged through a Swiss bank but held by a bank elsewhere.

STEP BY STEP

The following step-by-step procedure may help you to put things in their proper order when creating your own investment program.

1. Begin by determining how much money you have. Include all savings accounts and the *present market value* (not what you paid) of any investments you intend to get rid of. A few suggestions for raising more cash will be included in Chapter 36. Total the amount available to you.

2. Determine how much of that total is precious to you. Start the program with a foundation; place the precious funds in a Swiss bank. Put the amount that needs to be liquid in Swiss franc current accounts.

3. Decide how much income you need from the program, if any. If you don't need income from it now, ignore this step and emphasize other objectives instead.

If you need income, there are six possible sources: deposit accounts in Swiss banks, Swiss annuities, Swiss bonds, Eurocurrency contracts, certificates of deposit, and South African gold stocks. The banks can tell you the interest rates available, and you can determine the dividends on South African gold stocks by checking with a Swiss bank, an American stock broker, or by referring to a gold stock chart service. You can then determine how much of your funds must be used to produce the income you need from interest and/or dividends.

If you can't produce enough income through these means, consider making small periodic withdrawals from your capital (and, hopefully, from capital appreciation) without depleting your resources too quickly.

4. Determine how much life insurance protection must be provided for anyone important to you. You can do that in this way: (a) determine the amount in U.S. dollars that the beneficiary would require if you were to die this year; (b) convert that figure to Swiss francs at the present exchange rate (listed in daily newspapers or the *Wall Street Journal*); (c) add 20% for possible depreciation to the Swiss franc figure; (d) determine the premiums on that amount by writing to one of the Swiss life insurance companies mentioned in Chapter 33. You can arrange to have the premiums paid from a Swiss bank account.

5. Set aside any money you want to use for a retreat. You may want to start with only the basic requirements that will give you

a safe feeling. Additions to the minimum requirements can be made from future income.

6. Add the cost of coins you feel you need for emergency purchasing power. And set aside some dollars to be stored at home.

7. Choose the capital growth investments you feel most comfortable with. Don't pick one just because I recommend it or because a friend is excited about it. Choose the investment that makes the most sense to you. If you want to pay close attention to it, pick the one that interests you the most.

It's important to have capital growth in your program because you'll need increased purchasing power as currencies continue to depreciate.

8. If you've taken care of the needs that are important to you, you can use leftover funds for speculative purposes. Use conservative margin accounts if you want long-term growth without close attention. Use more liberal margin arrangements if you want to take bigger chances and are willing to feed the margin account with any additional funds necessary. If you want to play in the short term with money you can afford to lose, consider an interest in the futures market as a hobby.

9. To further protect against the unforeseeable, diversify to the extent appropriate for your funds. Use more than one investment, more than one currency, more than one Swiss bank, more than one storage place for coins and cash, etc.

The ultimate objective is to create a program that allows you to feel comfortable about the situation—knowing that you're protected against the risks that bother you most, and that you've acted upon the opportunities you think are most important.

Then when the next monetary crisis occurs, you'll probably observe that your reactions are different from what they were to previous crises. No longer will you get that sinking feeling in your stomach; no longer will you berate yourself for not having acted sooner.

You'll be excited because you've taken advantage of the situation and are ready to profit from it.

32

Sample Investment Programs

THE SAMPLE INVESTMENT programs in this chapter are offered only as *examples*—to help you visualize a distribution of your funds. Even if you find one that fits your situation, don't accept it *in toto*; examine it further, change it in ways that make it more comfortable for you.

There are fourteen different programs presented, to cover as many kinds of situations as possible. To avoid tiring you, there are several suggestions that aren't repeated in each place where they might be appropriate. So I suggest that you look at each program, even those that don't fit your situation, in case there are any ideas you may be able to adapt to your program. Mark any point you might want to consider later for your own program.

The programs fall into seven basic groups: safe, income, straddle, growth, go-for-broke, income protection, and what I call a 50/50 program.

Within the safe, growth, and go-for-broke groups, there are separate programs for different wealth categories.

Before investing in any of these items, reread the chapters that pertain to those investments (check the index for pages). *Be sure you understand what you're doing before you act.*

SAFE PROGRAMS

The first group of investment plans is for the individual who's concerned above all with preservation of the wealth he now has—no matter how little or how much. Since more diversity is possible in the higher asset brackets, it's necessary to separate examples for each bracket.

Safe—Tiny Assets: $500–$2,500

If your assets are $2,500 or less, you don't have a great deal to choose from, but you can still protect what you have. For maximum safety:

1. Keep 20% in U.S. currency at home; purchase silver coins with the entire remainder (store them yourself), *or*

2. Place the entire amount in a Swiss franc current account in a Swiss bank, *or*

3. Use any combination of 1 and 2.

Safe—Small Assets: $2,500–$15,000

Using $10,000 as an example:

Swiss franc current account	$ 5,000	50%
Silver coins at home [1]	2,500	25%
U.S. currency at home	500	5%
Retreat budget	2,000	20%

Safe—Medium Assets: $15,000–$100,000

With a program of this size, more than one Swiss bank is warranted for diversity. Also, the negative interest taxes on foreign currencies become important. Current accounts are limited to 100,000 Swiss francs (approximately $33,000); deposit accounts are limited to 50,000 Swiss francs (approximately $16,500) if they're to earn interest.

Using $40,000 as an example:

Swiss franc current account (Swiss bank #1)	$ 15,000	37½%
Dutch guilder current account (Swiss bank #2)	5,000	12½%

[1] All references to *at home* include the alternative of a safe deposit box.

Gold bullion or gold coins [2]		
(kept at one of the banks)	5,000	12½ %
Silver coins at home	7,500	18¾ %
U.S. currency at home	500	1¼ %
Retreat budget	7,000	17½ %

Safe—Large Assets: $100,000–$500,000

In this program, an Austrian bank is introduced for further diversity. Also, the amount of silver coins for storage at home may become prohibitive; so gold coins are used for half the budget.

Using $200,000 as an example:

At Swiss bank #1:
Swiss franc current account	$ 33,000	16½ %
Dutch guilder current account	20,000	10 %
Gold bullion or gold coins	35,000	17½ %

At Swiss bank #2:
Dutch guilder current account	20,000	10 %
Swiss franc deposit account	17,000	8½ %
Gold bullion or gold coins	15,000	7½ %

At Austrian bank:
Swiss franc current account	10,000	5 %

At home or partly in safe deposit boxes:
Silver coins	10,000	5 %
Gold coins	10,000	5 %
U.S. currency	5,000	2½ %
Retreat budget	25,000	12½ %

Safe—Extra Large Assets: $500,000 or More

In this program, many small accounts are required to avoid the negative interest tax. If your assets are other than one million dollars, don't go by the percentages shown for the currency accounts; use each account to the maximum allowable without negative interest. You can also have more accounts in

[2] Pre-1934 gold coins are the only legal way U.S. citizens can own gold.

one bank by using names, or combinations of names, of family members.

Using $1,000,000 as the example:

At Swiss bank #1:

Swiss franc current account	$ 33,000	3⅓ %
Swiss franc deposit account	17,000	1⅔ %
Dutch guilder current account	20,000	2 %
German mark deposit account	40,000	4 %
Belgian franc deposit account	15,000	1½ %
Gold bullion or gold coins	100,000	10 %

At Swiss bank #2:

The same as Swiss bank #1	225,000	22½ %

At Swiss bank #3:

Swiss franc current account	33,000	3⅓ %
Swiss franc deposit account	17,000	1⅔ %
Dutch guilder deposit account	20,000	2 %
German mark deposit account	30,000	3 %
Belgian franc current account	15,000	1½ %
Gold bullion or gold coins	75,000	7½ %

At Austrian bank:

Swiss franc current account	33,000	3⅓ %
Swiss franc deposit account	17,000	1⅔ %
Dutch guilder current account	20,000	2 %
German mark deposit account	25,000	2½ %
Austrian schilling current account	20,000	2 %
Austrian schilling deposit account	20,000	2 %
Silver bullion	50,000	5 %

At home or partly in safe deposit boxes:

Silver coins	10,000	1 %
Gold coins	45,000	4½ %
U.S. currency	20,000	2 %
Retreat budget	100,000	10 %

INCOME-PRODUCING PROGRAMS

If it's necessary to receive income from your investments, and you're concerned about safety, see the "safe" program in your asset category. Make the following changes:

1. Of the total funds in current and deposit accounts in your asset category, split the funds as follows:

Current accounts	25%
Deposit accounts	25%
Fixed deposit or savings accounts	50%

Limit each separate account in each bank to the amounts that will draw interest and/or not be subject to negative interest taxes. Of Swiss francs, Dutch guilders, Belgian francs, and German marks, lean more heavily to whichever currencies will earn the highest interest. But be sure to have no more than 30% in German marks; and be sure to have *at least* 35% in Swiss francs.

2. Ask the banks you deal with for information on Euro-currency contracts, certificates of deposit, and Swiss bonds. Each of these pays higher interest than the normal deposit accounts do. Don't put everything in these higher-interest alternatives, however; they aren't as safe as normal accounts. You might use one third of your funds for the high-interest alternatives, another third for deposit accounts, and a third for current accounts. The current accounts are required for liquidity. If you want to be safer, don't use Eurocurrency and certificates of deposit; use the allocation in item #1 instead.

3. If you're fifty-five or older, you might consider using a Swiss annuity for about half of your income requirements and use normal accounts for the other half.

4. Wherever gold bullion or gold coins (in a Swiss bank) are indicated in a "safe" program, use high-dividend South African gold stocks instead. Don't go beyond your income needs, however. Gold bullion and coins are safer than stocks.

LARGE OR EXTRA-LARGE STRADDLE PROGRAM

If you want to keep a position in the traditional investments (stock market, mutual funds, real estate, bonds, etc.), decide what percentage of your assets you want to use that way. Then refer to the "safe" investment program that applies to the amount of the remaining assets.

GROWTH PROGRAMS

The next three programs are designed for the conservative investor who wants his wealth to grow, but who doesn't want to take special risks.

Growth—Small Assets: $2,500–$15,000

Using $10,000 as an example:

Swiss franc current account	$ 2,000	20%
Growth gold stocks, silver bullion, silver coins, or gold coins; cash or 50% margin	3,000	30%
Silver coins at home	1,500	15%
Gold coins at home	2,000	20%
U.S. currency	500	5%
Retreat budget	1,000	10%

Growth—Medium Assets: $15,000–$100,000

Using $50,000 as an example:

Swiss franc current account	$ 10,000	20%
Dutch guilder current account	5,000	10%

Growth gold stocks, silver bullion, silver coins, or gold coins; cash or 50% margin	15,000	30%
Silver coins at home	5,000	10%
Gold coins at home	10,000	20%
U.S. currency at home	1,000	2%
Retreat budget	4,000	8%

Growth—Large and Extra Large Assets: $100,000 or More

Using $200,000 as an example:

Currency accounts (see previous programs for sample distributions)	$ 50,000	25 %
Gold bullion or gold coins (50% margin)	30,000	15 %
Silver bullion or silver coins (50% margin)	30,000	15 %
Growth gold stocks (50% margin)	20,000	10 %
Currency futures (20% margin) at a Swiss bank	30,000	15 %
Silver coins at home	5,000	2½ %
Gold coins at home	15,000	7½ %
U.S. currency at home	5,000	2½ %
Retreat budget	15,000	7½ %

GO-FOR-BROKE PROGRAMS

These programs are designed for the individual who's willing to bet all he has in hopes that he'll increase his wealth many times over. If that's for you, pick the speculative media according to your own taste.

Go-for-Broke—Small Assets: $2,000–$15,000

Using $10,000 as an example:

One currency futures contract (approximately 7% margin)	$ 5,000	50%
Margin account (25–40% margin)	5,000	50%

Go-for-Broke: Any Amount over $15,000

Using $50,000 as an example:

Currency futures (normal margin required)	$ 10,000	20%
Silver or gold futures (normal margin required)	10,000	20%
Margin accounts (maximum leverage) in gold coins, silver coins, silver bullion, or speculative gold stocks	15,000	30%
Cash in reserve to meet margin calls on all above accounts	15,000	30%

50/50 ACCOUNTS—ANY SIZE

It's unlikely that anyone who has accumulated very much wealth will want to risk it all in the go-for-broke way just indicated. A more likely possibility is that you might want to go for broke with *some* of your funds, but hold aside some assets. Then if you lose the speculative funds, you won't have to start over again from zero. To create such a program:

1. Decide how much you want to keep in safe reserve. Treat that as a separate budget and refer to the "safe" programs listed earlier in the chapter.

2. Use the rest—and additional funds that come in—for specu-

lative investments in the manner indicated in the "go-for-broke" programs. Obviously, how you speculate will depend upon your own taste. Investigate all the alternatives and decide on the one that looks likeliest to you, and which you'd enjoy following.

One other piece of advice: Make sure that you're serious when you say you'd be willing to lose some of your funds. Too often, an investor says that he's willing to take a chance, willing to lose what he has, but doesn't really mean it. He's operating on the unsaid assumption that he *won't* lose—not that he's willing to lose.

I suggest that you take thirty minutes or so and go off by yourself to a quiet place. Sit down and use your imagination. Picture yourself *without* the funds you're planning to use for speculation. Imagine that you've invested them and lost. Picture the situation in detail—the reactions of your family and others, your personal financial situation, the uses to which the money might have been put had you not lost the money. See how it feels. Make sure you really are prepared to lose the money before you risk it.

INCOME PROTECTION—ANY SIZE

If you're on a pension (or will be) that can't be cashed in, and you depend upon it for living expenses, refer to page 304 for an income protection plan using currency futures. Allocate sufficient assets to cover that program. Then use the rest as a separate budget to carry out one of the other programs—whichever fits the amount of money and your preference.

EXPANDING PROGRAMS

It's quite possible that you expect to have more money to put into an investment program within the next year or so. If that's the case, there are two basic ways to handle it:

1. Use a program appropriate to the amount you have now. As you receive more funds to use, add to each of the investments to bring them up to proportions appropriate to a larger-sized budget.

2. Assume the larger assets you expect to be able to use later, and establish the program immediately on that basis. Number the components of the program in order of importance. Begin with the most important investment, and add the other investments as the funds become available.

As you choose the order of importance, take into consideration future vulnerabilities—such as limitations on sending money overseas, etc. Try to do now what you might not be able to do later.

YOUR IDEAS

I hate to keep repeating myself, but it must be emphasized that these budgets are only examples to help you visualize what can be done. As you look at an appropriate program, notice any part of it that makes you feel uncomfortable. Alter the budget to eliminate that discomfort.

If you feel like arguing with me over any of the allocations I've made—*good*. That just proves that you have ideas of your own. *Use them*. It's *your* life and wealth that are involved, not mine. Don't let anyone tell you what you "must" do.

If you have a program of your own in mind already, it should still be helpful to go through all the programs listed—hunting for ideas. Some of the alternatives might trigger ideas of your own. Use anything appropriate to stimulate your imagination and attention to the task at hand.[3]

[3] On October 1, 1973 (after this book had been set in type), the Swiss government ended the negative interest tax. Now, unlimited funds can be kept in an account, but interest is available only up to 50,000 francs. The suggestions of this chapter can now be altered to eliminate the use of German marks in long-term plans; I suggest sticking with the Swiss franc and the Dutch guilder. Continue to diversify, although less diversification will be needed now. Write to a Swiss bank for up-to-date data regarding interest available from the different currencies.

33
Where to Go for Help

YOU MAY FEEL that I'm sending you out into an unfamiliar world in which you'll be all by yourself. No longer will you have your friendly, confident, on-top-of-it-all broker to tell you that everything's going to be all right if you just hang on. Gone will be the benevolent old banker who's seen your family and your father's family through thick and thin.

Now you have to cope with Swiss bank statements (if you can *find* a Swiss bank), and try to make sense out of a silver bullion margin account.

But it really isn't difficult. The principles and mechanics of investments are substantially the same—whatever the medium, wherever the locale.

And there are people in business who make their profits catering to your needs in this new investment world, just as there are stock brokers and bankers. As I've already mentioned, we're seeing a slowly dying economy, rather than one that expires with a sudden crash. This has provided time for suppliers to evolve to solve the problems of people who want to take protective measures. Many of them saw these crises coming years ago, and have established profit-making ways of helping people to cope with them.

In addition, there are protective institutions (like Swiss banks) that have been around a long time—because crises aren't a new phenomenon; for ages, they've been regular occurrences in other parts of the world.

I've been asked often *what* bank I recommend, *which* gold stock I think is best, *where* one should buy silver coins, etc.

I've had personal dealings with many firms, and I've recommended many to my clients. I'm willing to pass these recommendations on to you—hoping you'll accept the condition attached to the recommendations.

A company's relationship with each customer is an individual matter. One customer can be satisfied with a company, another might not be. Many factors enter into such a relationship: the personality of the salesman you deal with, the emphasis the company places upon certain services to the exclusion of others, your own desire for the reassurance of bigness or the wish for more individualized service.

There are companies with whom I get along well, and in whom I have confidence. But a client I refer there may not be as pleased. He may have been looking for something a little different.

In addition, there's no way I can guarantee a company's future business policy, solvency, or attitude.

So the condition I attach to the recommendations is that you'll have to decide for yourself whether you want to do business with any of these companies. But, of course, I've been saying throughout the book that you have to make your own decisions.

This chapter will suggest some places to look for the things you might want. If you find they provide what you want, good. If you don't, I hope that will inspire you to look further; you'll already know more than you had known before you started looking.

SWISS BANKS

There are over 400 banks in Switzerland, so there's no shortage of possibilities. However, many of them would be unsuitable for the purposes covered in this book. On the other hand, there are certainly other appropriate banks, in addition to the few I'm going to mention, so you don't need to stop with this list.

Foreign Commerce Bank
Bellariastrasse 82
8038 Zurich, Switzerland

I've dealt with this bank for many years, with excellent results. It's a medium-sized, newer bank whose managers have made it a practice to cater to the needs of non-Swiss residents, especially Americans. The managers have gone to a great deal of trouble to make their statements and communications intelligible to those of us who don't speak eight languages fluently. Also, they're able to service most of the investments covered in this book.

Bank Leu
Bahnhofstrasse 32
8001 Zurich, Switzerland

This bank could be called medium-sized, considerably smaller than the "big three" but larger than many others. It's an older bank that's well equipped to handle the traditional Swiss services for foreigners.

Each of the "big three" banks is prepared to serve foreign customers by mail. You'll probably find it harder to get individualized service, and that could be important, but that's sometimes offset by slightly better prices.

Union Bank of Switzerland
Bahnhofstrasse 45
8021 Zurich, Switzerland

To me, the Union Bank is the most impressive of the big three. The service is good and the financial statement is particularly attractive—high reserves and a low percentage of unsecured loans. However, you should investigate for yourself which of the three seems best suited for you. The other two are:

Swiss Bank Corporation   Swiss Credit Bank
Aeschenvorstadt 1   Paradeplatz
4002 Basel, Switzerland   8022 Zurich, Switzerland

You can also consider the use of an intermediary to help set up your account. It's helpful to deal with North Americans who understand the Swiss laws and banking procedures, and are continually aware of changes and new alternatives. One company of this type is:

Economic Research Counselors
1760 Marine Drive—Suite 2-12
West Vancouver, British Columbia, Canada
(604) 926-5476

I've known these people for many years and, in fact, worked with them during the late 1960s. They probably agree with 90% of the things I've said in this book. They can advise you of banks that will provide what you're looking for; and they can assist you when you have difficulties of any kind. They operate by mail and by telephone, since most of their clients are scattered all over North America.

The company receives a finder's fee from the banks it deals with, so you pay nothing for the service while still receiving the same terms from the bank that you'd get otherwise. In addition, they offer recommended investments in gold and silver, and charge you only if you profit.

AUSTRIAN BANK

For a bank outside of Switzerland, you can try:

Bankhaus Deak & Co.
Rathausstrasse 20
1011 Wien, Austria (Vienna)

This bank provides the normal current and deposit accounts, as well as margin accounts in silver and gold.

LEBANESE BANKS

Here are two Lebanese banks that accept current or deposit accounts from non-residents, and also offer futures contracts in the Lebanese pound. You can get one-year contracts, minimum $100,000, with 10–20% margin. Write for details.

Chemical Bank
Riad Solh Street
P.O. Box 7286
Beirut, Lebanon

Bank of Nova Scotia
Riad Solh Street
P.O. Box 4446
Beirut, Lebanon

OTHER BANKS

This is only a small list out of many banks that might be just what you're looking for. There are a number of different banking directories that list banks in many nations. You'll probably find at least one of them at the local library. You can write to any bank to see what it offers.

SWISS ATTORNEYS

If you have a large volume of business to be channeled through Switzerland, it's helpful to have a Swiss attorney working for you. An attorney can serve as a mail route, act as a go-between for sensitive matters concerning numbered accounts, and perform many other worthwhile services.

It would defeat the purpose to name attorneys here because one of their assets is their anonymity. However, you can ask any Swiss bank you deal with to recommend one. Also, if you go to Switzerland you can talk to a few yourself and then pick one who would serve your purpose.

SILVER COINS AND GOLD COINS

Many neighborhood coin dealers offer "junk" silver—pre-1965 U.S. silver coins in bulk. And some sell the recommended gold coins. Because the small dealers do this only as a sideline, their prices might be more or less than the norm.

There are several large dealers that have sprung up in the past three years or so offering silver and gold coins exclusively. Some are more knowledgeable than others. They're the best sources for coins; but be sure you get exactly what you ask for and compare prices. To my knowledge, the largest coin dealer in the United States is:

Pacific Coast Coin Exchange
3713 Long Beach Blvd.
Long Beach, California 90807
(213) 595-6311

The company has been in business since 1966 and has an annual volume of around $300 million. I've had numerous dealings with it and have never had reason to complain. They have offices throughout North America and the company can deliver anywhere. It's a good source for silver coins, gold coins, and silver bullion—on a cash or margin basis.

You can also buy gold coins and small gold bars in most metropolitan branches throughout Canada of:

Bank of Nova Scotia
602 W. Hastings St.
Vancouver, British Columbia, Canada
(604) 684-0272

Silver coins can be purchased at the New York Mercantile Exchange through any commodity broker. The prices are usually a little lower than through a coin dealer, but the lower price is offset by the requirement to deal in 10-bag lots and the bother of arranging delivery.

SILVER BULLION

As mentioned in Chapter 26, some Swiss banks will buy silver bullion for you on a cash or margin basis. Others will purchase only through forward or claims contracts. Ask any bank you correspond with how it handles such purchases. Also, Economic Research Counselors (see page 326) deals with banks that handle silver on a cash or margin basis. For delivery in the U.S., try the Pacific Coast Coin Exchange (mentioned on page 328).

GOLD STOCKS

There are brokers who specialize in mining stocks, and a few who specialize in South African gold stocks. I wouldn't rely upon a brokerage house's research service for recommendations; their reasons for selections may not be the same as yours.

If you discuss your objectives in person with a broker who specializes in gold stocks, you can probably decide for yourself whether he's operating on the same premises you are. For several years, I've made my selections with the help of:

John H. Weber
Investors Financial Services
14545 Victory Blvd.—Suite 1416
Van Nuys, California 91401
(213) 873-2277

He has numerous clients in other parts of the country.

INVESTMENT COUNSELORS

An investment counselor who has more faith in gold than in the paper pyramids of Wall Street is a rare find. I've met a few who have appeared quite sound to me. Unfortunately, however, I haven't known them well enough to recommend them. There are a few sources I can direct you to, though, if you feel the need for professional advice or financial management.

American Institute Counselors, Inc.
Great Barrington, Massachusetts 01230

This company is operated by sound money men who relate their understanding of economics to specific investment decisions. The institute offers several plans of its own to cope with a self-destructing dollar. Charges are nominal—usually ⅓% of the assets involved.

Also, you might consult with Economic Research Counselors (see page 326).

One of the best known gold advocates, and probably the most expensive, is:

Franz Pick
21 West Street—Suite 2512
New York, New York 10006
(212) 944-5960

I know of no one who has a greater knowledge of every currency in the world. His current rates are $400 per half-hour, so you'd better be sure your questions are phrased concisely.

As for me, I still do some counseling, but very little. And I, too, am expensive. I'll consult with a client on a one-time basis to help him arrange a long-term investment program he can live with without constant supervision. Such consultations last about four hours, and the fee (in 1973) was $1,750. I won't guarantee to be available for follow-up questions and problems, and I don't provide continuing account supervision. My address is 1126 Crestline Road, West Vancouver, British Columbia, Canada.

INVESTMENT NEWSLETTERS

I haven't subscribed to many investment newsletters, so there may be some good ones I haven't seen. There are several that specialize in gold and silver investments, but they often recommend investments that are much too sophisticated and speculative for the part-time investor; they rely too much on "inside" information; and I suspect they feel their existence wouldn't be justified by recommending long-term investments that need no further comment or attention.

I wouldn't let this stop you, however. Most newsletters will send you a sample copy or two if you write to them. Do so whenever you run across one that appears to lean toward the recommended investments. You may find some good ones I haven't seen—and you may also find good things in some that I *have* seen.

In my opinion, the best services a newsletter can offer are: a continuing presentation of economic understanding to explain the long-term forces at work leading to inevitable conclusions (forces that don't change every time a new issue is published); information that's relevant to the investor and is public knowledge, but may not have come to the reader's attention previously; and alternatives for investing that the investor may not have known of previously.

Two that I've read and appreciated are:

Investment Bulletin
American Institute Counselors
Great Barrington,
Massachusetts 01230
$10 per year

Market Perspective
Economic Research Corp.
Rennweg 42-44
8001 Zurich, Switzerland
$96 per year; $24 for
3 months

PRICE INFORMATION

Many metropolitan daily newspapers carry gold and silver prices, and a few list foreign currency prices. For regular information on most of the recommended investments, the best source is the *Wall Street Journal*. The articles are interesting; the forecasts of no importance. But the *Journal's* best service is the availability of prices and matters of record in one place. You can subscribe by mail (issues normally arrive one day late) for $35 per year.

The Wall Street Journal
22 Cortlandt Street
New York, New York 10007

If you don't want to be flooded with newspapers, you can get much of the price information on a weekly basis by subscribing to *Barron's* for $21 per year.

Barron's
22 Cortlandt Street
New York, New York 10007

If you're interested in South African gold stocks, the *Kaffir Chart Service* is a helpful tool. The twelve-page publication is mailed to you weekly. It lists the daily prices of all important South African gold stocks—together with a chart for the past six months, recent years' highs and lows, and dividend and earnings information.

Kaffir Chart Service
Indicator Chart Service
Palisades Park, New Jersey 07650
$75 per year; $45 for 6 months

SWISS ANNUITIES AND LIFE INSURANCE

The services described in Chapter 30 are available from at least two large life insurance companies:

Geneva Life Insurance Co.   Swiss Life Insurance Co.
Obstgartenstrasse 7   General Guisan Quai 40
8035 Zurich, Switzerland   8022 Zurich, Switzerland

SAFE DEPOSIT COMPANIES

When I mentioned, in the *Devaluation* book, that there are non-banking safe deposit companies in major cities, I was flooded with letters from readers who said they'd never heard of them and couldn't find them. I began to think maybe I'd dreamed up the idea—including the one I deal with. But a look in the Yellow Pages for several cities (under "Safe Deposit Companies") produced quite a number of them. I won't mention those in Chicago—because over a dozen were listed.[1] But here are a few others:

Safe Deposit Co. of New York   Standard Safe Deposit Co.
120 Broadway   25 Broad Street
New York, New York 10005   New York, New York 10004
(212) 227-1326   (212) 422-2570

Missouri Safe Deposit Co.   Fred E. Causey Co.
920 Walnut Street   1806 Layton Street
Kansas City, Missouri 64106   Fort Worth, Texas 76117
(816) 842-5740   (817) 831-1036

[1] In case it occurs to you, these are the only sources listed in the book that were taken from telephone books.

Day & Night Safe Deposit
   Vaults
507 Third Avenue
Seattle, Washington 98104
(206) 622-0722

First Safe Deposit Co.
210 West Seventh Street
Los Angeles, California 90014
(213) 627-1370

RETREAT

There isn't as much ready help available to create a retreat. There are numerous useful books, and there are suppliers of appropriate individual products and services. But very few of them are designed specifically for retreat purposes. So you have to collect the information and supplies from numerous different sources. I know of one consultant who makes recommendations for acquiring land, provides checklists of things to get, and offers help in solving technical problems. He is:

Don Stephens
P.O. Box 141
Glendale, California 91209

In addition, here are three companies that provide bulk food supplies for long-term storage. Each of them has created packages of food appropriate for retreat purposes, and each ships anywhere in North America.

Nevada Coin Exchange
P.O. Box 485
Carson City, Nevada 89701
(702) 882-2483
(also sells gold coins)

FSP Foods
P.O. Box 6128
Albany, California 94706
(415) 524-8131

Sam Andy
P.O. Box 1042
Chula Vista, California 92012
(714) 428-1861

BOOKS

There are a number of books than can enhance your knowledge of the various subjects covered by this book. They're listed in the Recommended Reading section in the Appendix.

THERE ARE MORE

The individuals and companies listed in this chapter are only a few of many potential suppliers and advisers. You may have noticed that many of the companies mentioned are in California. That's because most of my investment experience was there. So there are undoubtedly many other useful sources in other parts of North America.

The more you think about your investments, and the more you inquire about them, the more you'll know just what (and whom) you're looking for, and you'll be able to judge how appropriate any supplier is for you.

Most important, *you* have to decide what you're going to do. Don't ask a salesman or broker what to do. Tell him what you want, and he can tell you what he can do to facilitate that. He can inform you of alternatives you may not have known about before.

If you ask a coin dealer what you should do, he may tell you that you should have 80% of your assets in coins, and perhaps the other 20% in stocks. A stock broker might see it just the opposite way. It isn't only self-interest that prompts such reactions; from his vantage point, it may make the most sense. But he isn't you. And that's why you have to decide.

But as you can see, there are plenty of people to help you —once you've decided what you want to do.

34
When to Sell

A VALUABLE INVESTMENT RULE says: Never make an investment without deciding in advance at what point you'll sell it.

Most investors reconsider such questions every day because they didn't have a firm potential in mind when they bought. As a result, there's no precise standard by which to judge a proper selling point, and they reopen the question each day. Usually in such cases, the investment is finally sold because of an emotional reaction to a news item or downside fluctuation, or because of impatience.

If you choose an investment because of sound economic potential, you should be able to tell when that potential is reached. If you sell it before it reaches its full potential, it will be because you had set a time limit for that potential and the time is up.

Before then, you won't sell just because of a temporary downward fluctuation. You'll sell only if there are *significant* changes in conditions that alter the potential.

WHEN?

When should you sell the investments recommended in this book? The basic answer is: When the monetary crises have ended. No one can tell you *when* that will be. But as long as the crises continue, the investments will continue to appreciate; and until they end, these investments will be the surest means of protection.

There will be many calm periods in the midst of the turmoil. Agreements will be reached between governments, new "stable" monetary systems will be created, crises will occur, and grand solutions will be enacted for them.

But there are several things that must happen before the crises will truly end. Those requirements were listed in Chapter 16. Any time it appears that the worst is over, reread that chapter to see how many of the requirements for long-term tranquility have come to pass.

For example, at some time the prevailing opinion may be that the dollar is finally at a stable level, or even that it's undervalued. But if the dollar isn't convertible to gold, it will continue to depreciate in terms of gold, gold-backed currencies, and silver.

No government solution can change the fact that human beings only produce and exchange when it will lead ultimately to something they want.

In American history, there have been banking crises, panics, depressions, even some localized runaway inflations. Usually after each crisis, long-term tranquility ensued. That was because the crisis occurred when conditions called for it. Today, however, the U.S. government has developed ways of prolonging inflationary conditions far beyond the former crisis points. As a result, the final crises are bound to be far more painful and prolonged —and more extreme measures will be necessary to return to normality. We may see a complete washout of the system, instead of a minor cleansing.

During former crises, for example, the price of gold didn't necessarily rise to a level that allowed for all the previous inflation. This was partly because deflations were chosen as a way of avoiding bad consequences. Now, however, the price of gold may have to rise to a level equivalent to all the past currency depreciation.

POTENTIALS

Because no one can know exactly when the crises will end, no one can know how high in price the recommended investments can go. The potentials I've quoted in this book are estimates based wholly upon the present state of affairs. The longer the crises are allowed to continue unsolved, the higher the potentials will have to be.

Because you may feel cheated otherwise, I'll offer some guesses for these potentials. But don't consider these to be predictions; no one can make predictions when there are so many variables involved. I won't be shocked if these guesses don't prove to be correct.

Gold: $200 per ounce by the end of 1974; $300 sometime during 1974 or 1975; $500–$1,000 by the end of 1978.

Silver: $4 per ounce by the end of 1974; $6 by the end of 1975; $10–$15 by 1978.

Swiss francs: $.50 by the end of 1974; $1.00–$2.00 sometime between 1975 and 1978.

Other recommended foreign currencies: increases of 50% from mid-1973 levels by the end of 1974; increases of 100% by the end of 1975; approximate ultimate potentials by 1978.

Gold British sovereigns: $60 each by the end of 1974; $85 sometime during 1974 or 1975; $125–$250 by the end of 1978.

Gold Mexican 50-peso pieces: $275 by the end of 1974; $400 sometime during 1974 or 1975; $700–$1,400 by the end of 1978.

U.S. silver coins: $3,000 per bag by the end of 1974; $4,500 by the end of 1975; $7,500–$12,000 by 1978.

The guesses most likely to prove wrong are the short-term potentials. The longer the period of time involved, the more likely that the *broad* changes will occur in somewhat predictable ways. In the short term, any combination of events could delay the natural processes.

Also, these estimates are based upon *present* conditions. If the government continues to aggravate the situation, each of the prices could go much higher. And if there's a runaway inflation, the prices in dollars will be so high as to be meaningless. But the investments themselves will protect your wealth throughout the chaos.

CONTRARY ACTIONS AND OPINIONS

Much may be done to try to hold these prices down. Governments may dump gold on the market in a foolish, desperate attempt to make their currencies look better. But that will simply make the ultimate value of gold that much greater.

And those governments with strong currencies may fight to keep their currencies from rising too much against the dollar. However, that cannot go on indefinitely. Either the dollar will undergo a gigantic devaluation or the currencies will eventually be set entirely free to explode upwards or the governments involved will ruin their own currencies.

Another possibility is that all the governments will devalue their currencies by substantial amounts—to make the "official" gold price more realistic when compared with the actual free market price. Don't be shocked if that happens. Most likely, the stronger currencies will be devalued by amounts proportionately less than the U.S. dollar. That will leave the foreign currency prices (when measured against dollars) unaltered or higher than they were prior to the devaluations.

Keep the ultimate potentials in mind, and don't be swayed until you have positive evidence that the foreign currencies have been debased so significantly that the picture has been radically altered. As long as the strong currencies have at least twice the gold-backing percentage of the dollar, they will appreciate upward.

As for silver, there are bound to be reports in the future that it's priced too high and will have to come down. And, of course, there *will* be downward fluctuations—as there are with any investment.

But there's a sure way to know when the price of silver has reached its full economic potential. When the production of silver and the consumption of silver are approximately equal, a somewhat stable price will have been reached. *Not* when you hear that consumption is dropping (it's *bound* to), and not when you hear that production is increasing (it probably will). Only when consumption has dropped to the rate of production will the price level off.

If you're investing for the long term, don't be dismayed by fluctuations in the recommended investments—or by news reports or predictions.

FUTURE CHANGES IN INVESTMENTS

As conditions worsen, your concern for future economic freedom and safety will be greater. The first investments to sell will be those that are more vulnerable to governmental intervention. These might include gold stocks, margin accounts in the United States, and futures contracts.

The strong foreign currencies are relatively invulnerable for the next few years. But if the governments continue to play games with their currencies, they may become vulnerable after a few years. So consider converting currencies to gold and silver stored in a Swiss bank after a couple of years or so.

Also, after profits have been made, convert some of your holdings to silver coins and gold coins stored where you have access to them.

Keep in a Swiss bank those long-term assets that you can ignore until a new economic world opens up. And keep close to you those assets you'll need for short-term economic survival and profit.

As prices go up, sell off parts of a coin margin account and use the proceeds to pay down the loan. When you're finally on a cash basis, take delivery of the coins and keep them with you.

These alterations and any need you might have for spending

money are the only reasons to sell investments—until the crises are over.

If there's a runaway inflation, don't sell any of your investments for dollars. Make conversions into foreign currencies or gold only. You probably won't need to sell anything *during* a runaway inflation—except that you might use silver coins as spending money.

During the runaway inflation, don't try to bring home anything you have in Switzerland. If you're worried about the runaway inflation spreading to other currencies, instruct the bank to convert any currency holdings to gold to be kept in a custodial account. But don't try to bring any assets home until order is reestablished and a sound currency is available—or until you've moved to a country in which those conditions exist.

Overall, you're most likely to go wrong selling gold and silver too soon rather than too late.

And, returning to the present, you're more likely to be sorry if you buy too late than if you buy too soon.

35

If You Think
You're Too Late

BY THIS TIME, I hope you're convinced that you're not too late to protect yourself and to use the opportunities at hand. Even if you're reading this book many years after I wrote it, there are still things you can do to help yourself—provided you understand the economic causes of the crises and you turn to the investments that offer actual protection.

But in case you haven't read the preceding thirty-four chapters (maybe you're reading this chapter in a bookstore trying to decide whether to buy the book), I suggest you look at Chapter 16 and read the list of events that must occur before the crises will end. Anything less than those requirements will provide only a temporary interlude between crises. So if the required solutions haven't been effected, you're not too late.

You may wish you'd acted three years ago, but that's pointless. There's much that's yet to come. You should feel pained only if you knew what was coming and failed to do anything about it.

If you wonder if it's too late to act, ask yourself:

1. Has gold reached $300 per ounce yet? If not, it certainly has quite a ways to go upward—well past $300.

2. Has silver reached $7 per ounce? If not, there's profit to be made—for it should go beyond $10.

3. Is the Swiss franc at $1? If not, it will probably at least double from wherever it is now.

4. Is there still a U.S. currency operative? If so, you can trade for silver coins and gold coins to protect yourself against the possibility that there might not be a useful currency in the future.

LATE ACTIONS

No matter how late you may feel you are, there's always something you can do to save yourself. Here are some suggestions that should be appropriate *whenever* you read this:

1. Trade what you have—paper money, real estate, other properties—for silver coins. They'll take you a long way.

2. Send some money out of the country. If it's still legal to do so, it will be easy enough. If it's no longer legal, all the more reason you may want to take the risk. Take some money to Canada or Mexico, and send it from there to a Swiss bank. Or find someone who will make a black market transfer. Or put the wealth into silver and gold coins.

3. If you still have a good deal of wealth, trade something for gold coins. Store them someplace where they'll hold your wealth until better days.

4. Find a retreat somewhere and provide it with the means to see you through the worst of the crises.

5. If the economy is still in one piece, do something now about your employment situation. Find a way of making a living that isn't vulnerable to the problems the government has created.

6. If the economy isn't still in one piece, if times are very bad and so is your condition, find somebody who needs a service you can provide—not necessarily the service you've always provided in the past.

If you're concerned enough about the problem to read a book like this, you're probably a little ways ahead of most everyone else. That may mean that most people haven't yet realized the long-term significance of gold and silver. Perhaps you can trade something you have for gold or silver coins.

Most likely, you're reading this book early in the period of crises—in which case most of the recommendations summarized in Chapter 31 are still available to you. If any of those investments have become impossible or illegal, you can undoubtedly use other recommendations instead.

Above all, don't waste time and attention wishing you'd acted sooner. The past is gone and won't be coming this way again.

And don't wish you'd been born in a happier time. What we're going through is nothing new. The last generation faced the 1930s; and now we must face the 1970s. There have always been governments; there have always been economic revolutions.

But with the knowledge and the determination to survive —and survive well—you're equipped to face whatever the 1970s have to offer.

36

How to Raise Cash

PERHAPS YOU FEEL that you don't have enough money to give you the kind of protection you think necessary. Or maybe you just wish you could take greater advantage of the opportunities of the future.

Either way, you probably have more resources than you realize. The question, however, is: *Is it really important to you?*

Plenty of opportunities present themselves to an individual in a lifetime. Most of the opportunities are noticed and then forgotten because they really aren't that important to him. There are other things he'd rather do with his resources.

If you aren't convinced that the events described in this book will come to pass, the amount of cash you have doesn't matter; you won't act on the suggestions anyway.

But if you are convinced, *whatever* you have to work with will provide a big step forward. You'll do *something*—and as indicated in Chapter 32, even $500 can accomplish a lot.

Most important, once you're started you'll be motivated to increase your positions in the recommended investments. You'll find ways to make that possible.

You may think you're short of cash, but you're probably not devoid of wealth. The issue involved is whether or not you're motivated enough to turn some of your wealth into buying power.

There's no magic way to turn potatoes into gold bricks; but once you're motivated you'll think of countless ways to scrape up more cash to increase your stake. Just to trigger your imagination, here are some things you might consider:

1. Sell things you no longer use. Maybe at first glance you

can't spot more than $100 market value in what you have to sell. But if you only have $500 to start with, $100 is a 20% improvement.

2. Sell things you like owning, but which you aren't using very much right now—a second car, a vacation home, paintings that no longer excite you, unneeded stereo equipment or furniture, your private box at the stadium, anything you don't use regularly. There will be plenty of time to enjoy those things later—after you've established a more reassuring security for yourself.

3. Of course, sell any traditional investments that don't fit the requirements of the future—even if they're presently worth less than you paid for them.

4. Consider selling your home; and find a suitable house to rent. If you've been counting your home as part of your financial empire, you may be in for a disappointment anyway. If you really can sell your house today for what you think it's worth, this would be a good time to do it. Turn the equity into the recommended investments and you may be able to buy a much better home in a few years.

5. Borrow from your company retirement fund or credit union—if you can repay the debt from working income. Don't borrow with the intention of repaying from profits. Use the proceeds for the safer investments—in case you have to liquidate the investment later to repay the debt.

6. Consider taking extra jobs for a while—placing all proceeds earned into a special investment fund as soon as you receive them.

7. If you have money coming in the future that you wish you could use now, consider buying a Swiss franc futures contract equivalent to the amount involved. That will at least protect the purchasing power of the money until you receive it.

It's amazing how many more opportunities you can see after you start the effort. I once wallowed in debt for years because I couldn't see how any special effort would make a dent in the total. But once I finally made up my mind to reduce the debt by *any* amount I could divert to it, a strange thing happened to me—I became excited about the task.

I kept a running balance of the total debt and I felt a special thrill from knocking even $100 off the total—even though the debt was many thousands of dollars.

Every time I reduced the total I'd rack my brain to think of a way to reduce it by another $100 or $200. And when the total was appreciably smaller, my motivation accelerated. From then on I was obsessed with the fun of seeing my debts diminish.

The debt was completely liquidated in about one quarter of the time I'd expected. I even felt a little let down when it happened, I'd enjoyed it so much. So I kept up the momentum a while longer and added extra funds to my investments.

You might do the same thing. Set a target for yourself—even if it's only $5,000. Steal money from your own budget, delay purchases, set aside other long-term projects. Put every dollar you can into a special fund and keep a running total of your progress. Change the total every time you make a contribution to the fund—even if it's only $20. See if that doesn't help your enthusiasm—and your imagination.

If you're thinking you're different from me, you're probably right. You're most likely more energetic than I am, more ambitious, harder working. You probably don't spend half your day lying on the couch reading or listening to music. You probably have a family and responsibilities that motivate you to work harder.

So you'll probably accomplish more sooner.

I can't tell you where the cash is coming from. But I can assure you it's there someplace you haven't been noticing.

37
Other Considerations

THERE ARE A FEW other miscellaneous matters that should be covered before we close this part.

PRIVACY

I always argue with myself over the word that should be used—*privacy* or *secrecy*. The first sounds honorable, the second mischievous. But whichever word is used, there's no reason why an individual shouldn't want to keep his affairs to himself—especially since he doesn't know what the government will decide to confiscate tomorrow.

The more private you keep your affairs today, the more latitude you'll have in making decisions tomorrow. You can't know exactly what the government will decide to do in the future. Privacy preserves the opportunity to decide *later* whether or not you'll go along with a new government edict. If you forsake that privacy now, you'll have no choice but to go along later.

The really useful and imaginative ways to protect your privacy are those you think of yourself. And those quiet ideas, unpublicized, will probably remain useful permanently. But the popular ideas that are used too widely become vulnerable to government crackdowns.[1]

[1] That's one reason why I've never participated in organized tax protests and tax evasion schemes.

348

However, there are a few general guidelines that can be offered here without fear of compromising them. Some have been covered earlier and are here only as reminders.

1. You can purchase coins from a coin dealer on a cash basis without using a check or your name.

2. You can ask the Swiss bank to hold all correspondence so that you receive no mail from it. Normally, this isn't necessary because, as far as I've seen, a Swiss bank doesn't put its name on an envelope—only a return address.

3. You can arrange with an individual in Switzerland to handle your affairs for you. Instruct the bank to send your correspondence to him, and he can get in touch with you only if there's a problem.

4. As of July 1, 1972, Americans are required by law to report to the government all transmissions overseas of over $5,000. As of 1973, you can avoid this requirement by mailing $5,000 bank money orders in separate envelopes on separate days—as many times as necessary to transmit an amount over $5,000.

5. You can transfer money overseas by taking a short vacation to Canada or Mexico. Once there, you can purchase a bank money order and mail your remittance, or you can wire the money from any bank. As of 1973, banks in those countries are not required to keep microfilmed records, as American banks are. And a large sum of money would have to be involved for the U.S. government to put pressure on the Canadian government to uncover such a transaction. Understand, however, that you break United States law if you take over $5,000 across the border without reporting it. And understand, too, that there's no law preventing you from taking money out of the U.S. (as of September 1973)—only a law requiring you to report such transfers of over $5,000.

6. You can buy a bank money order in the United States without giving your name. Once you have established a Swiss bank account, you can mail a money order to the bank with only your account number attached to it.

7. You can open a numbered account by going to the Swiss

bank in person, but it probably isn't necessary unless a great deal of money is involved.

It's up to you to decide whether or not to do any of these things, of course. Don't let anyone tell you that you have to be secretive or that you have to break laws. On the other hand, don't let anyone tell you that your country comes first and that you must obey the law. Don't confuse your country with the government; they're not the same. So find out what your legal position is, and then do what your own rules and emotions permit.

I'm often asked what an individual should do about the question on income tax returns asking if you have any foreign bank accounts. Obviously, I can't answer for anyone else. You have to do what will make you feel the least discomfort. Although it is illegal to make a false statement on your income tax return, I know individuals who answer it truthfully, others who answer it falsely, and others who don't answer it at all. I report my foreign bank accounts; but then I live outside the United States, so I'm not so vulnerable to future laws.

TAX CONSIDERATIONS

The recommended investments have the same income tax considerations as normal investments. If you hold one of them over six months, it becomes a long-term capital gain—taxable at lower rates. No investment is taxable until you sell it.

Interest on a margin account can be deducted as a personal expense in the year that you pay it, no matter when you eventually sell the investment. Other expenses involving the investment aren't usually deductible until the investment is sold. At that time, you can deduct anything facilitating the investment —storage fees, commissions, etc. Any year in which you report investments on your tax return, you can deduct other items that relate to your investment future—such as the purchase of this book.

In other words, there's no difference between these investments and the traditional ones as far as income tax liabilities are concerned.

RUMORS

Once you've made your investments invulnerable to dollar decay, you'll be able to relax, and that means you'll be able to ignore the many rumors that circulate. For when you've already transferred a large part of your wealth outside the country, and you no longer have holdings in dollars, 90% of the rumors will be of no consequence to you.

A typical rumor circulating these days suggests that the government has already printed new paper money to replace the present greenbacks. The new money is said to be of many colors (except green) and will be good only in the United States. Foreigners will continue to receive greenbacks which will be ultimately redeemable for gold. But the colored money won't be redeemable, and so it will have no value outside the United States. Thus, people will be prevented from sending dollars abroad.

I have no idea whether the rumor is true. But I do know that it won't affect you if you use the recommended investments. For your assets won't be in dollars; they'll be in Swiss francs, gold, or silver. What difference will it make if dollars are restricted?

In the same way, other such threats will be relatively insignificant once you've made yourself invulnerable to the problems of the dollar. And so if you hear a "terrifying" rumor, think it through. Will it really affect *you*?

OPINIONS

And lastly, don't be distressed by what someone else thinks the future will bring—no matter who he may be or how "important" he's considered to be. Investment markets exist largely *because* of differences of opinion; without differences, there'd be no one from whom you could buy what you want.

The next time you hear a statement or a forecast that shakes your faith, look over these statements that were made by people "in the know" during 1970 and 1971. How right were they?

Mexican Finance Minister Hugo Margain, December 30, 1970: "In my lexicon the word devaluation does not exist. . . . The dollar, the pound, the mark, the Mexican peso are among the twelve hard currencies of the world."[2] (The Mexican peso was devalued by 7.89% on December 22, 1971. Hugo Margain must have changed his lexicon; he was still Finance Minister.)

Los Angeles *Times*, May 4, 1971: "Chairman Paul W. McCracken of the Council of Economic Advisers said there are 'heartening signs that the worst may be over' where outflows of capital are concerned." Los Angeles *Times*, May 5, 1971: "The U.S. dollar's market value dropped abruptly Tuesday in frantic speculative trading on the world's currency exchanges."

Israel's Finance Minister Pinhas Sapir, August 18, 1971: "I have no intention of proposing a devaluation of the Israeli pound."[3] (The Israeli pound was devalued by 20% four days later.)

Worden's Weekly Reports, "Sophisticated Computer Studies for Aggressive Investors," May 8, 1971: "The dollar is 'toppling, floundering, sinking, bowing, drowning, being humiliated, yielding, gasping, and biting the dust.' It is under 'attack!' They're going to revalue the mark or somebody's franc 'against' the exhausted and defeated dollar. This is the sort of thing you've been reading this week—all stuff and nonsense. The dollar is *not* under attack. *The dollar is the attacker* . . . somebody—one wonders who and how—some mastermind in Washington, D.C., has engineered (and is close to pulling off) the most subtle and sophisticated monetary power play in history. . . . In any event, and it is important to understand this, as far as the international

[2] *The News*, Mexico City, December 31, 1970.
[3] Los Angeles *Times*, August 24, 1971.

monetary situation is concerned things have been going rather well for the United States."

Economist and syndicated investment writer Eliot Janeway, December 10, 1970: "The only thing that's holding gold where it is, is the guarantee by the U.S. government, which I think is an ill-advised guarantee, to pay $35 for it. Gold is a snare and a delusion. . . . The only run to do with the dollar is not any fancied run out of the dollar, it's a run into the dollar. The dollar is strong. . . . The advice to take money out of American banks and put it into Swiss banks is irresponsible—irresponsible as well as impractical."[4]

Chicago *Tribune,* September 6, 1971: "A White House spokesman, however, has stated: 'It is not our intention to change the price of gold either up or down.'" (The devaluation occurred three months later.)

Richard M. Nixon (announcement suspending the convertibility of the dollar, August 15, 1971): "Let me lay to rest the bugaboo of what is called devaluation. If you want to buy a foreign car or take a trip abroad, market conditions may cause your dollar to buy slightly less. But if you are among the overwhelming majority of Americans who buy American-made products in America, your dollar will be worth just as much tomorrow as it is today. The effect of this action, in other words, will be to stabilize the dollar."

And finally, one last reminder . . .

"The country can regard the present with satisfaction and anticipate the future with optimism."

—Calvin Coolidge
Final Message to Congress
December 4, 1928.

[4] Bob Grant radio program, WMCA, New York, December 10, 1970.

Epilogue

38

Your Future

WE'VE COVERED A GREAT DEAL in this book—economic principles, monetary systems, economic history, investment principles, critiques of investment alternatives, mechanical information, and a little advice. I can't blame you if you consider it a lot to digest.

However, much of the detail has been for purposes of illustration, precision, and clarification. Perhaps the entire book can be summarized as follows:

1. Human beings produce and exchange only when they believe it will lead ultimately to something they want.

2. The General Market is the summation of the billions of individual desires and plans. It is the visible expression of what people want.

3. Money is a commodity you are willing to accept in exchange because you're confident you can trade it for something you want at a later time.

4. The people of the world, in their daily decisions, have found gold to be the most useful money commodity—for a number of understandable reasons.

5. Currencies originate as paper receipts for gold.

6. Governments try to overrule the General Market because they want resources to be used in ways other than people want to use them. And the government finances its projects substantially through inflation—the printing of paper money receipts for which there's no gold in reserve.

7. Because the paper receipts lose the value they once had, individuals turn to gold for value and protection.

8. The government declares war upon gold (the "barbarous relic"), but the war is actually between the government and the people. The government is attempting, through its policies, to prevent people from acting in their own self-interests.

9. Thus, whenever the government acts, the General Market reacts—and always in a way opposite to the intention of the government's program.

10. Because the General Market expresses the self-interest of each individual within it, it cannot be repressed indefinitely. It will always seek to reassert itself.

11. When the General Market finally succeeds in overcoming the government, a depression results—an attempt to redirect the resources to uses chosen by the people.

12. The government, in the cloak of benevolence, intervenes to stop the depression, but succeeds only in prolonging it.

13. In any time of crisis, expect the government to be unsuccessful in its objectives. Never bet on it to succeed.

14. Look for protection to those things that have value in themselves—that is, they have been chosen by the General Market, not by artificial governmental stimulation. To preserve wealth, the easiest and safest to hold are gold, silver, and gold-backed currencies. There are always ways to obtain and hold these valuable commodities. An investment program can be built upon them.

15. The ultimate standard by which you should judge your protection program is: *Does it eliminate the discomfort?* And that's why you must select the program for yourself.

I freely acknowledge that there's been a good deal of repetition involved in presenting these points. The repetition was necessary because there's no way for you to ask questions if a given point isn't clear enough. Where you've noticed repetition, consider it the price you pay for detail and clarity elsewhere.

MY OPINIONS

There's no way I can tell you what's going to happen three months from now. There's no way I can know how the future will be altered by governmental policies yet to come. I can only present the principles that must govern the reactions of the General Market to those future policies. So don't consider this book to be a timetable for the future; it isn't. It's an attempt to help you understand the nature of the crisis and to acquaint you with the numerous alternatives available with which you can cope with the crisis.

But I can't possibly foresee it all. In the book, *How You Can Profit from the Coming Devaluation,* I assumed things that I don't assume now. For example, I expected the dollar to fall through one large devaluation. Instead it has fallen through devaluations, upvaluations, and a free float downward.

Also, I expected the depression to be ushered in with one gigantic crash. Instead, it is entering slowly and steadily, day by day, as inflation and shortages and the falling dollar make it harder and harder for most people to maintain their standards of living.

And too, as recently as January 1973, I forecast a price of $130–$140 for gold over a five-year period—and perhaps $200 in ten years. Obviously, I was short-sighted.

These errors haven't affected the recommended investments adversely. But they illustrate the fact that I'm learning as I go along. I can't postpone writing this book until my knowledge and understanding are total—for that day will never come. But three or four years from now, there may be statements I've made that I'd like to erase.

So don't consider this book to be either your last word or my last word on the subject. Learn in every way you can—as I'm doing. We each have enough knowledge already to take the necessary steps for survival, protection, and profit. But new opportunities will arise that I can't even imagine today.

TIMING

Don't wait for those opportunities before acting, however. The future may be unpredictable, but there are certain expectations that have overwhelming probabilities. Gold and silver will triumph; gold-backed currencies will be worth far more than unbacked paper promises. Those principles can be acted upon now—and *should* be acted upon now, while the opportunities to do so still exist.

What will happen to the recommended investments during the next few months is relatively unimportant. What is bound to happen to them over the next few years *is* important. If you wait a few months, hoping for a better time to buy, you may find only a worse time to buy—or no way to buy.

Even if the prices of the recommended investments go downward after you buy them your purchase will be vindicated soon enough. When the *Devaluation* book was published in 1970, the price of silver was in the $1.50–$1.70 range. Those who took the advice bought immediately. Others may have waited for the price to go down.

The price dropped to $1.29 in 1971, and then began a long rise upward—to the $2.50–$3.00 range as I wrote this. The drop to $1.29 may have convinced those who waited that they should *never* buy silver. But those who bought "too soon" now hold silver with a market price that's 50–100% higher than the price they paid for it. Had they known for sure that the price would drop to $1.29, would it have made that much difference to wait?

When you've decided that the investment provides the right long-term protection or opportunity for you, that's the time to buy. Not before then—and certainly not after then.

BE SELFISH

If it's ever true that you should put the government's interests ahead of your own, it certainly isn't true today. If you were to donate everything you own to the government, it wouldn't solve a single problem. And if everyone in the nation did the same thing, it would only serve to make the nation impoverished. If the government has used your money so unwisely in the past, subsidizing unpopular causes and foreign governments, why should it be trusted with your wealth in the future?

If there's ever to be a time to put yourself first, that time has arrived. You can't afford to be promiscuous with your wealth; you need it far too much for the protection of your own future. For without a future, what good are you to anyone?

The governments have created their own problems. They'll have to deal with those problems themselves. Unfortunately, governments have no resources except those they take from you—and that's where they'll turn as the problems become more critical. Your duty now is to prevent further confiscation of your wealth.

Unfortunately, too, it appears that this time the government has gone so far that normality may never return. Whatever the future holds, it will be quite different from what we've known in the past.

Whether there will even be a U.S. government ten years from now is difficult to know. Certainly, the present system is dying from an overdose of government. How long it will be before it expires completely is another unknown. But this time the seeds of destruction have been planted and the signs are unmistakable.

And as the U.S. government goes under, so will the many governments it has supported. The great economic revivals of Europe and Japan have been financed with resources wrenched from the American taxpayers. The so-called benevolence of the American people toward their former enemies has never existed.

In the first place, the money wasn't given voluntarily by the American people. And in the second, the "aid" will have caused more destruction in Europe than the havoc caused by a thousand nuclear bombs. The U.S. government has provided the socialist governments of Western Europe with the means to create gigantic distortions in the marketplaces of their countries.

Unfortunately, the lesson hasn't been learned—in Europe or the United States—that governments can't create prosperity or security. And so most people continue to put their faith in the insecure institutions of governments—and suffer when their faith proves to be unfounded.

OPPORTUNITY

The future isn't bleak, however. For the fall of a valueless currency or a destructive government *can* be the prelude to a better era—a period in which prosperity is measured by satisfaction of consumer desires instead of government-subsidized "housing starts." It's just possible—if only barely—that many people in the next generation might assert their desires for freedom more strongly and say to the government, "Leave us alone." But, frankly, that's only a hope.

Whatever the future, however, it doesn't have to be grim. Every crisis is a time of opportunity. For every opportunity is only the recognition of someone's need. If no one needed anything, there would be no opportunities. And a time of crisis is a time of great need.

Someday, someone is going to need your wealth. If you've protected it, it will be a valuable, marketable asset. The gold you will have hoarded in such miserly fashion will be needed to help rebuild an economy and establish a useful means of exchange. Fortunately, you *will* have hoarded; otherwise, it might not be available to the community that needs it. You'll sell it, and you'll be rewarded well for the service you've performed.

It's hard for many people to realize that you can be benevolent only when you aren't threatened. Your good intentions toward others are meaningless unless you've created the wealth that can carry out those intentions. And you can't be protective toward others until you've created the protection to be protective with. As long as you're threatened by the crises, you can't be benevolent toward anyone.

So don't worry about others until you've taken care of yourself.

THE FUTURE

Whatever may happen, there will still be beauty and happiness in the world. There will still be wonderful things to see, beautiful things to enjoy, people to love, exciting ideas to explore, friendships to enhance your life, music to tug at your emotions, things to do, and places to go.

I want you to survive and prosper so that you can enjoy those things. I want you to trust yourself above all others. I want you to know that you can take care of yourself and those you love—no matter what happens.

That and the desire to take care of myself have prompted me to write this book. I hope that it's been useful to you.

And I hope that it will prove to be profitable to you beyond any expectations you have now.

September 9, 1973
West Vancouver, British Columbia

Appendix

Acknowledgments

I'LL ALWAYS BE GRATEFUL to Jerome F. Smith for helping me to realize that if the government is wrong in what it's
doing, there must be a way for an individual to profit by betting
against it. That simple observation converted my ideas from
intellectual curiosity to profit-making applications. The immense
profits made by myself and by readers of my *Devaluation* book
are due, in large part, to Jerome Smith's trailblazing.

I'm also grateful to Henry Hazlitt, Murray Rothbard, Alvin
Lowi, Andrew Galambos, and Robert LeFevre for helping to
educate me (some of them did so without knowing it). And to
Jack Williams and the Swiss bankers who have so patiently
taught me the mechanics of the recommended investments.

The editorial help given by Donna Rasnake and Mark
Corske was, as always, very useful.

And I'm certainly glad that Franz Pick has accumulated
such a vast store of knowledge regarding currencies; I relied
heavily upon the statistics he gathered as I evaluated the major
currencies.

And I'm especially grateful to Ingrid for tolerating me
while my attention was diverted to this book for two intense
months.

Obviously, these individuals have their own ideas, and I
have mine. They aren't responsible for anything said in this
book—right or wrong.

Glossary of Monetary and Investment Terms

American Depository Receipt (ADR): A receipt for shares of stock in a foreign company.

Bag: In silver coins, the basic unit of trading—composed of 10,000 dimes or 4,000 quarters ($1,000 face value).

Balance of payments: A nation's exports less its imports.

Banknote: A unit of currency in paper form, as opposed to a bank deposit.

Barter: The trading of one commodity for another; in modern usage, any exchange that doesn't involve the use of money or money substitutes.

Black market: A free market operating without the government's legal sanction.

Bullion: Refined bars of gold or silver.

Carrying charges: In futures trading, the difference between the spot price and a future price—usually equal to the costs of interest and storage for the period of time involved.

Cash: (1) Money substitutes in paper form. (2) The absence of credit.

Central bank: An agency created by a government to issue its currency and to supervise the nation's banking system.

Certificate of deposit: A deposit with a fixed time period and a fixed rate of interest.

Coin: Real money (gold or silver) transformed into a recognizable shape and weight in order to facilitate exchange.

Conservative: Involving a minimum of risk.

Consumption: The use or enjoyment of a product or service as an end in itself, rather than as a means to a further end.

Convertibility: The ability to receive gold in exchange for cur-

369

rency, at a stated rate of exchange, from the agency that issued the currency.

Currency: Correctly, receipts for real money in storage; in modern practice, any money substitutes in use—even if not backed by real money (synonymous with *paper money*).

Current account: A bank deposit that can be withdrawn by the depositor at any time.

Deflation: A decrease in the amount of money substitutes that have been issued in excess of the real money in storage. (See also *inflation.*)

Demand deposit: A bank deposit that can be withdrawn by the depositor at any time.

Deposit account: A bank deposit in which interest is earned and withdrawals are limited.

Depression: A period in which the General Market attempts to cleanse itself of the misguided uses of resources that have been encouraged by government intervention, and to redirect its resources to productive activity more desired by consumers. During that period, most people within the General Market find it impossible to maintain their previous standards of living—either because of unemployment, lower wage rates, higher prices, or shortages.

Devaluation: Repudiation of the government's promise to redeem its money substitutes at the stated rate of exchange.

Dirty float: A period during which the government intervenes in the foreign exchange market while claiming that it isn't. (See also *floating exchange rates* and *fixed exchange rates.*)

Downside risk: The possible depth to which the price of an investment can drop.

Economics: The study that seeks to allocate limited resources in ways that will provide maximum happiness (whether on a personal, commercial, national, or international scale); the art of making decisions.

Entrepreneur: An individual who forecasts future demand for a product or service and arranges a business enterprise to respond to that demand.

Equity: The value of an investment after deduction of all claims against it—loan amount, interest, commissions, and any other fees.

Eurocurrency: Currency that is circulating outside the nation where it was issued.

Exchange controls: Governmental regulations limiting or prohibiting the exporting or importing of currencies.

Exchange rate: The price of a currency as expressed in units of another currency. (Synonymous with *foreign exchange rate.*)

Face value: The legal tender value of a coin, token, or banknote.

Fiat money: Paper money without gold or silver to back it, enforced as legal tender by governmental fiat or edict.

Fineness: The extent to which bullion is pure gold or silver, expressed as a decimal of the total gross weight involved. For example, gold bullion of .995 fineness means that 99.5% of the total weight is pure gold.

Fixed deposit account: A bank deposit for a fixed period of time.

Fixed exchange rates: Currency exchange rates that are prevented from fluctuating by governmental purchases and sales of the currencies involved.

Floating exchange rates: Currency exchange rates that fluctuate freely because governments are *not* stabilizing the rates through purchases and sales. (See *dirty float* and *fixed exchange rates.*)

Fluctuation: A change in price—upward or downward.

Foreign exchange rate: The price of a currency as expressed in units of another currency. (Synonymous with *exchange rate.*)

Fractional reserve banking: A banking system in which money that is payable upon demand to depositors is lent to others by the bank; in other words, a system in which the bank doesn't maintain 100% reserves against demand deposits.

Free market: A market free of governmental intervention.

Futures contract: A contract for delivery of a commodity or currency in the future at a price determined in the present.

General Market: The sum of all individual markets; the totality of all individual desires compared with the totality of products and services available.

General price level: A theoretical average of all prices in the marketplace; the total money supply divided by the available products and services.

Government: An agency of coercion that is accepted as necessary by most people within its area of influence.

Grain: Used in coin weights; there are 15.432 grains to a gram, 480 grains to a troy ounce.

Gram: Used in gold weights; there are 31.1042 grams to a troy ounce; one gram = .03215 troy ounces. A kilogram is 1,000 grams; there are 1,000 milligrams to a gram.

Hard money: Gold or silver.

Income (investment): Dividends or interest received from an investment.

Inconvertibility: The inability to receive gold in exchange for currency from the agency that issued the currency.

Inflation: An increase in money substitutes above the stored stock of real money; the counterfeiting of money receipts.

Inflationary depression: A depression within a period of inflation.

Interest differential: See *carrying charges.*

Legal tender: A form of money that an individual is legally required to accept in payment of debts.

Leverage: In investments, the ability to purchase more than a monetary investment could purchase on a cash basis.

Liquidation: Normally, the sale of an investment. With regard to depressions, *liquidation* refers to the acceptance of losses and the closing of businesses that existed only because of the miscalculations caused by inflation.

Liquidity: The availability of spending money.

Long: The expectation that a price will go up; buying before selling. (See also *short.*)

Lot: In gold coins, the basic unit of trading. A lot contains 100 British Sovereigns, 20 Mexican 50-peso pieces, or 20 U.S. Double Eagles.

Margin: In a margin account, the amount of one's equity expressed as a percentage of the total current market value of the investment; also, it can refer to the amount of cash invested.

Margin account: An investment account in which the investment purchase is increased by borrowing money and using the investment as collateral.

Margin call: In a margin account, a request by the lender to deposit additional money so that the loan amount will remain well below the total current market value of the investment.

Market: (1) An opportunity to exchange. (2) A group of exchanges unified by common factors of geography or items traded.

Marketable: Capable of being sold at a price that covers all costs and a profit.

Marketplace: The General Market.

Money: A commodity that is accepted in exchange by an individual who intends to trade it for something else.

Money receipt: A receipt that can be exchanged for real money.

Money substitute: A money receipt or a demand deposit that can be used in exchange, in place of real money.

Money supply: The total of all money and money substitutes (demand deposits and currency outside of banks).

Paper money: Any money substitutes (even if not backed by real money).

Part-time investor: An individual investor whose profession is other than investments.

Premium: (1) In a coin, the difference between the market value of the coin and the market value of its metallic content. (2) More generally, any increased value above normal.

Production: Energy expended to create a product or service.

Real money: Gold or silver.

Redemption: The payment of gold in exchange for currency by the agency that originally issued the currency as a receipt for gold. (See also *convertibility*.)

Resources: (1) *Natural resources:* land, minerals, vegetables, and animals. (2) *Human resources:* time, effort, and knowledge. (3) *Secondary resources:* property created by the application of human resources to natural resources.

Revaluation: A change in the rate at which a government will redeem its currency with gold. In normal usage, *revaluation* means *upvaluation*—an increase in the amount of gold payable per currency unit.

Runaway inflation: An inflationary period in which the paper money supply increases fast enough to cause all retail prices to change daily or more often.

Short: The expectation that a price will drop; the sale of a commodity the seller doesn't own, with the expectation of buying the commodity at a lower price later. (See also *long.*)

Special Drawing Rights (SDRs): A currency issued by the International Monetary Fund, used only by governments in place of gold as a monetary reserve.

Specie: Gold or silver.

Speculative: Involving more than a minimum of risk.

Subsidy: Payment to an individual or a company by other than a customer or investor; or a purchase at a price higher than the market price; or a loan that doesn't carry a rate of interest commensurate with normal marketplace interest for the risk involved.

Swaps: An arrangement by which one government borrows another government's currency in order to buy its own currency in the marketplace—in order to keep its own currency from sinking in price.

Tax: Property coercively taken from its owner by a government.

Term insurance: Insurance in which the benefits are payable only upon the death of the insured.

Time deposit: A bank deposit that isn't payable on demand.

Token: A money substitute in metallic form (includes gold and silver if the legal tender face value of the token is considerably above the market value of the gold or silver content).

Troy ounce: A system of weights in which twelve ounces are equal to a pound (gold and silver are always measured in troy ounces).

Upside potential: The higher price to which an investment has a reasonable opportunity to appreciate.

Upvaluation: A governmental decision to pay *more* gold than originally promised in exchange for the money substitutes it has issued (the opposite of a *devaluation*).

Wealth: Resources that can be used or marketed.

Recommended Reading

Included herein are a number of books that I've found useful. I've grouped them according to subject matter, and placed those that are particularly technical at the end of the list. The rest should be easy enough to read and profit from.

Some of the books are now out of print; but you may be surprised to learn how easy it is to obtain an out-of-print book through a used book dealer who will locate it for you. If a book is very old, it will cost a little more than what a comparable new book would sell for; if the book is less than fifty years old, it may sell for less than it did when new. For each out-of-print book, I've indicated a price quotation I received in 1973 which you can use as a guide.

GOLD AS AN INVESTMENT

Gold—How and Where to Buy and Hold It by Franz Pick. This may tell you more than you want to know about gold, and at a higher price than you want to spend. But this 70-page booklet contains valuable information for the gold buff—price histories, American gold regulations, ways to buy and sell, etc. (Cardcover: Pick Publishing Corp., 21 West St., New York, N.Y. 10006; $45.)

How to Invest in Gold Stocks and Avoid the Pitfalls by Donald J. Hoppe. If you intend to select your own gold stocks,

APPENDIX

this book can be helpful. Among other things, it provides detailed background information for all of the major South African gold mining companies. (Arlington House, 81 Centre Avenue, New Rochelle, N.Y. 10801; $9.95.)

SILVER AS AN INVESTMENT

Silver Profits in the Seventies by Jerome F. Smith. The most complete source of information on silver—supply and demand figures, history of government intervention, etc., plus a great deal of statistical information concerning the international monetary situation. (Cardcover: ERC Publishing Company, P.O. Box 91491, West Vancouver, British Columbia, Canada; $12.50.)

CURRENCIES

Pick's Currency Yearbook by Franz Pick. A unique reference work—listing background information, statistics, devaluation records, etc. for each currency in the world. A new edition is published every year. (Pick Publishing Corp., 21 West St., New York, N.Y. 10006; $90.)

Pick's Currency Reports. The cost of this monthly report makes it prohibitive for all except those who need a convenient source of up-to-date information concerning currency price changes, developments, and anything affecting short-term currency trading. (Pick Publishing Corp., 21 West St., New York, N.Y. 10006; $300 per year.)

SWISS BANKS

The Swiss Banks by T. R. Fehrenbach. Published in 1966, this is still the best source of background information on Swiss banks and Switzerland. Written in an interesting and absorbing style, the book makes it easy to understand why Switzerland is the money haven of the world and will continue to be. (McGraw-Hill Book Co., 1221 Avenue of the Americas, New York, N.Y. 10020; $7.95. Published in England under the title *The Gnomes of Zurich*.)

The Banking System of Switzerland by Hans J. Bär. Perhaps the best explanation of the Swiss banking system—but, alas, it is only published in Switzerland (although in English). If you're interested in the details of the system, it might be worth your while to try to get it. (Schulthess Polygraphischer Verlag, AG, Zurich, Switzerland; 9 Swiss francs.)

Switzerland: An International Banking and Finance Center by Max Ilké. Another good book explaining the details of the banking system. (Dowden, Hutchinson & Ross, Inc., 10 N. Seventh St., Stroudsburg, Pa. 18360; $7.)

RETREATS

The Retreater's Bibliography by Don and Barbie Stephens. A useful compilation of books and sources for retreat supplies. The only book of its kind I've seen. (Don Stephens, Box 141, Glendale, Calif. 91209; $9.50.)

INVESTMENT MARKETS

Supermoney by "Adam Smith". An excellent job of unraveling the fallacies of the investment world—especially valuable for its explanations of the banking and stock market crises of 1971. (Random House, 201 E. 50 St., New York, N.Y. 10022; $8.95.)

The Money Game by "Adam Smith". Although not quite as valuable as *Supermoney*, this book will help you understand why so many things go wrong in the investment world. (Hardcover: Random House, 201 E. 50 St., New York, N.Y. 10022; $6.95.

Paperback: Dell Publishing Co., 750 Third Ave., New York, N.Y. 10017; $1.25.)

The Second Crash by Charles D. Ellis. A good book, in that it indicates how vulnerable the stock market is to an unexpected crash. The author's hopes for stock market reform are meaningless, however. (Simon and Schuster, 630 Fifth Ave., New York, N.Y. 10020; $5.95.)

MONEY

How You Can Profit from the Coming Devaluation by Harry Browne. Although the investment recommendations are superseded by the present book, there is a much more detailed explanation of the reasons why gold will not be dethroned, how inflation is created, and other monetary matters. (Hardcover: Arlington House, 81 Centre Ave., New Rochelle, N.Y. 10801; $5.95. Paperback: Avon Books, 959 Eighth Ave., New York, N.Y. 10019; $1.25.)

What Has Government Done to Our Money? by Murray N. Rothbard. A short, but valuable, 49-page booklet outlining the role of money and its perversion by governments. (Cardcover: Rampart College, 102 W. 4 St., Santa Ana, California; $1.)

What You Should Know About Inflation by Henry Hazlitt. An excellent, easy-to-read primer for anyone interested in the subjects of money and inflation. Henry Hazlitt is a master of clear writing. (Hardcover: D. Van Nostrand Co., 450 W. 33 St., New York, N.Y. 10001; $4.95. Paperback: Funk & Wagnalls, Inc., 53 E. 77 St., New York, N.Y. 10021; $.95.)

13 Curious Errors About Money by Paul Bakewell, Jr. A clarification of several important misconceptions that most people have about money. Very easy to read and follow. (Paperback: Caxton Printers, Ltd., Caldwell, Idaho 83605; $2.)

ECONOMICS

Essentials of Economics by Faustino Ballvé. A very good introduction to economics—providing a great many valuable truths in less than 100 pages. (Foundation for Economic Education, Irvington-on-Hudson, N.Y. 10533; hardcover $3; cardcover $1.50.)

The New Approach to Freedom by E. C. Riegel. The best explanation of the free market I've seen. Unfortunately, it's coupled with a suggestion for an unworkable money system. (Cardcover: The Heather Foundation, Box 48, San Pedro, Calif. 90733; $1.)

Economics in One Lesson by Henry Hazlitt. A valuable book that demolishes many popular economic fallacies. (Hardcover: Harper & Row, 49 E. 33 St., New York, N.Y. 10016; $4.95. Paperback: Macfadden Publications, Inc., 205 E. 42 St., New York, N.Y. 10017; $.50.)

The Great Idea by Henry Hazlitt. A novel in which the plot is little more than a setting for the economic ideas that are explained. Unusual and helpful because it works backward from the present popular fallacies to the truth. (Appleton-Century-Crofts, 1951, out of print; approximately $5.)

Anything That's Peaceful by Leonard E. Read. A well considered presentation demonstrating the nature of government enterprises and the harm they do to the economy. (Foundation for Economic Education, Irvington-on-Hudson, N.Y. 10533; hardcover $3.50; cardcover $2.50.)

University Economics: Elements of Inquiry by Armen A. Alchian and William R. Allen. For the serious student of the subject only. This is one of the few college economics textbooks that present a realistic view of the consequences of governmental intervention. (Wadsworth Publishing Co., Inc., Belmont, Calif. 94002; $17.25.)

1929 DEPRESSION

America's Great Depression by Murray N. Rothbard. The definitive monetary history of the United States from 1921 to 1933. The book is not easy reading; it's a textbook. But it provides a great deal of useful information for anyone who wants to understand the causes of the 1929 depression. (Nash Publishing Corp., 9255 Sunset Blvd., Los Angeles, Calif. 90069; $10.)

28 Days by C. C. Colt and N. Keith. A day-by-day summary of the events of the banking crisis of 1933, including the bank holidays and Roosevelt's totalitarian solutions. The authors praise the solutions, but the book is still useful for details of the era that I haven't found elsewhere. (Greenberg Publishers, N.Y., 1933, out of print; approximately $8.)

Oh Yeah? edited by Edward Angly. An amusing compilation of statements made by public officials from 1928 to 1931—all forecasting prosperity just around the corner. A sure antidote for anyone inclined to believe what he hears. (Viking Press, N.Y., 1931, out of print; approximately $8.)

RUNAWAY INFLATIONS

The Economics of Inflation by Costantino Bresciani-Turroni. A detailed and lengthy summary of the German inflation of 1914–1923. It includes extensive tables of price indexes month-by-month for consumer items, wholesale prices, foreign currencies, stock prices, etc. (John Dickens & Co., Northamton, England, 1937, out of print; approximately $12.)

Fiat Money Inflation in France by Andrew Dickson White. The classic book on runaway inflation, it explains how governmental policies were incapable of overcoming the General Market during the famous runaway inflation during the French Revolution. (Cardcover: Caxton Printers, Ltd., Caldwell, Idaho 83605; $1.)

Inflation and the Investor, an Axe-Houghton Economic Study. A summary of the French and German inflations, showing how they affected various types of investments. (E. W. Axe & Co., Inc., 400 Benedict Avenue, Tarrytown, N.Y.; $1.)

The Financier and the Finances of the American Revolution by William Graham Sumner. A detailed study of the famous

"Continentals" runaway inflation during the American Revolution. (Augustus M. Kelley, Publishers, 305 Allwood Rd., Clifton, N.J. 07012; 2 volumes; $20.)

U.S. ECONOMIC HISTORY

Past and Present Facts About Money in the United States by Paul Bakewell, Jr. An easy-to-follow summary of U.S. monetary history. (Macmillan Publishing Co., N.Y., 1936, out of print; approximately $10.)

The Triumph of Conservatism by Gabriel Kolko. A review of the "Progressive Era," showing that antitrust legislation was designed to benefit large companies at the expense of the consumer, not vice-versa. (Free Press, 866 Third Ave., New York, N.Y. 10022; $8.95.)

Railroads and Regulation, 1877–1916 by Gabriel Kolko. Similar to *The Triumph of Conservatism,* but dealing specifically with the railroads. (Princeton University Press, Princeton, N.J. 08540; $8.50.)

PRICE CONTROLS

The Vampire Economy by Guenter Reimann. A thorough review of price controls, wage controls, production quotas—in other words, fascism—in Nazi Germany. (Vanguard Press, N.Y., 1939, out of print; approximately $8.)

MISCELLANEOUS

How I Found Freedom in an Unfree World by Harry Browne. This may help you to understand yourself better, so that you can better define your own investment objectives. It also contains suggestions for minimizing government interference in your own life. (Macmillan Publishing Co., 866 Third Ave., New York, N.Y. 10022; $7.95.)

How to Keep Your Money and Freedom by Harry D. Schultz. A small 87-page booklet that reviews taxing and residency policies in most of the major countries of the world. Helpful for anyone looking for a new nation to live in or for the opportunity to avoid taxes through the creation of foreign corporations. (Harry D. Schultz, 170 Sloane St., London S.W.1, England; $8.)

The Lusitania by Colin Simpson. An interesting exposé of the efforts by the United States and British governments to bring the U.S. into World War I.[1] (Little Brown and Co., 34 Beacon St., Boston, Mass. 03106; $8.95.)

TEXTBOOKS

The following books are useful sources for anyone undertaking a serious study of money or monetary history. For the casual reader, they aren't recommended.

World Monetary History

All the Monies of the World by Franz Pick and René Sédillot (Pick Publishing Corp., 21 West St., New York, N.Y. 10006; $80.)

History of Monetary Systems by Alexander Del Mar (Augustus M. Kelley, Publishers, 305 Allwood Rd., Clifton, N.J. 07012; $15.)

The History of Foreign Exchange by Paul Einzig (St. Martin's Press, 175 Fifth Ave., New York, N.Y. 10010; $13.95.)

U.S. Monetary History

A Monetary History of the United States, 1867–1960 by Milton Friedman and Anna Jacobson Schwartz (Paperback: Princeton University Press, Princeton, N.J. 08540; $4.95.)

---

[1] There are also numerous books covering the same situation for World War II —too many and too far afield to go into here.

The Financial History of the United States by Albert S. Bolles (Augustus M. Kelley, Publishers, 305 Allwood Rd., Clifton, N.J. 07012; 3 volumes; $45.)

A History of the Greenbacks with Special Reference to the Economic Consequences of Their Issue: 1862–1865 by Wesley Clair Mitchell (University of Chicago Press, 5801 Ellis Ave., Chicago, Ill. 60637; $12.50.)

The Memoirs of Herbert Hoover, The Great Depression 1929–1941 (Macmillan Publishing Co., out of print; approximately $10.)

The American Revolution

Seedtime of the Republic by Clinton Rossiter (Harcourt Brace Jovanovich, 757 Third Ave., New York, N.Y. 10017; $10.75.)

The First Congress by Robert P. Williams (Exposition Press, Inc., 50 Jericho Turnpike, Jericho, N.Y. 11753; $12.50.)

The Great Frontier by Walter Prescott Webb (University of Texas Press, Box 7819, University Station, Austin, Texas 78712; $8.50.)

Sources of Charts and Tables

Land, Stocks, and Mutual Funds—page 6

Stocks: Standard & Poors' stock averages.

Mutual Funds: The information was calculated from data appearing in *Investment Companies, 1973 Edition*—a yearly review of mutual fund performance published by Wisenberger Services, Inc., 1 New York Plaza, New York, N.Y. 10004 ($60). From the average appreciations of the different types of funds, an overall average was derived—weighted by asset size.

Land: Percentages were developed from statistical information for land costs for residential dwellings in the United States provided by the Department of Housing and Urban Development, Seattle office.

Gold, Silver, Gold Stocks, and Swiss Francs—page 7

Gold bullion: London daily price fixing as published by the *Wall Street Journal.*

Silver bullion: London daily price fixing as published by the *Wall Street Journal.*

Gold stocks: The *Financial Times* index of South African gold stocks as published by the *Wall Street Journal* and *Kaffir Chart Service.*

Swiss francs: Exchange rate in dollars as published by the *Wall Street Journal.*

Gold Backing of Twenty-Six Currencies—pages 216–217

Figures for Demand Deposits, Currency Outside Banks, and Gold Reserves were published in reports issued by the central banks of each nation. The figures were collected by Franz Pick. Gold reserve figures were provided in U.S. dollars and I translated them into each currency by using the prevailing official exchange rate on December 31, 1972.

Potential Currency Changes—page 221

Currency prices for June 18, 1973, were published in the *Wall Street Journal* on June 19, 1973, with the exception of Ireland, Lebanon, New Zealand, Turkey, and Yugoslavia—which were obtained from *Pick's Currency Reports* (prices for end of June).

Actual Units per Ounce figures were obtained by dividing the number of gold ounces in reserve (*gold reserve* in table on pages 216–217 divided by official gold rate) into the total money substitutes (also in table on pages 216–217).

Actual $ Value was derived by dividing the *Actual Units per Ounce* figure into 1,120.93 (the number of dollars issued per ounce of gold held by the U.S. Treasury).

Change Necessary Against $ was computed by dividing the June 18, 1973, price into the *Actual $ Value* figure and subtracting 1.00.

Change Necessary Against All was computed by dividing the *Change Necessary Against $* figure plus 100 by 238.26 and subtracting 100 from the answer. The average change against the dollar was +138.26%. The calculations are unworkable unless 100 is added to each figure and subtracted from the result.

Currency Price Changes—page 223

Prices for June 30, 1970 and June 18, 1973, were published in the *Wall Street Journal* on the following business days—with the exception of Ireland, Lebanon, New Zealand, Turkey, and Yugoslavia, which were obtained from *Pick's Currency Yearbook, 1972* and *Pick's Currency Reports,* July 1973.

THE AUTHOR

HARRY BROWNE, born in 1933, spent most of his forty years in the Los Angeles area. After graduating from high school, he tried twice to go through college, but quit after a few days because he couldn't stay awake in class.

He decided to educate himself and found all subjects except economics interesting. Economic textbooks proved to be as tranquilizing as college classrooms were. Around 1960, he discovered that economics was actually an exciting subject. And he realized that most people can understand economics if it isn't taught as a mysterious world apart from human action.

In 1964, he began giving courses in economics to paying customers. In 1967, he applied his understanding to specific investments and began showing investment clients how to carry out the recommendations made in this book.

In 1970, his first book, *How You Can Profit from the Coming Devaluation,* was published. It became a best-seller; and between his royalties and his personal investment success, he saw no need to continue working as an investment counselor. In 1973, his second book, *How I Found Freedom in an Unfree World,* was published and it, too, was a big seller.

In 1971, he moved from Los Angeles to Vancouver, British Columbia, where he still lives. Unmarried, he says that his principal interests are opera, classical music, travelling, love, playing with speculative investments, making money, reading and lying on the couch—not necessarily in that order

Index